Orthodoxy and Psychoanalysis

European University Studies

Europäische Hochschulschriften

Publications Universitaires Européennes

Series XXIII Theology

Reihe XXIII Theologie

Série XXIII Théologie

Volume/Band **938**

Petru Cazacu

Orthodoxy and Psychoanalysis

Dirge or Polychronion to the Centuries-Old Tradition?

Elaborating on the Views of Basil Thermos

PL ACADEMIC RESEARCH

Bibliographic Information published by the Deutsche Nationalbibliothek
The Deutsche Nationalbibliothek lists this publication in the Deutsche Nationalbibliografie; detailed bibliographic data is available in the internet at http://dnb.d-nb.de.

ISSN 0721-3409
ISBN 978-3-631-64416-4 (Print)
E-ISBN 978-3-653-03005-1 (E-Book)
DOI 10.3726/978-3-653-03005-1

PL Academic Research is an Imprint of Peter Lang GmbH.
Peter Lang – Frankfurt am Main · Bern · Bruxelles · New York · Oxford · Warszawa · Wien

www.peterlang.de

Prolegomenon

I.

The world in 2013 is more complex than it ever was before. Some cite the amount and speed of technology for this state, others see industrialization as a cause, while yet others believe it is related to a denial of death — a consequence of a culture that no longer deals with death daily and even dresses up death to mask its existence. Our secular society characterizes itself as post-modern and post-Christian. This society finds itself in unchartered waters and is unsure of its path or future. Today, people enter puberty earlier than ever before and life's complexities prolong adolescence into the late twenties. Modern youth are unable to cope with interpersonal relationships and ill prepared to make a living. In general, people are less mature and less responsible than at any other time in modern history. Our secular society is struggling with the economic, sociological and psychological impacts of these changes in its culture. A secular society that is post-Christian also needs to redefine what is right and wrong as well as what is normative and acceptable. The Church in this time is challenged by the fact that its members live in this secular and post-Christian world. Even if we are not of this world, we certainly are in it. Our people are more familiar with the language and frames of secular society and the social sciences than with the narratives and truths of Orthodoxy. Let us ask how we are to respond. Should we as a Church interact with social scientists, secularists and modern governments? And, if so, how? What language should we speak with people, even our own people, who are better versed in secularism than in Christianity? Can we learn from modern frames and sciences? Can we — and should we — witness to them? How can we help immature clergy and faithful grow and / or repent and better serve the Church?

Some have attempted to use theological language to understand modern social sciences. Others have used psychological language to understand theology. I find both of these approaches unsatisfying as they compromise their own definitions. I rather understand the interaction of Orthodoxy and the social sciences as a conversation. The pastoral-theologian or pastor can learn frames to help him understand some of his own complexities or immaturities and those of people he serves. Likewise, the psychologist or social scientist can learn what Orthodoxy teaches to better serve Orthodox Christians, and perhaps everyone else too, by coming to understand what the Church really says about mankind and all of our relationships. A clergyman can use modern tools to communicate the Gospel and reconcile God's people to Himself and each other.

Petru Cazacu shows us that the work of Fr. Basil Thermos is a successful conversation between Orthodox Theology and the social sciences. Cazacu shows that Thermos could utilize the language and frames of modern psychology without compromising the teachings of the Orthodox faith or straying from the goals of deification through our Saviour, Jesus Christ. He has also shown how psychoanalysis can be useful in examining and preparing clergy for Church service and serving the faithful.

I believe this book to be a valuable contribution to the conversation between the Orthodox Church and modern social science, useful for seminarians and Church leaders alike. It offers the reader some practical ways of using the social sciences and shows how our Church Fathers have understood the complexities of the human condition to help people repent, grow and heal.

15th April 2013 Bishop JOHN (Abdalah)

Auxiliary Bishop-Diocese of Worcester and New England
Antiochian Orthodox Christian Archdiocese of North America

II.

Pastoral issues have always been the central topic of study on the Balamandian hill. The St. John of Damascus Institute of Theology has offered important contributions to Orthodoxy to improve pastoral ministry within the Orthodox Church.

Petru Cazacu is one of our graduate students who has devoted himself entirely to studying the key pastoral issue: the advisability of using psychoanalysis in the Orthodox pastoral ministry. The present book is the result of Cazacu's research work since his theological studies in Russia, Greece and the Lebanon. Cazacu has set himself firmly on the road of acquiring the conceptual and practical theological treasures of these three Orthodox pastoral traditions. Although they are diverse in practice, they nevertheless converge in comprehension because of their common deep roots. Now, Cazacu has also come to the fore with the additional experience of being part of the Orthodox diaspora in Western Europe, an experience which has enriched and refined the present condition of his research. Having been one of his professors and a member of the assessment board of examiners, I know in detail Cazacu's progress during its Balamandian period.

Rev. Basil Thermos is a well-known Greek Orthodox priest, a child and adolescent psychiatrist and a prolific writer in the realm of pastoral theology. His theological approaches to psychoanalysis seem to have begun influencing considerably modern Orthodox pastoral care. Importantly, Thermos recommends the use of psychological knowledge in pastoral counselling and, simultaneously, rightly avers that psychological maturity is not a condition for holiness. As a result, not only psychologically mature persons are called to be saved. However, maturity is an essential condition to be a successful church minister. Church ministers must seek to fathom the unconscious spheres of their soul in order to perform their pastoral duties effectively.

Cazacu questions whether Orthodox pastoral counselling could profit from implementing modern psychoanalytic practices used by Thermos to investigate the pastoral problems in the Orthodox Church. Cazacu deals with two key pastoral problems according to the way Thermos approaches and solves them: the vocation of pastoral work and the ineffectiveness of modern pastoral ministers. In doing so, Cazacu endeavours to verify whether the paradigm propounded by Thermos, as a way of solving these problems, can be applied. Cazacu's work is, on the one hand, sufficiently based on a thorough knowledge of psychoanalytic theory and the principles of Orthodox pastoral theology. And, on the other, the reader is given the opportunity to profit from the pragmatic conclusions justifying concrete measures to ensure clergy effectiveness in carrying out congregational work.

Indeed, the present research belongs to the line of contemporary Orthodox studies which offer a dynamic approach to the present encounter between Orthodox pastoral theology and psychological sciences.

University of Balamand, the Lebanon
15th April 2013

Prof. Daniel Alberto Ayuch

Author's Note

This study is a fully-revised and updated version of a MTh thesis in Orthodox pastoral theology presented to the St John of Damascus Institute of Theology at the University of Balamand (the Lebanon) in June 2004. The original title was "Orthodox Pastoral Theology and Psychoanalysis in the Works of Basil Thermos: Hypothetic paradigm of interaction".

I proposed the topic to the administration of the Institute. His Beatitude John X (Yazigi), the present Greek Orthodox Patriarch of Antioch and all the East, the Dean, at that time, of the St John of Damascus Institute of Theology, readily endorsed the proposal. His Grace Bishop John (Abdalah) of Worcester and New England (USA) kindly agreed to supervise my research at the St John of Damascus Institute of Theology. Professor Daniel Ayuch (Balamand University, the Lebanon), the Very Reverend Archimandrite Dr. Jack (Khalil) and Professor Vasilios Makrides (University of Erfurt) provided me with helpful feedback on certain issues within the work. Dr. David West, Mr. Curtis Magnuson and Ms. Julie Anne Zein carefully examined the completed work, offering constructive criticism and useful suggestions; they aided me in securely holding my ambition from outdistancing my means. The Very Reverend Dr. Basil Thermos readily agreed to provide me with all his recent and relevant research papers. The meticulous preparations for the publication of this book were financially supported by His Grace Irenaeus (Tafunea) of Orsk (Russia). It would have been difficult to accomplish these preparations without the database of the University of Münster, and for this opportunity I owe a heartfelt thanks to the Renovabis, a charitable organization of the Roman Catholic Church in Germany.

Professor Assaad Elias Kattan (University of Münster, Germany) encouraged me to revise as well as update the work, and to submit it to the present Dean of the St John of Damascus Institute of Theology, His Grace Ghattas (Hazim), for the necessary permission to publish. His Grace Bishop John (Abdalah) of Worcester and New England (USA) very kindly provided this study with a prolegomenon. Prof. Daniel Alberto Ayuch amiably wrote a recommendatory word to the book as well.

I owe special thanks to His Eminence Archbishop Eugenius (Reshetnikoff), the Principal of the Moscow Theological Academy, for recommending me to His Holiness Alexius II (Ridiger), the *inoubliable* Patriarch of Moscow and All Russia, who introduced me to the administration of the University of Balamand. My warmest thanks, however, go to His Beatitude Ignatius IV (Hazim) of blessed memory, the Greek Orthodox Patriarch of Antioch and all the East, for allowing me to broaden my theological knowledge at the St John of Damascus Institute of Theology between 2001 and 2004. To all those mentioned here and to many others who helped me I wish to extend many thanks.

Petru Mikhail Cazacu

Contents

1. Introduction

To the eternal memory of my spiritual father,
Bishop Dorimedont (Chekan)

"Throughout the contemporary Christian world there is a thirst for spiritual guidance and at the same time a severe dearth of persons blessed by the Holy Spirit to serve as guides" (Ware 62). Only a few Orthodox theologians would doubt the value of these words, but many would not scruple to voice their dissension at the accompanying suggestions about how best meet this huge challenge. Following extensive discussions, Greek theologians have recently suggested utilizing the expertise and knowledge available in the fields of psychology, psychiatry and psychotherapy. Grafting such expertise and counsels onto the body of knowledge and experience of the modern Orthodox priest would thereby equip him with additional knowledge of the human soul. Greater cooperation between ecclesiastical and secular knowledge promises to counter the "severe dearth of persons blessed by the Holy Spirit to serve as guides", a dearth which threatens to depopulate the Church in the future. Such effectual cooperation promises to render spiritual counsel a singularly rewarding activity.[1]

The seriousness of this issue urgently requires effective measures to address the pressing problem of an inscrutable Providence withholding spiritual favours from the ordained minister. Taking sides instead of preserving traditions that are held dearest represents a quandary for present day Orthodox theology. The predicament for the Orthodox mind is this: firstly, close cooperation between ecclesiastical and secular knowledge might imply that the Church, as the Body of Christ, lacks its own means to solve the problem of the priest's spiritual immaturity and his concomitant incapacity to guide Christ's people. The minister endowed with abundant spiritual qualities is replaced by the quasi-pastor who lacks knowledge of the human soul, and lacks the ability to discern spirits, to prophesize and to interpret. As a result, some in the Church resort to expertise which derives from the secular, a-theist realm rather than its own theocentric frame of reference. Additional problems arise within Orthodox anthropology when the immediate necessity for greater elaboration[2] impels the deliberate,

---

1 Kornarakis says: "In the case that a pastor is not a spiritual father endowed with the gift of spiritual insight he must, nevertheless, being the instrument of the divine grace, resort to the use of human possibilities in order to collaborate creatively with divine grace; psychological knowledge is God's indirect gift to the wise collaborator" (*Έγχειρίδιον* 15).

2 Metropolitan Ware says: "Our theology of human personhood needs to be much more fully elaborated … Such elaboration is possibly the special task that will confront Orthodox theology in the coming century … Certainly what Florovsky used to say about our Orthodox ecclesiology - that it is 'still *im Werden*, in the process of formation' – is even more true of our Orthodox anthropology" (78).

functional and epigenetic interlacing of both anthropological frames of reference, secular and sacred, causing Orthodox anthropology to implode. Finally, the progressive depletion in knowledgeable, skilled spiritual shepherds is a matter that allows no delay, because the increasing commodification of spiritual care[3] helps to legitimize and sustain the desacralisation of the Church.

The Very Reverend Basil Thermos is in the vanguard of attempts to obtain revealing insights into a possible dialogue between Orthodox pastoral theology and psychology, psychiatry, and psychotherapy. The decision to analyze and evaluate the tendency to rapprochement and interaction between theology and "anthropological (in the sense of the psychological and social behaviour of humans) sciences" by way of Thermos's thought appears promising. Thermos is an accomplished theologian with a Th.D. degree earned for the study — *Ἡ Ἱερατική κλίση ὡς ψυχολογικό γεγονός* (The Hieratic Vocation as Psychological Event) — and has received medical education in the field of psychiatry. In addition, he is the author of many books and articles which form a repository, on the basis of which meaningful dialogue between Orthodox theology and the psychological sciences could be established. Within this repository, Thermos is prepared to grapple seriously with the problem of spiritual immaturity among Christian ministers, an immaturity which makes such ministers ineffective and improper guides for their Orthodox congregations. The reason for some priests' spiritual immaturity and consequent ineffectiveness can be attributed to a pastoral vocation problem. Some priests, although physiologically mature, evidence regrettable psychological immaturity. By means of the psychological sciences Thermos seeks to explain why these priests swerve from their initial intention to act according to the highest sense of their vocation.

In the context of this problem, it is important to ascertain precisely which paradigm of interaction between Orthodox pastoral theology and psychoanalysis Thermos suggests. How does he manage to maintain the necessary balance of mutual inviolability between the realms of theological and psychological knowledge? It seems also of key importance to determine what Thermos understands under Orthodox pastoral theology and psychoanalysis. Does he tolerate the scientific insufficiency of the psychoanalytic method? What arguments does

---

3 " … In the coming century the devotion to the traditional religion or the religion of revelation will play not a great role. Devotion is peculiar to the historical religions alone. What will count is the certain power of religion or its components to gratify the needs of individuals and small communities; among the needs of religiously active people it is the necessity of psychological and corporeal health that reigns supreme" (Mitrī 117-8). Augustidis claims something very consonant with Mıtrī's opinion. He says: "It will be very regrettable, if tomorrow we shall face a phenomenon, whereby the parish will be considered capable of gratifying religious needs alone, while devising solutions for personal and family problems will fall within the ambit of the municipal psychological health care centre business, because only the latter is able ostensibly to afford understanding and elimination of personal problems" (Αὐγουστίδης 101).

he put forward in favour of interaction between psychoanalytic and theological knowledge? And does he raise counterarguments to this? Is it expedient for Orthodox theology to pursue a model of the human being obtained from a deterministic anthropological approach?

To answer these questions the present study will proceed from the following thesis statement: **Thermos presents a powerful and well-grounded argument for the interaction between Orthodox pastoral theology and psychoanalysis.** The above statement rests on the following assertions:

I. The importance of the human component in pastoral vocation arises from the epistemology which psychoanalysis inhabits; however, this epistemology is not foundational to the ultimate destiny of the Orthodox priesthood.

II. Apart from the practice of the spiritual life, the effectiveness of the modern Christian priest is dependent on minimizing the influence of the unconscious and promoting self-knowledge.

III. Thermos strips the methodological insufficiencies and philosophical biases of psychoanalysis to their essentials, and constructs a standard Orthodox model of the human entity.

IV. It is necessary to encourage better interaction between Orthodox pastoral theology and psychoanalysis. Any divergence between the two can probably be attributed to the failure to acknowledge the mutual lack of expertise in each other's respective fields rather than to an inherent incompatibility.

These assertions will be confirmed with the help of writings on the topic by a relatively large cross-section of theologians and thinkers: Thermos, Bendaly, Matsukas, Ricœur, Kornarakis, Tselengidis, Staniloae, Romanidis, Evmenius, Florovsky, Freud, Jung, Manzat, Jaspers, and Dansereau, to name a few. Selected translations of the Greek Fathers which are pertinent to this topic have also been undertaken. Importantly, neither English nor French academic texts quoted in Greek by Thermos have been checked against their original versions but rather directly translated from the Greek text, because it is Thermos's entire model and not his academic reliability that is of most importance here. The present study follows the MLA referencing style (7th edition 2009 with small adaptations made to it by the University of Balamand Libraries, Style Manuals 6th edition 2011).

In terms of epistemological tools, translation, periphrasis, description, analysis, comparison, example and illustration should help build a better understanding of the subject.

The primary objectives of the study are:

I. To confirm whether Thermos advances an acceptable paradigm of interaction between Orthodox pastoral theology and psychoanalysis.

II. To determine the admissible limits of interaction between these two spheres of knowledge.

These two objectives should contribute to forming a rationale for the possibility and advisability of repairing to psychoanalysis in default of efficient solutions for pastoral problems within the Orthodox Church.

This study will develop an argument in support of the four assertions outlined above. It begins with a concise reconstruction of the pastoral vocation problem and Thermos's suggested solution to this. The reconstruction adheres closely in argument and description to the tenets contained in Thermos's text. After outlining this initial problem, that of pastoral vocation, the paper goes on to examine and explain the reasons for the *many* pastoral vocation problems present in ecclesiastical life not only by emphasizing the responsibility of the Church authorities but also by establishing the importance of the quality of the psychological atmosphere within the Christian family. The latter is essential to the initiation of future clergymen into a life of love and interpersonal solidarity in the Church. Next, the study suggests reasons for and the causes of the failures in effectiveness among established priests. The suggestion is made that the balance of responsibility should be shared by particular ecclesiastics and the Church authorities. Finally, the paper examines the theoretical underpinnings of Thermos's paradigm, from the perspectives of psychoanalysis and Orthodox anthropology, with preliminary discussion focusing on the advantages and disadvantages of psychoanalytic discoveries for Orthodox pastoral theology.

2. The pastoral vocation problem and its solution according to Thermos

2.1. Introduction to the issue

In recasting the pastoral vocation problem in terms of psychoanalysis, the Very Reverend Thermos initiated the central paradigm of a new movement within the Orthodox Church. He wrote about the pressing problem of pastoral vocation in his study *Ἡ Ἱερατική κλίση ὡς ψυχολογικό γεγονός* [Hieratic Vocation as Psychological Event].

At the beginning of his study, Thermos (*Ἡ Ἱερατική*) notes that certain Orthodox theologians hold to the majority opinion that the pastoral vocation is exclusively theocentric in character. *C'est-a-dire*, God alone calls the candidate to the priesthood pursuant to the ancient precedent of the prophets and apostles who were called by God to the hieratic ministry (Θερμός, *Ἡ Ἱερατική*). In Thermos's account (*Ἡ Ἱερατική*), the Divine vocation may certainly take a different, mediated form, cloaking its "pursuits" by acting either through competent proper ecclesiastics or the faithful within the bastion of the Church. However, as he claims, even in such instances, candidates to the priesthood acknowledge that, apart from an indirect or direct call to the Divine vocation, there is also the personal desire to become a priest (Θερμός, *Ἡ Ἱερατική*). The importance of personal desire in the hieratic vocation can also be found in the age-old standpoint of the Church as revealed in the canonic warrant for a candidate's aspiration: "my spiritual son *came … asking to take* the foremost rank of priesthood … " (Νικοδήμου Ἁγιορείτου 758). The message of this testimony is that the candidate at one and the same time *seeks* to become a priest and reveals the completion of an inward, though not always conscious, process during which his vocation matured (Θερμός, *Ἡ Ἱερατική*).

Thermos (*Ἡ Ἱερατική*) claims that there are two terms in the Greek language which suggest two distinct strands in pastoral vocation: 1) *κλήση* (derived from the verb—*καλώ*), and 2) *κλίση* (from *κλίνω*). The first term refers to "vocation", and implies the gracious providence of almighty God, who attracts the human person to His ministry. The second term denotes "inclination, bent of heart / mind to something", and is applied to the idea of a propensity inside a particular person to become a servant of God (Θερμός, *Ἡ Ἱερατική* 38).

It is obvious from the title of Thermos's study that his primary aim is to investigate the vocation termed *κλίση*. In other words, he is concerned with a detailed analysis of the psychological dimensions of the hieratic vocation. Thermos underscores the fact that, as much as the division between divine and human strands is necessary, it is also certainly artificial, because to separate the inscrutable divine strand (*κλήση*) from a human inclination is inconceivable. In this respect, the last chapter of his study contains an interesting and detailed analysis of the dialogue concerning divine vocation which takes place between the individual and God. Ultimately, Thermos (*Ἡ Ἱερατική* 39) draws on the psychological dimension since his specific objective is to comprehend the human aspect of the sacerdotal vocation. Such comprehension should facilitate the called candidate's effective cooperation with divine grace. The separate analysis of the psychological dimension should lead to a restoration of the necessary balance between both dimensions of the vocation. This is important because it is growing ever more apparent that candidates may consider their leanings toward hieratic ministry as evidence of divine vocation, whereas they are really "developing their own inclination for priesthood" (Θερμός, *Ἡ Ἱερατική* 39). Thermos (*Ἡ Ἱερατική* 39) asserts that such self-delusion may lead to unfortunate consequences both for the candidates (or even priests) and their congregation.

Thermos seeks answers to the following concrete questions: what crucial psychological factors are at play in forming a vocation (*κλίση*)? What are the necessary psychological conditions for the emergence, development and increase or decrease of a sense of vocation? Does the proper or improper pursuit of a hieratic vocation cue the appropriate authorities to deliver impartial moral, and spiritual judgment only, or oblige them also to offer reasonable psychological interpretation? What are the strict psychological criteria for interpreting psychologically certain hieratic vocations? Should one conjecture that there are "sham" vocations (*κλίση*)? (Θερμός, *Ἡ Ἱερατική* 40)

After establishing the reality and immanent force of the psychological dimension of a hieratic vocation, Thermos (*Ἡ Ἱερατική* 40) then discusses the questions: Is it possible to transform, improve and change the psychological risk factors so that the negative be rendered positive? What independent standpoint concerning the psychological dimension of the hieratic vocation should the Church adopt? At what point is direct intervention in the development of vocation by appropriate ecclesiastical authorities justified? How should the Church deal with harmful psychological misuse of the hieratic vocation and should it establish clear guidelines to manage such misuse?

Apart from drawing on the fullness of his intellectual and Orthodox theological knowledge, Thermos also refers to the findings of Protestant and Catholic studies. According to Thermos (*Ἡ Ἱερατική* 13), such an inter-confessional approach to the above problem should help repair the current Orthodox scientific hiatus in research into the psychological dimension of the hieratic vocation. For those who oppose or even demonize such scientific inter-confessional cross-studies, Thermos (*Ἡ Ἱερατική* 13), in considering the issues of the non-Orthodox experience being grafted into the Orthodox domain, states that this issue does not concern the realm of ecclesiology, but the ecclesiastical which addresses the faithful as individuals. In relation to the individual, Thermos (*Ἡ Ἱερατική* 13) avers that the sinfulness of human nature is ubiquitous. Hence there is no canonical obstacle to inter-confessional cross-research and studies which effectively tackle common anthropological issues.

It will be immediately noted that Thermos (*Ἡ Ἱερατική* 11) makes recourse not only to psychoanalysis, but to other currents in psychology as well: pastoral psychology, "ego" psychology, family psychology, occupational psychology, social psychology and the psychology of religion.

2.2. The Essence of Human Component (*κλίση*[4])

In his discussion, Thermos attempts to define which psychological factors contribute to a sense of hieratic vocation.

In order to analyze and extrapolate these psychological factors, it will initially be necessary to present the psychological model of the individual which underlies Thermos's conceptual schema. There is good reason to maintain that Thermos has adopted the psychological model constructed by Freud. Specifically, the Freudian notions of "ego", "id", "superego", "mechanisms of defence" ("identification", "repression", and many others), "ideal ego", and "narcissism" underpin Thermos's model (Θερμός, *Ἡ Ἱερατική* 46-94).

2.2.1. "Ideal ego", "mechanisms of identifications" and "formation of identity"

Thermos claims that there are three main psychological factors at play in forming the vocation: "ideal ego", "mechanisms of identification" and "formation of identity" (*Ἡ Ἱερατική* 46-94).

Rycroft's (40) psychoanalytic dictionary defines the notion "ideal ego" as follows: "individual's self-perception in consort with his own expectative self-image" (qtd. Θερμός, *Ἡ Ἱερατική* 49). Blos ("The function" 95) affirms that "ideal ego" formulates the desired objective; with the fulfillment of this objective, the human soul proceeds to identify other new objectives (qtd. Θερμός, *Ἡ Ἱερατική* 49). Thermos (*Ἡ Ἱερατική*) states that the impetus toward lofty ambition for new objectives is the distinctive characteristic of true ideals. Kyriazis and Sakellaropulos (279) claim that "ideal ego is foundational to choosing a sphere of activity. As a consequence, the human person invests the energy of his libido into his activity, during which his self-sensation (narcissism) will be formed, depending on whether he is successful in it or not" (qtd. Θερμός, *Ἡ Ἱερατική*). Thermos (50) notes that the realization of the "ideal ego" results in the pleasant sensation of satisfactions and a feeling of self-esteem, whereas failure to meet the demands of the "ideal ego" results in shame. According to Kohut (1966), development and education interact with each other in order to combine the "ego" of the individual with the ideal so that the "values of this ideal are harmonized with 'ego's' psychical structure and are acceptable for this 'ego'"

---

4 From here on, the word vocation will be used in the sense of the Greek term *κλίση*, i.e., the human component of pastoral vocation.

(qtd. Godin 70). According to Thermos, the coordination of the values of the "ideal ego" with the actual "ego" is a pressing matter, because many unattainable or sham ideals can often be espoused within an individual, and lead him to unsuccessful activity. Kyriazis and Sakellaropulos provide the following definition of identification:

> Identification is a psychical process, during which the individual adopts a not-his-own streak in his character, in other words, standards of behaviour which belong to another human person. As a result, the individual changes himself partially or completely, actualizing the borrowed character. Identification is not only a mechanism of defence or mere imitation of others' behaviour, but an independent, mainly unconscious, function promoting development and maturing of the human ego as well as the modeling of human behaviour. (Κυριαζῆ and Σακελλαροπούλου 70)

There are several kinds of identification: primary identification, secondary identification, projection and introjection. In his study, Thermos discusses only secondary identification and introjection.

> The former is a process of identification with an object that is acknowledged by the individual himself as a distinct person (as opposed to primary identification in which there is no such acknowledgement). This sort of identification stands for a defence since it decreases the aggressiveness of the individual toward the object and grants him the possibility of separating from it (object). Introjection is a process of identification with everything assimilated by the individual. It is also a state in which the individual considers there to be another within himself, another who becomes part of the individual. (Θερμός, *Ἡ Ἱερατική* 58)

With the activation of introjection, the individual interpolates the external object and assimilates its features. From this, Thermos concludes that the "super ego" must be the result of introjection (Θερμός, *Ἡ Ἱερατική* 58).

Thermos's idea of an external object harks back to psychoanalysis. Interestingly, Thermos does not completely explain the idea of external object. He says that "object" means person (Θερμός, *Ἡ Ἱερατική* 58). However, Freud intentionally designated "another person" as "object", since he considered another person to be an object of instinctive powers, solely the work of the imagination (Freud, *Psychopathologie* 276-277). In this regard, Delacampagne articulates the following idea: "Freud's meta-psychology, according to Lang's remark, matters only at the individual level. It does not take into account such ideas as 'thee' and 'ye', in contrast to M. Buber, L. Feuerbach and Parkinson. This meta-psychology does not possess any means to express the meeting between 'I' and 'he '"[5] (52).

These forms of identification are the basis for identity formation. Rycroft (68) puts it as follows: "Self-identity is a sense of continuity within 'ego's' syn-

---

5 Author's translation from the French

thetic methods, a human person's individual style. Moreover, it is a sense that the style of an individual corresponds with his idea of those people who are of great importance to him" (qtd. Θερμός, *Η Ἱερατική* 66). The foregoing definition of self-identity as suggested by Rycroft is fairly difficult to comprehend. Thermos interprets the idea in the following way: "Self-identity means that a human person realizes who he[6] is and keeps up this idea about himself for a long time" (Θερμός, *Η Ἱερατική* 66). The process of self-identity formation begins simultaneously with the cessation of perceiving identification as useful. ... Childish identifications are partly abandoned as unnecessary and partly assimilated by the individual's new image. This process depends on how society identifies the new individual. On the one hand, it acknowledges him as the one whom he should become; on the other hand, the individual can pin hope on societal empathy with him only if he attains his stated objectives (Θερμός, *Η Ἱερατική* 66-7). Kyriazis and Sakellaropulos (1985) believe that self-identity is manifest in behaviour, and emanates from two realms: (1) sexual identification and (2) professional, social, ideological identification. The development of identity in accordance with these two realms takes place chiefly during adolescence, a time during which, according to Thermos (*Η Ἱερατική*), the individual chooses his vocation. This choice of vocation is described by Blos in the following terms (*On Adolescence* 124): "during the time of adolescence the human person begins to imagine himself in the certain role, say as an engineer or a mother" (qtd. Θερμός, *Η Ἱερατική* 67). Today, due to teenagers' late maturity and, consequently, deliberately postponed choices for their future, it comes as no surprise that the period during which a sense of vocation is formed can last until the age of twenty-five or even later (Θερμός, *Η Ἱερατική* 67). However, as Blos (*On Adolescence* 149) says: "the most important and substantial changes of 'ego' occur after the perturbations of the adolescent state break down" (qtd. Θερμός, *Η Ἱερατική* 67). This issue concerns the processes of sweeping aside some possibilities of "ego", and advancing others. The given selection (unconscious in many events) reaches its climax in the sphere of occupational vocation (Θερμός, *Η Ἱερατική* 68).

The next question that Thermos raises is: by which psychological premises does this vocation emerge, develop, and become consolidated or substantially weakened in the individual?

The birth of vocation is directly linked with the emergence and development of "ideal ego" (the ideals). Thermos (*Η Ἱερατική* 51) reckons that "ideal ego" is closely interlaced with the "principle of reality" which helps the "ego" to resign itself to this principle. "Ideal ego" is a sort of mirror, within which "ego", with all its virtues and shortcomings, is able to appreciate itself (Θερμός, *Η Ἱερατική*

---

6 Only for the sake of brevity the pronouns referring to feminine nouns are here not provided. Yet, it is meant to connote them always throughout the text wherever the discussed issue concerns the one and same human nature.

51). Thermos avers that "ideal ego" is called to carry out the crucial task of maintaining the balance of the narcissism of the soul.[7]

It is growing ever more apparent in the epistemological realm of psychoanalysis that there is a point in the individual's early period of life in which he becomes aware of the gradual loss of the sense of his omnipotence (Θερμός, *Ή Ἱερατική* 52). This awareness creates great anxiety which shakes the balance of a child's narcissism. The "good object" loses its immutable character and, moreover, mixes with the "bad object"; in other words, the child begins to perceive these different objects as real things (Θερμός, *Ή Ἱερατική* 52). Yet, "the most good" qualities begin to project upon the "ideal ego", and the latter is thus shaped (Θερμός, *Ή Ἱερατική* 52). The supply of feelings which the child invests in shaping his "ideal ego" restores to his narcissism the proper balance of positive and negative sensations, which had been upset by the emergence of the reality principle (Θερμός, *Ή Ἱερατική* 52). Thus, the "ideal ego" becomes a successor to lost first narcissism (Θερμός, *Ή Ἱερατική* 52). It is obvious that, when the gradual loss of the sense of omnipotence by the child occurs naturally, the great and perfect (ideal) is located in the exterior, as distinct from the interior, world; as a result, the child becomes inclined to aspire toward this individual, but external, "ego" (Θερμός, *Ή Ἱερατική* 52-3).

Thermos (*Ή Ἱερατική* 52) notes that, in shaping the "ideal ego", "faultinesses" may arise, which means that the great and perfect qualities aspired to, instead of being projected onto the external world, "reside" within the human person. In such a case, narcissistic fantasies arise and contribute to the emergence of the pathological phenomenon of an idealized ego (Θερμός, *Ή Ἱερατική* 52-3).

The inherent limits between the mature and immature "ideal ego" (natural and pathological narcissism) are often hard to define (Θερμός, *Ή Ἱερατική* 53). "The 'ideal ego' is mature when it debars idealizations and inculcates both real self-perception and objective perception of others" (Θερμός, *Ή Ἱερατική* 53). No matter how high or low its levels of maturity, "ideal ego" participates, according to Thermos (*Ή Ἱερατική* 53), in each creative action. To support his assertion Thermos refers to Kohut's ("The disorders" 74) discovery that "each creative action represents the transfiguration of narcissism" (qtd. Θερμός, *Ή Ἱερατική* 53).

The process of forming human ideals (the "ideal ego") is dependent on external influences (Θερμός, *Ή Ἱερατική* 54-7). Such external influences are at work in the framework created by parents, relatives and the school environment. It is, however, the parents who leave a lasting imprint on their children's ideals

7 Thermos (*Ή Ιερατική* 51) specifies what sort of narcissism he means to introduce into his research. This narcissism has a psychoanalytic bearing, as distinct from the moral one. One necessitates an elementary supply of love and esteem toward his own self; however, in the event that this supply is absent or decreases, the particular person is subject to depression or other serious psychopathologies.

(Θερμός, *Ἡ Ἱερατική* 53-5). Kaplan and Whitman ("The negative" 185) state that the child introjects parental positive and negative qualities, a process which culminates in a positive (or negative) 'ideal ego' (qtd. Θερμός, *Ἡ Ἱερατική* 53). Milrod (48) notes that, "when a parent is extremely exalted in his child's eyes, because of the former's ostensible good qualities, the child's 'ideal ego' acquires imitating, impersonal and immature inclinations which are prejudicial to his developing judgment. The child considers unconsciously that he has magically come into possession of the parent's desirable qualities" (qtd. Θερμός, *Ἡ Ἱερατική* 53). In such cases, the ideals stay immature and "external" (imitative) or "non-attendant upon 'ego' ideals"; it is necessary then to form ideals which differ from parental ideals (Θερμός, *Ἡ Ἱερατική* 54).

During adolescence, it is necessary that parents progressively lose their supreme position in the eyes of their children, so that the children can substitute real, mature judgments for infantile ones. Blos (*On Adolescence* 184) avers that "there are forerunners of 'ideal ego' even during pre-adolescence" (qtd. Θερμός, *Ἡ Ἱερατική* 54). However, "the formation of 'ideal ego' begins at the end of the first phase of adolescence, and by the end of adolescence, teenagers should have usually formed their self-perception, other perception, and 'ideal ego'" (Θερμός, *Ἡ Ἱερατική* 54).

Adolescence is therefore of vital importance in the shaping of ideals and the forming of vocation. With respect to this, Thermos claims that "many pastoral vocations emerge during adolescence" (*Ἡ Ἱερατική* 54*)*. This period in human development summons to action both the theology and the pastoral care of the Orthodox Church. Therefore, the latter ought to show much gravity, prudence and wisdom in dealing with this period.

The need for wisdom and prudence is urged by Thermos (*Ἡ Ἱερατική* 55) in his reference to Laufer's observations, according to which there is a high probability that a teenager will develop a sham "ideal ego", if he proves incapable of overcoming inner psychological conflicts. It is argued that a teenager may experience deep anxieties because of conflicts with, and levels of dependency on, his parents. To overcome these psychological tensions, the teenager often resorts to defensive measures which can cause him to assimilate ideals and patterns from the external world, in a superficial and insincere manner (Θερμός, *Ἡ Ἱερατική* 55). In being thus assimilated, out of inner compulsion, such ideals are doomed, according to Thermos, since they solely serve to reduce the "individual's anxiety and to maintain the balance of his narcissistic self-esteem" (*Ἡ Ἱερατική* 55).

The group is another major factor that shapes ideals. The wane of parental influence is accompanied by the increasing adoption by children of other frames of reference. The individual starts to adopt values and ideals from his circle of acquaintances, friends and society (Θερμός, *Ἡ Ἱερατική* 56). If he assimilates ideals from any of these milieus, then his own "ideal ego" will certainly be constituted by the relevant milieu /s (Θερμός, *Ἡ Ἱερατική* 56). According to Milrod

(56), the individual sets up the group leader as an idol, and his desired self-perception, which does not have deeply assimilated values, is replaced by the new idol.

Milrod explains the ideas of idol and pattern as follows: "Idols are personalities, whereas patterns are faceless and embody the 'ideal ego'" (56). As a consequence, "any young man who experiences a strong inclination toward the priesthood because of a priest-"idol" and not because of the priesthood will face, according to Thermos, a crisis of vocation at some stage" (*Ἡ Ἱερατική* 56).

Thermos states that the narcissist has two potential defences: "the individual 'ideal ego' and the collective one" (*Ἡ Ἱερατική* 56). The collective defence reduces not only feelings of guilt but also raises self-esteem (Θερμός, *Ἡ Ἱερατική* 56). Thermos shows, however, that there is a real probability of "conflict between the individual 'ideal ego' and the desired self-perception" (*Ἡ Ἱερατική* 56), when the latter is challenged by the group. For instance, a teenager may have already taken on certain religious ideals, whereas his environment wishes to inculcate in him a different set of ideals (Θερμός, *Ἡ Ἱερατική* 56). Thus, a conflict occurs: the teenager needs to hold to his own individual ideals and, simultaneously, needs the recognition of his friends to maintain his own inner balance. It is a serious conflict because it jeopardizes the individual's ideals and sometimes even causes their suppression and obliteration. Yet, as Blos ("The genealogy" 86) puts it: "the grandeur of human person is reflected exactly in such situations, wherein he prefers to die rather than to bury his ideals" (qtd. Θερμός, *Ἡ Ἱερατική* 57).

Thermos then prescinds from the human ideal formation and turns his attention to the issue of identification. He argues that identification performs a prominent function in the formation of the hieratic vocation (Θερμός, *Ἡ Ἱερατική* 59-60). What is of key importance in relation to the concept of identification is that it raises the issue of mature and immature identification and the significance of ecclesiastical patterns.

Drawing on a study by Rulla (*Depth* 308), Thermos discusses three ways in which identification can occur: 1) "the individual endeavours to be like the person referred to as a pattern; 2) the individual behaves according to the prescribed pattern, attempting not to disappoint the hopes of the person / pattern while seeking to satisfy his own feelings and needs; 3) the individual owns objectives and behavioural patterns which are approved by a particular group" (*Ἡ Ἱερατική* 60). Thermos (*Ἡ Ἱερατική* 61) attributes the second and the third case to immature identification. He argues that the individual's conscious and unconscious conformism to the "idol" or the group arises from his need to secure the group's / idol's approval and recognition. These two cases may be subsumed under the rubric of sham vocations which appear to be cultivated either by certain eminent ecclesiastics or particular parishes (Θερμός, *Ἡ Ἱερατική* 61). However, even the first case referred to above may lead to false identification and dictated choice (Θερμός, *Ἡ Ἱερατική* 61).

Kohut and Wolf (191) describe persons "thirsty for ideals" in the following way: they cannot appease their particular "thirst" for a role model "to which they get attached and whose ideals they earnestly assimilate; they justify their own existence inasmuch as they channel their entire love to this role model; the developing relationship may last or deteriorate and breakdown. In the event that a total breakdown in the relationship cannot be prevented such persons look for another role model" (qtd. Θερμός, *Ἡ Ἱερατική* 61). In terms of an agreed ecclesiastical agenda for the promotion of healthy vocations, Thermos (*Ἡ Ἱερατική* 61) voices criticism of the practice of attachment to various role models, a practice which is unfortunately tolerated and even encouraged by certain ecclesiastics. Rejection of the practice of attachment to idealized role models should be observed by every spiritual father because an "immature character may goad a spiritual father into undesirable behaviour" (Θερμός, *Ἡ Ἱερατική* 61).

Lorand (51-2) emphasizes that there are many cases whereby identification with ecclesiastics reflects psychological defence. This is a defence against the unsuccessful resolution of conflicts between the instinctive drive's demand for satisfaction and the coercion of a non-compromising "super ego" (Lorand 51-2). The failure to resolve these inner conflicts leads, in Lorand's opinion (51-2), to assimilating ecclesiastical role models and their values. As a result, the repression becomes consolidated and the "ego" gains relief. Thermos holds that the "conscious desire of such people is to realize the moral values and ideals inculcated by the ecclesiastics, while their unconscious drive arises from dependence on their mother" (*Ἡ Ἱερατική* 62). Externally, a person with such infantile dependencies seems to follow his vocation, whereas, internally, he leads a different life, catering to suppressed needs, and being subject to continuing inner conflict (Θερμός, *Ἡ Ἱερατική* 62).

Thermos follows Kohut's and Wolf's observations (187) that "when an individual lives under the suzerainty of idealized things for a long time, he slowly begins, at the level of his unconscious life, to perceive this suzerainty as a threat to the narcissist balance within his inner world; as a consequence, the lofty ambition to succeed in important objectives refrains from burning and the gratification through the experience of precedent successes becomes languid" (qtd. Θερμός, *Ἡ Ἱερατική* 62). The negative consequences of such identification "significantly increases the responsibility of priests", because sometimes, being in charge of ecclesiastical communities, they participate, however unintentionally, in such "romantic" acts whereby they at once embody the "ideal ego" of community and dominate it without being aware of this (Θερμός, *Ἡ Ἱερατική* 62-3). Thermos claims that "identification is often at work in such acts without the priest's really understanding it" (*Ἡ Ἱερατική* 63). When a priest cultivates an idealized self-image, he may, according to Thermos (*Ἡ Ἱερατική* 63), debar certain young people from following the hieratic vocation experienced by them in their innermost world.

The importance of Church patterns for the formation of hieratic vocation is another serious issue which should be addressed. Thermos takes advantage of Dittes's expertise (154) in his consideration of this issue. The latter asserts that there are "several deciding factors in the emergence of the aspiration to become priest: 1) parents and clergy; 2) familial attitude toward the Church; and 3) the individual's participation in diverse parochial activities" (qtd. Θερμός, *Ἡ Ἱερατική* 63-4).

Theoharis's study shows that a "virtuous and accomplished priest attracts to himself young people and, consequently, becomes a role model (an example for emulation)" (qtd. Θερμός, *Ἡ Ἱερατική* 64). In the same way, the personality of such a priest can be instrumental in replacing and doing away with an individual's previous negative identification (Θερμός, *Ἡ Ἱερατική* 64). Diverse church activities — such as "church youth movements, parish schools, and camps"— can, according to Strunk (433), also contribute to and have a beneficial effect on an emerging vocation to the priesthood (qtd. Θερμός, *Ἡ Ἱερατική* 64).

Cardwell and Hunt (127) have found a correlation between the frequent transfers of priests and a decline in the number of young people wishing to become priests. Apart from the continuing tenure of a priest in a parish, another critical factor in the process of the development of a sense of vocation is proper identity formation during adolescence. Relying on Houts and Marcia's research, Thermos (*Ἡ Ἱερατική* 69) discusses several points with regard to adolescent identity formation and the development of vocation: the maturity of the candidate's identity and "self-perception", and the impact these have on the candidate during the process of the formation of vocation. He lists several categories of identity and the criteria by which they are defined:

> **1.** '*Identity achievement*': The individual has undergone life crises which he has overcome and assimilated to his experience. Such an individual is considered psychologically mature and is able to endure sudden environmental changes, to meet binding commitments, and to forge enduring relationships with others. **2.** '*Foreclosure*': The individual has a vocation to the priesthood, but he has been unable to resolve personal crises. His choices match his parents' choices or those of other important persons, with no substantial difference. Characteristic of such persons is their lack of resourcefulness. Their entering an environment in which parental values are abandoned may precipitate a sense of great frustration. **3.** '*Moratorium*': The individual cannot relinquish inner conflict; neither his decisions nor acknowledgments manifest steadfastness. It might be that he abjures any notion of personal disorder. **4.** '*Diffusion*': The lack of resoluteness reigns supreme; such persons stand out through apparent disorganization of thought and blurred limits of 'ego'. (qtd. Θερμός, *Ἡ Ἱερατική* 69)

If a decision for the priesthood is not founded on a fully formed identity, but rather on an identity which has not grappled with and overcome life crises, then the decision is hasty, bad and fateful (Θερμός, *Ἡ Ἱερατική* 69).

"Self-perception" concerns the way the priest or the candidate for the priesthood regards himself and feels about his vision of his own self (Θερμός, *Ἡ Ἱερατική* 70-1). Thermos (*Ἡ Ἱερατική* 71) affirms that the words "regard" and "feel" include the realm of unconscious as well; in other words, the priest is not always conscious of certain aspects of his own self-perception (Θερμός, *Ἡ Ἱερατική* 71). Nevertheless, this lack of awareness "does not prevent his self-perception impacting heavily on his pastoral activity" (Θερμός, *Ἡ Ἱερατική* 71). Much as the idea that "the competencies of priests are determined not by their actual faculties but by their self-perception" seems to be odd, it is nevertheless an established fact that the individual as he actually is and his perception of himself, his self-perception, may have nothing in common (Θερμός, *Ἡ Ἱερατική* 71). According to Crawford (49), even in the direct dialogue between a priest and his parishioner, "six individuals are involved: 1) the real priest; 2) the priest's self-perception; 3) the parishioner's perception of the priest; 4) the real parishioner; 5) the parishioner's self-perception; 6) the priest's perception of the parishioner; thus apart from the two individuals, parishioner and priest, there are another imaginary four individuals present in the dialogue" (qtd. Θερμός, *Ἡ Ἱερατική* 71).

It is important to note that, just as the self-perception of the priest or sacerdotal candidate can be in error, so can the parishioner's perception of the priest be in error. An individual's imagination may reflect reality accurately or distort it (Θερμός, *Ἡ Ἱερατική* 71). More important, however, according to Thermos is that

> the problem here consists not in ascertaining whether these imaginative perceptions are good or bad but whether the priest knows them or, at least, wishes to gain knowledge of them. Significantly, the sacerdotal candidate's lack of awareness of the subjectivity of his own self-perceptions and of the way others perceive him may pose serious problems for his future pastoral duties. Worse still, this self-ignorance may constitute the very foundation of his conviction concerning hieratic vocation. (Θερμός, *Ἡ Ἱερατική* 71)

Basically, this "ignorance of self" arises from unreal ideals, immature identifications, and a hastily and pathologically formed identity (Θερμός, *Ἡ Ἱερατική* 72). Thermos refers to Walsh's criteria (38-9) for diagnosing whether or not the hieratic candidate is mature in his self-identity:

> The candidate must accept his present self. He too must accept his sexuality, and be able to direct it from the biological sphere to the one of the human relationship. He should perceive in an indulgent manner his exteriority, i.e. his corporeal constitution along with all its possible disadvantages. He should be content with all his talents, know his limitations, aspire to increase all his capabilities … and recognize his limits as well. (qtd. Θερμός, *Ἡ Ἱερατική* 72)

Moreover, O'Doherty (227) states: "The candidate should gain personal autonomy, see the positive and negative sides of his personality, learn to live alone, be able to respect the present reality, avoid fantasies and adolescent needs" (qtd. Θερμός, *Ἡ Ἱερατική* 72). Firm and respectable self-identity is, according to Coombs and Nemeck (119-20), all important to the sacerdotal vocation: "one has to possess himself ere he can grant this self to God" (qtd. Θερμός, *Ἡ Ἱερατική* 72).

Another major aspect in the formation of vocation is the issue of role. In coming to maturity, individuals choose to follow one or another occupation, generally for good. Each occupation sets out essential requirements that are called roles. "The role stands for the totality of guiding principles and special characteristics that regulate the acceptable behaviour of every individual in the group" (qtd. Θερμός, *Ἡ Ἱερατική* 74). Thermos (*Ἡ Ἱερατική* 78) claims that roles are assumed for the purposes of either living according to a self-sufficing ideal or sharing the set of values embodied in any given role. In the first case, it is the satisfaction of the needs of the individual that takes precedence. Adherence to and effectiveness in the chosen role depend on the eventual satisfaction of the individual's hidden needs (Θερμός, *Ἡ Ἱερατική* 78). In the second case, the individual chooses a particular role hoping to get close to the ideal behaviour pattern assigned to the role (Θερμός, *Ἡ Ἱερατική* 78). "The ideal behaviour pattern assists in realizing the values that supersede the role, values for the sake of which the role was ultimately assumed" (qtd. Θερμός, *Ἡ Ἱερατική* 78).

According to Thermos (*Ἡ Ἱερατική* 78-9), the maturity of vocation depends on the reciprocal relationship between role and values. In other words, in the event that the individual's choice of a sacerdotal role primarily satisfies his personal needs and only secondarily materializes the role, the vocation appears to be immature (Θερμός, *Ἡ Ἱερατική* 78). When this occurs, an enormous toll is exacted on the pastoral care and spiritual image of the priest, because, in extolling his role, the priest forges "relativistic morality", while, in emphasizing the values of the vocation, he contributes to "personal freedom" (Θερμός, *Ἡ Ἱερατική* 78-9). Thermos (*Ἡ Ἱερατική* 79) asserts that the priest can hold on to the values of the vocation to the extent that his self-perception is satisfied; in other words, "the compatibility of the desired self-perception with the values of vocation implies an increase in self-esteem and the advance of values assimilation" (Θερμός, *Ἡ Ἱερατική* 79). In the case of an undesired formation of vocation, certain candidates for the priesthood, and even priests, prove to have assimilated only particular values of vocation, values whose acquisition did not require great effort (Θερμός, *Ἡ Ἱερατική* 79).

Thermos seeks to underline that his critical remarks about the values inherent in a sense of vocation do not apply to the religious convictions of an individual, but to behavioural motives since, "with behaviour being a combination of many factors, values and motives flock together but rarely overlap" (Θερμός, *Ἡ*

Ἱερατική 79). He talks about two stages critical to the successful assimilation of the values inherent in a sense of vocation: 1) the pre-pubertal stage and 2) the adolescent and the adult stage (Θερμός, *Ἡ Ἱερατική* 79). During the first, pre-pubertal stage, the individual "conforms" to the group, while the second stage emerges after the individual has joined the group (Θερμός, *Ἡ Ἱερατική* 79). Both stages imply the enforced conformity of personal values to a collective pattern; the key difference between them, however, lies in the way in which each age achieves conformity to the ideals of the organization. The adolescent and adult possess more comprehension and awareness of personal responsibility toward the mission of the group than does the pre-pubescent. In making these psychological observations, Thermos (*Ἡ Ἱερατική* 79) assigns responsibility to the ecclesiastical authorities for the clergyman's assimilation of the values of pastoral vocation.

The last stage in the development of pastoral vocation is its full maturity. Thermos points to the inadmissibility of ignoring the conscious motives which urge the individual to choose the priesthood. Simultaneously, however, he calls his reader not to derogate the importance of unconscious motives in reaching a stage of maturity in pastoral vocation.

There are a great number of conscious motives. Thermos here underlines (1) "altruism"—the magnanimous concern for the good of others, (2) the desire "to remake the world" in order to improve it, and, finally, (3) "the sense of Divine vocation" (*Ἡ Ἱερατική* 83). He avers that the primary motivating factor determines the quality of the vocation. The force and influence of this factor is so great that it is able to control and even to change other attendant negative motives (Θερμός, *Ἡ Ἱερατική* 83-5). This psychological power draws on the "ego" of the individual.

Thermos's idea here is remarkable because it sharply differentiates itself from Freud's model of the human psyche, according to which the human "ego" has no trace of such autonomy. Relevantly, Ricœur (*De l'Interprétation* 474-5)[8] states:

> Freud himself formulated the task of psychoanalytic practice in the following words: "'Ego' should be wherever the 'id' has been already". Yet the task to become 'ego' finally is irreducible to the economy of desire within which this task is designed. As a matter of fact, this economy of desire presupposes that everything comes down to impulsive powers of 'id', which is the deep part of human psyche teeming with instincts and obeying the law of satisfaction alone. In such a case, a related question remains unanswered: how can mere prohibitions (which are comprehended as something proffered from outside) differentiate a valid desire, which could contribute to the transformation of 'id' into 'ego'? Thus, if psychoanalysis reveals "the archaic, infantile, instinctive, narcissistic and masochistic features of our pretended sublimity, one has to … surmise that,

8 Author's translation from the French

> contrary to the regressive stance taken by psychoanalysis as the foundation of its theory, there is a certain capability for progressing, which psychoanalytic practice is wont to use, while for psychoanalysis as theory this capability still remains the pending file. (qtd. Bendaly 1: 94)

The maturing of an individual's motives goes through several stages which match those of general physical growth (Θερμός, *Ή Ίερατική* 86). Godin (30) points out that these stages are "bound to evolving maturity in the sexual and emotional spheres" (qtd. Θερμός, *Ή Ίερατική* 87-9). Thermos (*Ή Ίερατική* 87-9) asserts that the path to maturity lies in the unique personal emotional experiences of egocentrism, idealization or openness toward other people and social objectives. Further, one comes to the formation of "a personal pattern for imitation", a pattern which egocentrism and idealization alike still inhabit. When the emulation of the role model becomes a fossilized invariant pattern of behavior, the individual uses this pattern as a mechanism to cope with all situations (Θερμός, *Ή Ίερατική* 87-9*)*. However, in emulating the role model or its values, the individual does not nullify his autonomy. Ultimately, the individual assumes a certain professional role that strengthens the sense of vocation. The path through all these stages may take varying amounts of time (Θερμός, *Ή Ίερατική* 87-9*)*.

In addition to the stages involved in the maturing of motives, the sense of vocation passes through several stages. Thermos (*Ή Ίερατική* 89) states that vocation is mature when it has "successfully passed through the following stages: 1) the choice of vocation; 2) devotion to the particular choice; 3) effectiveness in work; 4) comprehension of the work" (Θερμός, *Ή Ίερατική* 89). The successful negotiation of one stage does not predict successful negotiation of the next stage (Θερμός, *Ή Ίερατική* 89). Therefore each stage must be considered and addressed as a separate "problem" (Θερμός, *Ή Ίερατική* 89). Accordingly, one can speak about individuals who experienced failure during any of these stages. Thermos (*Ή Ίερατική* 89) classifies individuals who do not successfully negotiate the stages in the following way: 1) renegades—are those who followed the pastoral vocation but left it at a particular stage; 2) scroungers—are those who follow their vocation but are ineffective; 3) myrmidons—are those effective priests who, however, do not find meaning in their activity. From this, Thermos concludes that pastoral vocation represents a long-term phenomenon whereby the reaching of one stage further is unique and determinative for the ultimate accomplishment of this vocation (Θερμός, *Ή Ίερατική* 89).

Stavropoulos (23-4) describes the criteria for determining a candidate's maturity for the priesthood as follows: "It should be established that a candidate is able to live in a collective as one of its members, to react appropriately to circumstances and situations that change as quickly as lightning, and, finally, to comprehend persons unlike himself" (qtd.Θερμός, *Ή Ίερατική* 89).

Thus, taken in its psychological hypostasis, vocation to the priesthood develops according to the psychological development of the human personality. In other words, the peak of human psychological development is conterminous with the advent of a mature vocation.

2.2.2. Healthy and unhealthy condition of vocation

Having established the significance of ideals, group (coterie), identification, the psychological maturity of a candidates' identity, self-perception, the impact of self-perception on the formation of vocation, and the function of roles, values, maturity of conscious motives, and psychological stages of vocation for the emergence, development, and effectiveness / ineffectiveness of vocation, Thermos seeks to answer the following question: Does a healthy or an unhealthy condition of vocation necessitate moral and spiritual reflection, only, or does it oblige one to offer an alternative psychological interpretation? What would the psychological criteria be for such an interpretation?

In speaking of a healthy or an unhealthy sense of vocation, Thermos (*Ἡ Ἱερατική* 97-105) is in actual fact referring to an immature or mature sense of vocation. The identifying features of a mature vocation include the ability of the "ego" (in the psychoanalytic sense) to be in connection with the world and to adapt to changing environments. The importance of this ability for a successful ministry clearly demonstrates that a vocation to the priesthood falls within the scope of both the spiritual and psychological domains. Rulla indicates that "the mature (harmonic) vocation debars the notion of dissension (conflicts) within the deeper psychic life. At least, when such dissension is attendant, it is a superficial, conscious dissension. As to immature (disharmonic) vocations, they are distinguished by the unconsciousness of their dissension" (qtd. Θερμός, *Ἡ Ἱερατική* 105). Thermos (*Ἡ Ἱερατική* 105) indicates to the reader that dissensions in a mature vocation can be propitiated by accepting the favourable influence of the environment[9]. This suggests to the intellectually inconsistent person the solution for dissensions. Not so with the dissensions of the immature, disharmonic vocation. Such a vocation does not tolerate any salvage operation offered by the environment, and is finally only able to adopt partial, non-permanent solutions (Θερμός, *Ἡ Ἱερατική* 105-6). If environmental circumstances conspire against unconscious dissension, the dynamic of the dissensions erupts (Θερμός, *Ἡ Ἱερατική* 106-7). Assaulted by unconscious dissension, the individual combats this, according to Thermos (*Ἡ Ἱερατική* 105-7), not by way of reasoning, but by repressive measures and defence mechanisms. This strategy is driven by emotional needs and avoids getting to the root of the problem. This explains why such individuals never succeed in coping with their frustrations by learning from

9 Favourable influence of the environment is taken to mean the benevolent intervention of relatives, friends / cooperators by way of valuable advice.

previous experience (Θερμός, *Ἡ Ἱερατική* 105-7). In this context, Thermos (*Ἡ Ἱερατική* 105-7) considers that a vocation to the priesthood may be used to manage inner conflict. Being affected by the unconscious dissension, the individual may simulate the presence of a hieratic vocation in order to reduce the pressure caused by inner conflicts (Θερμός, *Ἡ Ἱερατική* 105-6). Thus, the hieratic vocation comes across as an unconscious desire for psychological relief which, once delivered, is more of a palliative that alleviates suffering but does not heal (Θερμός, *Ἡ Ἱερατική* 105-7). Such an approach ignores the problem's source, and, therefore, causes the conflict to lay deep roots. Thermos (*Ἡ Ἱερατική* 106) is convinced that the difference between a person with a healthy vocation and one with an unhealthy vocation lies in their motives. "The motive of a harmonic character is flexible, deeply conscious, and corresponds to his age, while the contrary one is inflexible, reserved, almost autonomous, and, to a considerable extent, unconscious. The origin of the latter can be traced back to the early stages of life and, practically, always carries something infantile" (Θερμός, *Ἡ Ἱερατική* 106). Thus, the detection of a healthy or an unhealthy state of vocation largely depends on inferences drawn from psychological knowledge and interpretation, since the quality of vocation is determined both by the potential of the human "ego" and the content of the unconscious.

The key criteria used in making an accurate psychological assessment of the development of vocation in a candidate, include the trinity "values – attitudes – needs", as well as role, narcissism, defence mechanisms and family dynamics.

Thermos states that there are three factors in the human psyche that decisively influence whether a vocation to the priesthood will be healthy or unhealthy: "values, attitudes and needs" (*Ἡ Ἱερατική* 111). The values are "the individual's firm abstract ideals, which are connected with behavioural manners and the ultimate aims of existence …" (Θερμός, *Ἡ Ἱερατική* 111). Attitudes are the predispositions by which the individual responds and is ready to react to external and internal stimuli (Θερμός, *Ἡ Ἱερατική* 111). Thus, attitudes consist of mentalities and behaviours and can be intellectual or emotional in nature (Θερμός, *Ἡ Ἱερατική* 111). The former (mentalities) constitute personal opinion and point of view, while the latter (behaviours) consist of spontaneous friendliness or unfriendliness (Θερμός, *Ἡ Ἱερατική* 111). Attitudes are important in that they can either consolidate a set of values or destroy them (Θερμός, *Ἡ Ἱερατική* 111). The individual usually "has a bulk of attitudes, and, simultaneously, seems to possess only a scanty number of values" (Θερμός, *Ἡ Ἱερατική* 111). With relation to needs, it is important to know that these are "inner inclinations common to all human persons, inclinations which are primordial sources of such motives as aggressiveness, success, obedience, attachment to one's self, autonomy, ascendency, curiosity, flexibility, recreation, orderliness, rivalry, sexual satisfaction, acceptance of certain people's caresses and delivery of the same to others ..." (Θερμός, *Ἡ Ἱερατική* 111). Thermos (*Ἡ Ἱερατική* 112) states that needs and values engender attitudes. Another way of viewing this is to consider attitudes as relevant to the "ego", needs to the "id", and values to the "superego"; the "ego" acts in everyday life, but is shaped by both the "id" and "superego" (Cazacu, Letter to the Author). Thereby, "the ideals may become a kind of mirror, a resort to discern in another person his latent, inner inhabiter" (Θερμός, *Ἡ Ἱερατική* 112). Relying on Rulla et al.'s case histories (*Entering* 75), Thermos (*Ἡ Ἱερατική* 112) declares that people serving as trusted counsellors and tutors to future priests must contribute to unmasking cases of disharmonic (immature) vocation in order to reduce the risk of permanent harm to the ecclesiastical organism. The detection of disharmony ought to be done by investigating an individual's attitudes and needs. The condition of these is the benchmark for the presence of harmony or disharmony. The gravity of the issue of disharmony, notwithstanding the ostensive preponderance of some moral values, demands that counter-measures be taken promptly (Θερμός, *Ἡ Ἱερατική* 112-4).

The transformation of attitudes into values poses a serious problem, because the individual thereby does not develop but stagnates, retaining an immature attitude toward the external environment (Θερμός, *Ἡ Ἱερατική* 113-4). When attitudes dominate and overshadow values, a personal commitment to serving others becomes a defensive measure (Θερμός, *Ἡ Ἱερατική* 113, 134). The pretended philanthropy is expected to satisfy the individual's personal need in that other people should feel that this individual is necessary for them (Θερμός, *Ἡ Ἱερατική* 113). In similar cases, an attitude is equated with a value, which precludes the acquisition of the real values which should have provided the underlying motive for the attitude (Θερμός, *Ἡ Ἱερατική* 113-4).

This tendency—"to overlay values with something else"—is an essential feature of our modern society (Θερμός, *Ἡ Ἱερατική* 114). Importantly, modern society has experienced the overall impoverishment of values and attitudes, while psychological needs have grown stronger (Θερμός, *Ἡ Ἱερατική* 114). This rampant demoralization will certainly not spare vocations to the priesthood, which in consequence may see a long-term decline culminating in a drastic reduction in the number of true and effective vocations.

Thermos (*Ἡ Ἱερατική* 114) is convinced that, if a candidate to the priesthood has psychological disharmony, any endeavour to assimilate the values of the vocation will eventually be reduced to a minimum, notwithstanding the sublimity of any values instilled by the candidate's ecclesiastical mentors; he too is convinced that an inability to assimilate the values of vocation takes place in particular candidates for the priesthood when they are compelled to embody such values independently in their life. This is a fact ecclesiastical mentors should be aware of (Θερμός, *Ἡ Ἱερατική* 114). The effective assimilation of values occurs only if the individual's attitudes arise from a Christian system of values and are independent of any external source of encouragement (Θερμός, *Ἡ Ἱερατική* 114). "It is only the person devoid of any (unconscious) disharmony that is certainly capable of changing himself and acquiring evermore new valuable experience from life" (Θερμός, *Ἡ Ἱερατική* 114).

A healthy or an unhealthy state of vocation also depends on an individual's attitude toward his own role, since, according to Thermos (*Ἡ Ἱερατική* 115-20), the experience of any motive as a source of inspiration emanates from cognition of role and cognition of its function; most importantly, no work can be carried out without an attached role (Θερμός, *Ἡ Ἱερατική* 115-20). However, priests practising a role, and candidates imagining themselves within it, may face the problem whereby the self-sufficiency of role constitutes an obstacle to the priest's and the candidate's true realization of vocational values. Such an obstacle may lead to unavoidable delays in the journey toward personal maturity and effective work (Θερμός, *Ἡ Ἱερατική* 115-20).

Thermos (*Ἡ Ἱερατική* 119-20) maintains that there is a danger that the priest will cleave to his role and that such rigid adherence may have an alienating impact on his personality. Thermos states that the immature person is usually tempted to try to find himself within the role, a statement which agrees with the following remarks of the American psychoanalyst Becker (65-7):

> Teenagers endeavor to find their personal identity by experimenting with roles. Yet, at a greater distance in time they abandon all imitations. In such instances they become able to assimilate properly the role, i.e. not as a kind of own self-perception, but as a part of inner person or of self … Extreme identification with the hieratic role makes a kind of clergyman who is inflexible and psychologically unadapted, and deprived of a mature sense of self. The ordination of such a person may make the ministry insipid, and lead him to psychological exhaustion and disappointment. (qtd. Θερμός, *Ἡ Ἱερατική* 129-30)

Thermos (*Ἡ Ἱερατική* 129-30) holds that weak self-perception leads to extreme identification with a role. The basic criterion to detect whether such identification is present is a display of self-aggrandizement which tolerates no questions (Θερμός, *Ἡ Ἱερατική* 129-30).

The experience of disharmony in vocation makes an individual seek satisfaction in the role rather than in faithfulness to a set of values. The satisfaction derived from faithfulness to one's values requires the hard, demanding work of personal change (thought + behaviour), whereas the satisfaction derived from the practice of a role—only conformism (behaviour) (Θερμός, *Ἡ Ἱερατική* 130-6).

Thermos (*Ἡ Ἱερατική*) explicitly warns against expecting psychological maturity and assimilation of the values of vocation from the candidate for the priesthood after his ordination as priest. For the full realization of the role, one must possess the ability to assimilate the values and attitudes associated with the role. The lack of awareness of this truth causes some ecclesiastics to experience unhealthy symptoms of frustration and failure (Θερμός, *Ἡ Ἱερατική* 130-1).

Granting any person premature acknowledgment as a role model within the Church may give ammunition to those looking to cause ecclesiastical upheaval.

The way a candidate for the priesthood apprehends the hieratic role may also have negative repercussions. Thermos (*Ἡ Ἱερατική* 130-42) considers that the effective or problematic performance of the role is inversely proportional to the candidate's knowledge of that particular role; in other words, if the candidate for the priesthood is not really conscious of all the aspects of the role, this lack of awareness will precipitate a crisis in his vocation at some point. The prevention of a professional crisis for an inexperienced priest is also the duty of the Church authorities. The choice of any profession places the individual both in front of and above the parapet of accountability since the choice between multiple occupations is guided *not only* by real knowledge of all aspects of a role or by an individual's profound self-knowledge and his knowledge of his suitability for a given occupation, *but* also by the candidate's emotional stance and empathy with a certain professional role (Θερμός, *Ἡ Ἱερατική* 118-31). The presence of objective and subjective constituents in the choice of a profession increases the scope for a subsequent crisis, because the discovery of the true, as opposed to the imaginary and the expected, content of the professional role usually compels withdrawal or perseverance. Both effects have very different implications for the Church: while withdrawal can impair pastoral care at the quantitative level, perseverance tainted by conformism can result in damage—at the qualitative level.

The maturity of vocation depends to a significant degree on the maturity of the narcissism (self-love) in the candidate for the priesthood. Maturity of narcissism is bound to the concepts of "ideal ego" and "idealized ego" (Θερμός, *Ἡ Ἱερατική* 130-1). The "ideal ego" is, according to Thermos (*Ἡ Ἱερατική* 131), a natural phenomenon that maintains inner equilibrium and assists in developing the person, while the "idealized ego" is a pathological aberration. The presence of an "idealized ego" within an individual is manifest in the appearance of unconscious fantasies of power, glory and recognition (Θερμός, *Ἡ Ἱερατική*). Thermos (*Ἡ Ἱερατική* 130-2) insists that the reader should not confound these unconscious fantasies of personal grandeur with "egoism", because the latter is found in a particular behaviour pattern while "idealized ego" does not necessarily manifest itself in behaviour.

These two concepts—"ideal ego" and "idealized ego"—have, however, several similarities (Θερμός, *Ἡ Ἱερατική* 124-31). Firstly, they are similar in name; secondly, they have idealization in common (Θερμός, *Ἡ Ἱερατική* 131). Idealization within the "idealized ego" pertains to the individual's self alone, while, in the "ideal ego", it seeks to localize the non-personal ideal without, not within, the individual. The emergence of the "idealized ego" is precipitated, in Thermos's opinion (*Ἡ Ἱερατική* 131), by traumas experienced during a child's psychological development. However, it is misleading to claim that trauma is identical with certain traumatic incidents in the individual history of a person

(Θερμός, *Η Ἱερατική* 124-31). Thermos (*Η Ἱερατική* 124-31) believes that trauma may occur in circumstances in which there is a lack of an emotionally positive atmosphere within the familial / social environment (this applies especially to kindred). An essential component underlying the various pathological manifestations of the narcissistic searching for missing self-esteem is the lack of an appropriate emotional atmosphere between parents and their children (Θερμός, *Η Ἱερατική* 124-31). This causes children to seek an alternative in the illusory products of the unconscious life.

Thermos (*Η Ἱερατική* 131-2) insists that people possessed by delusions of grandeur must be dissuaded from pursuing the priesthood, *or else* there is a strong probability that their hieratic vocation will become the embodiment of an exalted, imagined narcissistic self and of a certain omnipotence or even of Messianic vocation, *instead of* being a true vocation grounded in authentic ideals.

Thermos claims that "the more the individual's imagined self-perception differs from his own true inner state, the more haughtiness, avidity and touchiness will increase within him" (*Η Ἱερατική* 131). But this claim should not lead to biased perceptions. The point is that this haughtiness and avidity may not necessarily be manifested in the person's patterns of behaviour, because the person can follow the laws of haughtiness and avidity in his *inner* attitude toward the world (Θερμός, *Η Ἱερατική* 131).

Sometimes, the hieratic vocation may function as a kind of defence mechanism against overpowering biological urges. Thermos (*Η Ἱερατική* 132-3) says that the sense of vocation often emerges during adolescence and may be motivated by defences against biological urges and hostile feelings, rather than by a true sense of vocation. It is well known that, during adolescence, sexual urges and aggressiveness run high (Θερμός, *Η Ἱερατική* 132-3). These emotions sweep over the teenager's psyche and upset him. He fears either the punishment of these particular emotions or psychological implosion on account of the "threatening factors" (Θερμός, *Η Ἱερατική* 132-3). These two kinds of anxiety cause a spontaneous reaction within the teenager's "ego", whereby he repairs to a behaviour pattern which reduces the inward stress and suppresses the sense of threat (Θερμός, *Η Ἱερατική* 132-3). It is interesting that the asceticism and intellectualization of an adolescent may also show the symptoms of such behaviour. The asceticism of an adolescent can be attributed to the suppression different from ordinary repression of the biological urges in order to attain a certain emancipation of body (Θερμός, *Η Ἱερατική* 134-5). The possible solution to adolescent asceticism is twofold: 1) the gradual maturing of the young person, which results in the adoption of a fully cognizant asceticism; 2) the lifting of all previous prohibitions (Θερμός, *Η Ἱερατική* 134-5). In favouring the latter solution, the teenager or the young man will usually give himself over to every sort of shamelessness. What are the repercussions for the ecclesiastical community, if the second is chosen by particular clergy? Recent scandals in Western Christendom suggest only a negative outcome. In this context, Thermos (*Ἡ Ἱερατική* 134-135) articulates the idea that "ambition and avarice or prosperity that appear during a period of life in a priest are often the ominous harbinger of a sham (defensive) vocation which regrettably has never been sensed. It is needless to say how important it is to discern opportunely such kinds of vocations" (Θερμός, *Ἡ Ἱερατική* 135).

The intellectualization adopted by the adolescent is tantamount to steadfastly inhabiting his own thoughts, opinions and quests. In the event that the intellectualization is grossly disproportionate to the teenager's level of development and age, it is completely justified to wonder along with Thermos whether 'this intellectualization does not serve as a kind of defensive measure' (*Ἡ Ἱερατική* 136-7). Thermos (*Ἡ Ἱερατική* 137) points out that such a defensive measure may easily constitute the principal source of failure to distinguish between natural attributes of character and virtues. Accordingly, immaturity may appear as humbleness, ordinary emotionality as love, conformism as obedience, adolescent asceticism as abstinence (Θερμός, *Ἡ Ἱερατική* 134-42). In encountering such cases, an ordinary priest who is not thoroughly familiar with adolescent intellectualization and its products could envision such attributes as signs of a true and mature vocation (Θερμός, *Ἡ Ἱερατική* 134-42). What can the Church do to resolve this problem? Thermos (*Ἡ Ἱερατική* 137) believes that the best way to "forestall the pathological phenomenon of a vocation resolving into a certain mechanism of defence is to create healthy families both at home and within the Church (ecclesiastical family); an individual can learn his inner truth and live with dependence on God only within an environment that he accepts" (Θερμός, *Ἡ Ἱερατική* 137).

The entire complex dynamics of family life play an important role in the formation of vocation. Modern research suggests that there is a certain strong relationship between the frequency of the emergence of hieratic vocation and birth order (Θερμός, *Ἡ Ἱερατική* 174-6). Drawing on research carried out by Cardwell ("Persistence") and Godin (*The Psychology*), Thermos claims that the first child most frequently experiences a sense of hieratic vocation[10] (*Ἡ Ἱερατική* 176). He goes on to state that this phenomenon could be explained by "a clearer dominance of 'super ego'[11] within the psyche of first-borns" (*Ἡ Ἱερατική* 177).

---

10 Cp. (Ex 13.2)

11 In another place Thermos suggests an interesting interpretation for the mechanism of "super ego". He claims that there is a difference between the moral consciousness and "super ego"; the latter aims at chiefly maintaining self-esteem (natural narcissism) and at times even "idealized ego", when the individual comes into contact with unpleasant feelings (*Ἡ Ιερατική* 165). Therefore, "super ego" does not always lead to repentance, but it mobilizes the defence mechanisms of the "ego": the repression, sublimation, etc. This theologian argues that this issue concerns phenomena common to all mankind (Θερμος, *Ἡ Ιερατική* 165). Only perfect persons possess "healthy" moral consciousness able "to resist" the clash with unpleasant feelings (Θερμος, *Ἡ Ιερατική* 165).

For this is the reason why the first-born manifests unconscious "identification" and "conformism" to a higher extent than do their younger brothers. But then again, the true "adoption" of values should never be excluded among first-borns (Θερμός, *Ἡ Ἱερατική* 177).

The active involvement of parents in the religious life of the Church has a great impact on the rapid emergence of a hieratic vocation. Cardwell ("Persistence" 125-7) says that the religiosity of the mother has enormous importance for vocation to the priesthood; on the other hand, the religiosity of the father impedes the development of the vocation, whereas his indifference assists it (Θερμός, *Ἡ Ἱερατική* 178, 180-2, 183-8). In the *formation of vocation*, maternal religiosity reigns supreme but in a way which sometimes makes the paternal role in *this* appear inconspicuous (Θερμός, *Ἡ Ἱερατική* 180-2, 183-8). In such situations, it is increasingly probable that the mechanisms of identification with the mother will engulf the psyche of the teenager (Θερμός, *Ἡ Ἱερατική* 183-8). Identifying himself with the mother, he may appear to be serving the narcissistic expectations of his mother (Θερμός, *Ἡ Ἱερατική* 183-8). A close relationship between the teenager and his mother, which excludes others, and excessive interference in her son's private life by a mother, can be strong indicators for arrested personality formation in the son (Θερμός, *Ἡ Ἱερατική* 187). It is important to remark that the unconscious dominance of the mother within the inner world of the son produces an unenlightened conformism and a mentality of servile subordination to exterior institutions; a conformism and subordination which, in the case of some priests, may mean restricting their capacity for initiative and creativity, very necessary attributes during times of massive social upheaval (Θερμός, *Ἡ Ἱερατική* 187).

The development of a stable relationship between parents is equally important for the emergence of a healthy vocation to the priesthood. Troubled relationships between parents may precipitate a false sense of vocation; often the eldest child, a son, will be engaged in salvaging the family he lives in (Θερμός, *Ἡ Ἱερατική* 179-80). This is why Thermos (*Ἡ Ἱερατική* 179-80) sees common features between the phenomenon of the "saving" priest and the young person who has transformed his mission in the broken family into a personal vocation to the priesthood.

Thus, Thermos (*Ἡ Ἱερατική* 187) claims that the human component of hieratic vocation is influenced by three factors: "ideal ego", "mechanisms of identification", and "formation of identity". Whether an individual develops a healthy or an unhealthy sense of vocation is determined by the way in which he traverses and negotiates the path of psychological formation. In this respect, a key factor is the influence of environment. By exploring the path of psychological formation, one comes to the understanding that it is the interrelation between values, attitudes and needs that represents the real nexus of a healthy or an unhealthy vocation.

2.3. The solution to the pastoral vocation problem

Seeking to provide a solution to the pastoral vocation problem, Thermos embarks upon a discussion of the effective ways of altering, transforming and improving negative psychological factors linked to a sense of vocation.

Thermos maintains that a priest's effective engagement in pastoral care is directly correlated with "his mental harmony" (Θερμός, *Ἡ Ἱερατική* 224), and attributes the stability of this mental harmony to the condition of the individual's attitudes and needs, because "the decision to become a priest is founded on the individual's values, whereas his stay in the vocation as well as the effectiveness of his pastoral care depend on the existence and state of disharmony, i.e. on the priest's attitudes and needs" (Θερμός, *Ἡ Ἱερατική* 224). Elsewhere, Thermos (Cazacu, Letter to the author) says that inconsistencies (disharmony) are always intra-psychic and therefore very difficult to handle, because in most cases they are unconscious and consequently more pathogenic than are external conflicts (dilemmas).

2.3.1. Self-knowledge and the mobilization of psychological and spiritual factors

The existence of negative psychological factors in the emergence and development of hieratic vocation does not exclude the possibility of altering them. According to Thermos (*Ἡ Ἱερατική* 225), there are three means for positively avoiding any probable pathology playing a role in hieratic vocation: self-knowledge, the mobilization of psychological factors that can transform the hieratic vocation, and, correspondingly, the mobilization of appropriate spiritual factors.

Thermos lays stress on the importance of self-knowledge, because "the self of the priest remains the chief tool of pastoral care and therefore he should possess deepening self-knowledge, in order to make his ministry increasingly effective" (Θερμός, *Ἡ Ἱερατική* 158, 164, 245-52, 258, 262-63). Thermos (*Ἡ Ἱερατική* 245-52, 258, 262-63) believes that the capability to judge other people without condemnation, to be indulgent of human weakness, and to partake in other people's lives only for their own sake and not because of their social status constitutes the paradigm of an effective pastor. But how can one improve these capabilities? Thermos answers: "When the clergyman sincerely scrutinizes himself, his message will meet with a very warm response. People feel that he understands them, and therefore they are ready to confide in him" (Θερμός, *Ἡ Ἱερατική* 245-6). Thermos (*Ἡ Ἱερατική* 245-6) believes that self-knowledge is practically impossible without the assistance of a counsellor and a transformed spiritual life. The pastor can understand his flock only if he scrutinizes himself for sins in the act of his own confession (Θερμός, *Ἡ Ἱερατική*).

The pastor ought to find various ways of self-examination. The aims he sets at the beginning of his pastoral activity, however experienced he might be at that time, should be reconsidered and even changed over time (Θερμός, *Ἡ Ἱερατική* 240-8). Thermos refers to the ideas expressed by different thinkers saying that

> the pastor should be aware of all hidden motives that drive him, otherwise all his endeavours may prove useless, despite his devotion to the great cause … He ought also to be aware of his own defence mechanisms and unconscious inner conflicts … At times, he should stop, sit down and question himself. Importantly, many of the pastor's interpersonal relations, the confusion within various situations during his engagement with people, and many other difficulties relating to his duties underscore the importance of self-examination as a kind of subtle and necessary spiritual component for he who has been ordained a priest. The questions the priest should ask himself are: Who am I? Why do I act or did I act this way or another in a certain situation? Why do certain activities satisfy me or, to the contrary, distress me? Why do I sympathize or not sympathize with a particular person? And many other similar questions arise that must aid the priest in clarifying his inner world. All the related questions have the mission of keeping the priest in a condition of psychological and spiritual alertness, of preventing mistakes and of protecting him against serious dangers. (qtd. Θερμός, *Ἡ Ἱερατική* 247-8)

It is obvious that emotions and behaviour are the channels through which the priest is called on to attain the core of his inward life.

Thermos (*Ἡ Ἱερατική* 249-50) notes that self-knowledge is a difficult task, because there are many obstacles which appear on the path along with the decision to strive toward self-knowledge. He argues that priests are wont to confound psychological and spiritual phenomena (Θερμός, *Ἡ Ἱερατική* 250). Thermos (*Ἡ Ἱερατική* 250-1) means here that priests sometimes substitute theological rationalizations for the emotional problems which actually underlie inward conflict. According to Thermos (*Ἡ Ἱερατική* 250-1), theological conceptions and "spiritual" terminology[12] may become a kind of mechanism to evade the pain of introspection. Using such terminology all too often is a lucid signal of alienation, as the conceptions and words with imminent power to save turn into shackles and existential lies (Θερμός, *Ἡ Ἱερατική* 251). Another obstacle to personal self-knowledge may be the defence mechanisms which are usually mobilized if the narcissism of 'ego' is threatened with danger (Θερμός, *Ἡ Ἱερατική* 251). He considers that the priest and the flock often resort to the mechanisms of projection and *reaction formation*, by which blame is put on others (Church authorities, laymen, society, and state); such behaviour is used to help the individual to

12 There are several testimonies from the modern Orthodox theologians as well as Church Fathers that could support Thermos's standpoint. Kornarakis, for instance, says that a reaction caused by complex or a latent aggressiveness can express itself through the psychological 'dress' of virtue (Εγχειρίδιον (a) 14). Mark the Ascetic too states that there is room for situations in which "a particular person seems externally to fulfill a commandment of the Lord, whereas he really is acting out of passion. Thus, he ruins a virtuous deed by means of his sly thoughts" (Εγχειρίδιον (a) 38).

avoid the radical demands of self-knowledge (Θερμός, *Ἡ Ἱερατική* 251). The inner world adjusts the surroundings to itself in order to make these surroundings less unpleasant (Θερμός, *Ἡ Ἱερατική* 251). Sometimes, it seems difficult to check whether the quality of the candidate's hieratic vocation is valid, because the psychological endeavours undertaken to clarify this issue cause various reactions: "some people become panic-stricken, others categorically refuse to cooperate, while others start to argue that such checking is useless" (Θερμός, *Ἡ Ἱερατική* 251). Yet, many of those who agree to cooperate underscore the immutability of their initial choice; as a result, they repair only to the "technical" means that are expected to enable them to "attain their unattainable ideal" (Θερμός, *Ἡ Ἱερατική* 248-51). Thermos believes that, in such cases, "the inner organization remains inaccessible and there is only a transfer of symptoms … As if the face-to-face discussion about their *vocation* will destroy *it*" (Θερμός, *Ἡ Ἱερατική* 251).

The gradual transformation of pastoral vocation may be achieved by mobilizing certain psychological factors. Thermos (*Ἡ Ἱερατική* 254) considers that immaturity may co-exist with a true vocation and a precocious decision to become a priest does not exclude both the presence of a vocation and the possibility of maturing. There is always, according to Thermos (*Ἡ Ἱερατική* 254), a touch of immaturity and even pathology within a vocation. There is no vocation devoid of imperfection (Θερμός, *Ἡ Ἱερατική* 254). Yet, the crucial question to answer here is how the individual should face immaturity (Θερμός, *Ἡ Ἱερατική* 254). Rulla et al. (*Entering* 259) assert that "the psychological laws of vocation are formed by the potential of the individual's feelings … The individual himself does not bear responsibility for this potential, but for his attitude toward it, i.e., whether he tries to change it or not" (qtd. Θερμός, *Ἡ Ἱερατική* 254).

Thermos (*Ἡ Ἱερατική* 254) considers that within the psyche there are psychological and spiritual powers which are able to effect change in the character of a vocation from the pathological to the healthy. These powers are embodied in ideals and values (Θερμός, *Ἡ Ἱερατική* 254). "The awakening of these powers means the initiation of personal transformation in the candidate or the clergyman" (Θερμός, *Ἡ Ἱερατική* 254). Petroutsou (13-15) claims that "the transformation of pastoral vocation may be effected, if disease is apprehended, and the confusion between true and sham values, neurosis and self-abnegation, inferiority complexes and Christian humbleness is cleared up" (qtd. Θερμός, *Ἡ Ἱερατική* 255). Beside the intensive spiritual life and divine grace, Petroutsou (11-15) also suggests the following means to reach this "transformation": one has "to divest himself of the fetters of unconscious[13], to maintain self-control and goodwill, to

13 "The psychotherapist establishes the content of an unconscious sphere of human psyche, using four methods: method of associations, symptom analysis, anamnesis analysis and analysis of the unconscious. The method of associations reveals the chief complexes of patient. These complexes are revealed by the psychotherapist during the experience of as-

define the goal toward which one should work, to be in contact with people who are apt to give this release" (qtd. Θερμός, *Ἡ Ἱερατική* 255).

The foregoing ideas warrant the observation that many candidates or clergymen can be aware, partially aware or sometimes even unaware of an urgent desire for self-change (Θερμός, *Ἡ Ἱερατική* 255). Yet, what psychological road is necessary in order to meet or achieve this urgent desire? Thermos (*Ἡ Ἱερατική* 255) considers that this road quite often runs through the immense suffering inflicted by a crisis of vocation or, rather, the beginning of this road is based on this suffering. He says: "The process of healing is usually possible only if the conflicts are not deeply unconscious. Most importantly, this process is of a long duration, and therefore a clergyman is compelled to waste a lot of power, which correspondingly decreases the effectiveness of his ministry" (Θερμός, *Ἡ Ἱερατική* 255).

Thermos (*Ἡ Ἱερατική* 256) expresses the opinion that, if there are not deep unconscious conflicts within a candidate or clergyman, the proper way for a clergyman to heal his vocation is to cultivate the values of vocation by means of role. However, the "time spent by a person in any role does not guarantee one's

---

sociation, when the complexes become apparent as reactions. The symptom analysis consists in the psychotherapist's hypnotic pressure on the patient. A specialist expects that all his questions should reveal whatever reminiscences are hidden within the patient's unconscious. The anamnesis method consists of reproducing the development of neurosis by remembering it. A particular patient gives an account of all the facts connected with the disease to the psychotherapist. An experienced specialist resorts to the assistance of leading questions, which can make a point fairly more clear. This method has a therapeutic value, since a patient begins to understand the main reasons for his disorder as well as its motivating forces. Then he is able to see himself in a new way and to appreciate the events of his life. The last method – analysis of the unconscious – is essentially different from the previous others. This method does not take into consideration the conscious sphere of the patient's psyche. It is used, when the information brought by the consciousness is impoverished or proves to be insufficient for understanding the reasons for the patient's conflicts. The essence of this method is closely connected with dreams. Dreams contain inside themselves the totality of ideas that reflect, to a greater or lesser extent, real events from a particular person's life, i.e., Freud considered that the dreams are integral parts of human life" (Μπαλογιάννης 111). "Among other ideas, there is, according to S. Freud, one idea that stays apart and seems to be in contradiction to others; this idea expresses as a rule the patient's certain desire, which cannot be realized in the real life. Therefore, this desire finds asylum in the world of dreams and becomes its power kernel. Thus, the dreams are a particular place where the suppressed desires are fulfilled. These desires become apparent in dreams, since the mechanisms of defence are disconnected during sleep. When a man sleeps, paramount ideas are remade and regrouped with other secondary ideas. Therefore, the symbolic character of the paramount ideas gains strength. Thus, the analysis and interpretation of dreams lead to investigation of the unconscious" (Κορναράκη, *Το Πρόβλημα* 11-2). Thermos believes that "the purification of the unconscious is conterminous with the course toward the sanctity and passes obligatorily through the vigilance" (Θερμος, *Ομοιοπαθείς* 39).

development which may be interpreted as a flowering of vocational values" (Θερμός, *Η Ἱερατική* 256). Concerning this issue, it is "not time but the way in which one makes use of role that counts; if this is used in a passive way, no progress is made" (Θερμός, *Η Ἱερατική* 256). Thermos substantiates his view with reference to Ziller (174) who states that

> a change of values, attitudes, behaviours and roles should be in line with a change in self-concept. The foregoing change is the highest stage in an individual's personal change. Any modification in other psychological components becomes mercurial without a change in self-concept; and the person gravitates toward a return to his initial inner state. (qtd. Θερμός, *Η Ἱερατική* 256-7)

Commenting on the statement above, Thermos says that, "if there is no change in the way a candidate or clergyman sees his current condition, and if he does not seek to transform this condition to how it should be (something called '*μετάνοια*'—repentance in terms of Christian ascetic life), any ostensive change remains superficial and volatile" (Θερμός, *Η Ἱερατική* 257).

Speaking of the content of the transformative experience that every candidate or clergyman seeking personal change should undergo, McAllister says: "The aim of introspection (self-knowledge) is to make a person feel that he is really becoming more and more master and "owner" of his feelings and decisions" (qtd. Θερμός, *Η Ἱερατική* 258).

The most significant factor in this context concerning the improvement of character and the state of vocation is the suggestion that psychological knowledge and practice could assist. Thermos, along with several non-Orthodox scholars such as Polock, Kennedy, Rulla et al., considers that psychological assistance has a double mission: diagnosis and healing (*Η Ἱερατική* 260-6). The specialist has to establish the full value and essential components of the candidate's faith in God as well as the way this faith has been shaped; then, he should foresee the development of this faith, being guided by the calculations with respect to its future openness to or, contrariwise, exclusiveness in, interpersonal relationships, since interpersonal relationships are part and parcel of pastoral activity (Θερμός, *Η Ἱερατική* 262-5). As a whole, psychological assistance is considered by Thermos (*Η Ἱερατική* 262-5) to be a tool which should assist the Church authorities in selecting capable candidates, attracting new ones, and preventing any ineffectiveness that is the result of the blocking of inner potential. Thermos (*Η Ἱερατική* 262-5) claims that psychologists and psychiatrists, whether they are clergymen or laymen, are the bearers of psychological assistance. This assistance may be offered, in response to a candidate's expressed inner need and personal request, and in special centres founded by Church authorities. The methods of psychological assistance consist in individual interviews, questionnaires, psychological testing and psychotherapy (Θερμός, *Η Ἱερατική* 263-5).

Furthermore, Thermos (*Ἡ Ἱερατική* 265-6) turns to the problem of personal information revealed by candidates to the specialist. Self-evidently, this information may be explosive and any mistake made in dealing with it would certainly cause irreversible damage to both candidate and Church (Θερμός, *Ἡ Ἱερατική* 266). Serious damage may occur when a specialist (without a thorough examination) hurriedly informs the ecclesiastical authorities of a candidate's psychological unsuitability for the hieratic ministry on the basis of insufficiently proved data (Θερμός, *Ἡ Ἱερατική* 266). Great damage to the Church may also occur when a specialist lopsidedly considers a candidate's psychological state to be healthy and does not accurately convey to the ecclesiastical mentors (the administrators of seminaries, eparchial bishops) why it could be necessary to dissuade a particular candidate from ordination (Θερμός, *Ἡ Ἱερατική* 266). Thermos (*Ἡ Ἱερατική* 266) states that such problems must be solved according to three principles: 1) the priesthood is not each individual's automatic right; the possibility that an inadequate person may seek to enter the pastoral ministry invalidates the supremacy of the principle of privacy in this case; 2) the right to refrain from releasing confidential information is founded on a demand for privacy common to all humans, and therefore each person is free to divulge or not divulge personal information; 3) the greatness of the ministry and the corporate interest of God's folk should be regarded as of paramount importance. Commenting on the combination of these principles, Thermos stresses that the psychiatrist or psychotherapist-in-charge should convey to the ecclesiastical authorities only the information that is absolutely necessary for them to accomplish their mission (preparation of healthy and effective priests) (Θερμός, *Ἡ Ἱερατική* 266).

It is therefore obvious that the principle of medical confidentiality is subject to conflicting demands. Thermos is aware of the considerable confusion surrounding the issue of privacy. Thus, he resorts to the experience of Western psychologists who offer a variety of opinions. The foregoing reflections do not offer a complete solution but rather point to the complexities which call for pastoral discernment in each particular case.

The chief reason for utilizing psychological assistance, according to Thermos (*Ἡ Ἱερατική* 269), is to reveal in a timely fashion psychopathological phenomena present in candidates for the priesthood. In achieving this, clinical diagnoses should be made by means of psychiatry or by means of psychodynamic diagnoses of personality which rely on psychological theories. Thermos shares the opinion of several non-Orthodox scholars that "the religious life may also attract a certain number of people with mental disorders" (Θερμός, *Ἡ Ἱερατική* 269). Research by non-Orthodox researchers has revealed symptoms of pathology among candidates for the priesthood; such pathology could include persons with schizoid and psychopathic disturbances as well as individuals prone to homosexuality, psychosomatic disorders, depression and even alcoholism (Θερμός, *Ἡ Ἱερατική* 269). Thermos depicts several psychopathological manifestations that certainly signal the need for psychological assistance: 1) "the presence of quick temper because of which the person in question has no friends; 2) the feeling of living more in the past than in the present, 3) complaints about loneliness and low spirits; 4) attitudes of dependency; 5) systematic absence from current situations and failures; 6) shame and proclivity for seclusion; 7) difficulty or fear in expressing one's self; 8) fear of and long-term opposition to the authorities; 9) terror; 10) tense sexual manifestations that cannot be publicly expressed" (*Ἱερατική* 270-1).

Psychodynamic diagnoses of personality are made with specific psychological tests. Personality tests differ from intelligence tests (Θερμός, *Ἡ Ἱερατική* 273-4). Personality tests measure and analyze the psychological organization of the individual; there are two kinds of personality test: 1) of the conscious, and 2) of the unconscious sphere of the human psyche (Θερμός, *Ἡ Ἱερατική* 274). The tests of the conscious sphere consist in a number of questionnaires such as the Edwards Personal Preference Schedule (EPPS) and the Minnesota Multiphasic Personality Inventory (MMPI) (Θερμός, *Ἡ Ἱερατική* 274). The EPPS does not measure pathology, but normal psychological data (Θερμός, *Ἡ Ἱερατική* 274). It evaluates motives by means of questions that request a respondent to choose between two occupations. The EPPS determines fifteen features of human character (Θερμός, *Ἡ Ἱερατική* 274). Thermos (*Ἡ Ἱερατική* 274) argues that using this questionnaire in the Orthodox seminaries has long been necessary.

The Minnesota Multiphasic Personality Inventory test is considered by psychologists to be less effective than the EPPS, due to difficulties in interpreting its results (Θερμός, *Ἡ Ἱερατική* 274). Generally speaking, Thermos considers these two questionnaires to be useful. He says: "The usefulness of these psychological tests lies not in the possibility of choosing or rejecting candidates, but in their potential for providing the candidates with valuable advice, expert guidance and comprehensive education" (Θερμός, *Ἡ Ἱερατική* 274). Yet, the questionnaires directed to investigate the candidate's conscious sphere are powerless to meet the fundamental need to unmask any pathology within him (Θερμός, *Ἡ Ἱερατική* 274). The insufficiency of these questionnaires has led psychologists to use so-called projective tests. In such tests, the candidate expounds his autobiography, describes his characteristics, undergoes a clinical interview; and, though these tests are able, it seems, to reveal the main conflicts and defence mechanisms of the unconscious, they are, according to Thermos (*Ἡ Ἱερατική* 274), unable to predict behaviour. Thermos considers that the value of personality tests depends on whether the psychiatrist who uses them is experienced and shares the interest of the candidate in the priesthood (Θερμός, *Ἡ Ἱερατική* 274). If this is the case, the psychiatrist could uncover insufficient and immature motives, but he must also be aware of the limited nature of these tests and at times be guided by his intuition (Θερμός, *Ἡ Ἱερατική* 274).

Notwithstanding the various tools offered by the psychological sciences, Thermos (*Ἡ Ἱερατική* 275-6) acknowledges that it is very difficult to judge the quality of vocation or to predict the vector of its development. These tests are only tools and aids and as such may prove effective only to a certain extent, and under particular circumstances (Θερμός, *Ἡ Ἱερατική* 275-6). Therefore, the rejection of candidates should not, in Thermos's opinion (*Ἡ Ἱερατική* 276), be based upon the data received from these tests. Only if a person is suffering from serious psychological problems that encumber his adaptation to society should he be dissuaded from aspiring to the priesthood (Θερμός, *Ἡ Ἱερατική* 276).

In discussing the mobilization of spiritual factors as another possible means by which the pastoral vocation could be improved, Thermos asks what standpoint the Church should take regarding the psychological component of vocation. At what point is intervention preferable? (Θερμός, *Ἡ Ἱερατική* 285-7)

He considers the psychological component of vocation to be directly related to the Church, because the Church can ensure the quality of pastoral care by devoting attention to the psychological maturity of both priests and candidates for the priesthood. The fundamental importance of psychological maturity increases the accountability of the Church authorities in the matter of ordination. Sufficient reason for such accountability is the authorities' special expertise in selecting candidates for the priesthood. Since he is expected to become a role model, the candidate for the priesthood has to show greater maturity than his peers. Yet, who can guarantee that immature individuals will not end up in hieratic schools? This is another considerable challenge for the Church authorities, because their expertise needs to be utilized in both screening out unsuitable individuals and in aiding those who have "mistakenly" enrolled in the school to acquire maturity. Maybe it is a unique feature of our time that there is a lack of mature young individuals. If it is, then the issue of quality may turn into the issue of quantity as well. Thermos (*Ἡ Ἱερατική* 285-7) claims that the mission of the Church (the ecclesiastical authorities, administration of priest schools, clergymen, mentors, etc.) is to struggle for the salvage of each belated vocation. This matter certainly implies and demands a kind of cooperation with parents, educators and all those who have an influence on young men with a vocation (Θερμός, *Ἡ Ἱερατική* 286-7). Anne and Jacques Gagey (1991, 15) consider that "the care of vocations means care of families, from which the vocations sprout" (qtd. Θερμός, *Ἡ Ἱερατική* 285).

The mutual relationship between a candidate for priesthood and Church authorities has a big impact on the development of vocation that a particular candidate experiences. The expectations, fantasies and feelings concerning this mutual relationship are absorbed by the candidate's psyche and influence the psychological development of his vocation (Θερμός, *Ἡ Ἱερατική* 286-7). Thermos (*Ἡ Ἱερατική* 286-7) considers that this mutual relationship may cause someone to experience his vocation and to try to realize it, while another's desire to be ordained fades away, and a third may feel no vocation at all. An absolute lack of vocation within a person who would have felt it had he lived at a time when other Church authorities were in place, or the sham impression of vocation within a person who has never experienced it at all — are the extremes of such mutual relationship (Θερμός, *Ἡ Ἱερατική* 287). The interstitial space between these two extremes is occupied, in Thermos's opinion (*Ἡ Ἱερατική* 287), by cases of a defensive character. The participation of Church authorities in this defensive process should be, according to Thermos (*Ἡ Ἱερατική* 287), taken seriously, since "in following a vocation within the Church, certain people are more inclined to attribute to the authorities the values and attitudes of their own ideals, than are those who follow any secular vocation" (Θερμός, *Ἡ Ἱερατική* 287). Thermos (*Ἡ Ἱερατική* 287) points to idealizations and projections as the defence mechanisms most often used by candidates. These two defence mechanisms are the principal driving sources of vocation (κλίση) during its formation (during adolescent immaturity). During this period, the individual's inner world maintains balance by making recourse to the defence mechanisms. As a result, a clear and accurate perception of reality, including a true image of Church authorities, may be destroyed for the sake of conforming to the vocation (Θερμός, *Ἡ Ἱερατική* 287).

When such candidates begin to grasp reality, this combination of idealizations and projections becomes a ticking time-bomb beneath the timeline of their vocation. Therefore, Thermos asks whether "the ecclesiastical authorities should in a timely fashion bring these candidates to reason, by aiding the gradual elimination of the candidates' idealizations?" (*Ἡ Ἱερατική* 290-1) He thinks that they should not, since defence mechanisms will always be at work within each candidate (Θερμός, *Ἡ Ἱερατική* 290-1). Consequently, it is Thermos's expectation that one day every priest may experience disillusionment with his idealizations and projections. However, this eventual disillusionment among future pastors does not reduce the immense importance of the mission of Church authorities. Their responsibility toward the Church in its entirety may be reduced to the following three tasks:

> 1) Transformation of the shortcomings (disharmonies) of candidates; 2) opportune preparation for a gradual de-idealization of the candidates' illusions about the Church authorities; preparation of such should exclude any attempt to defend those illusions; 3) the exertion of continuous self-criticism and voluntary self-reformation. (Θερμός, *Ἡ Ἱερατική* 290-1)

The responsibility of Church authorities concerning interaction between themselves and candidates for priesthood is described by Sakellariou as follows (95-97):

> The subsequent increasing or decreasing of vocations depends mainly on the way in which the ministering Church communicates with its future clergymen. It also depends on what the ministering Church promises its children and what they

> themselves see and feel with their heart, before they make this great and unique decision concerning their life. (qtd. Θερμός, *Η Ἱερατική* 290-1)

What is then the mission of Church authorities? What kind of problems do the authorities face? The mission of the Church in relation to vocation, according to Thermos (*Η Ἱερατική* 292-3), is to diagnose psychological problems and to heal them. The Church has to evaluate the candidate's psychological "foundations", since the establishment of a candidate's suitability to the requirements of vocation depends on whether or not he is driven by unconscious motives. The candidate could be either unable or unwilling to realize that he might be driven by his own unconscious motives, which may be revealed in the emerging gap between the ideal and the person's real self. This very notion of a gap presupposes an objective evaluator who can trace the line between these two sides in one self. The most appropriate and objective evaluator appears to be the Church authorities because they bear responsibility for assessing the suitability of clergymen.

Furthermore the ecclesiastical mentors should, according to Thermos (*Η Ἱερατική* 292), show understanding and assist in advancing the candidate's maturity. They ought to care for the candidates in such a way that they can decide of their own accord whether or not to become ordained priests. Importantly, Thermos (*Η Ἱερατική* 292) considers that there should be a personal relationship between the candidate for the priesthood and an ecclesiastical mentor. The latter should be older than the candidate and psychologically mature (Θερμός, *Η Ἱερατική* 292). This is immensely important especially when the candidate faces spiritual challenges which often comprise the urges of the flesh. However, this personal relationship is useless, if the mentor too has deep unconscious conflicts (*Η Ἱερατική* 292). Thermos (*Η Ἱερατική* 292) also considers that the active participation of the candidate in the life of the parish Church is a key factor in the promotion of his spiritual and psychological maturity, although this may not necessarily be the case. He points out that nobody ought to ignore the negative outcomes inherent in prematurely appointing a candidate to any Church role (Θερμός, *Η Ἱερατική* 292). Such a premature appointment may cause the candidate to minister in an alienating and defensive way.

According to Wicks (1-10), the Church authorities have to ascertain whether a candidate potentially possesses the flexibility to acknowledge any immature elements in his motivation to become a priest so that the mature elements of his motivation can be given opportunity to develop (Θερμός, *Η Ἱερατική* 292-3). Such opportunity as provided by the Church authorities is, in Wicks' opinion (1-10), extremely important as it often happens that "we are interested only in how the state of motivation is at the present moment, and therefore potentially good candidates may be rejected, whereas those who seem appropriate to the ministry at this instant, but who will prove to be psychologically inflexible, are encouraged to realize their vocation" (qtd. Θερμός, *Η Ἱερατική* 293). The offering of such an opportunity to candidates means that the ecclesiastical mentor knows existentially the dynamics of the human psyche or rather the notion of affect itself on the basis of their own experience.

To diagnose and heal unconscious disharmonies is a difficult task. "Kindred behaviours may have a different psychodynamic structure so that there are a number of serious problems originating in the issue of one or another candidate's suitableness to the priesthood" (Θερμός, *Ἡ Ἱερατική* 293).

Referring to Rulla et al.'s expertise (*Entering* 211, 218, 250) in the field, Thermos points out that psychological and spiritual assistance are often offered as though they represent different spheres, between which synthesis is impossible. Thermos affirms that unconscious conflicts remain prolonged in such circumstances,[14] and explains: "There is a need for a certain harmony between the spiritual values inculcated by the Church authorities, and the capability of a particular person to assimilate these values; otherwise the inculcated ideals become a source of failures rather than of maturity" (Θερμός, *Ἡ Ἱερατική* 293). Thermos is convinced that it is the Church authorities' urgent task to use spiritual edification and practice in such a way that it brings about psychological healing.

Rulla (1976, 259-260) asserts that the traditional way of preparing candidates for the priesthood and of developing vocation is effective only in relation to the conscious part of the psyche, while the unconscious sphere along with its problems remains untouched. He describes this phenomenon by comparing it with passing through a tunnel: "Many components of human personality change on sight, but in fact they have simply been concealed. Real life will later unmask these hidden components" (qtd. Θερμός, *Ἡ Ἱερατική* 293). Rulla et al. (*Entering* 324-327) offer the following principles as a guide for the pastoral psychology of vocation:

> There are four conditions ... concerning the experiences that a candidate for priesthood should acquire: **1)** *Existential experience.* A candidate for priesthood should be offered an opportunity to test himself in various kinds of tasks, and different life situations, which demand him to manifest initiative and personal responsibility. All this will endow the candidate with experience that will teach him what he is and what he is worthy of. This experience should reveal, as much as possible, the candidate's real self, personal abilities, values and inner needs. This experience too should expose the candidate to failures, fiascos, and feelings of loneliness. Only in these experiences will a candidate be made aware of the depths of his personality and be made able to accept them. He will understand the joy of being himself and in offering himself to others. As he is not yet engaged in the ministry permanently, his experience will not have negative repercussions for him. **2)** *Integrating experience.* A candidate for priesthood ought to try to obtain the integration of the following three levels of activity and inner life that are unique to each human being: psychosomatic, psychosocial and spiritual.

---

14 However, one has to acknowledge that Thermos, in his research, does not offer any way by which to combine these two kinds of assistance.

> Proceeding from each of these levels, each action should be in harmony with the other ones. This experience should be offered to each candidate for the priesthood, because every success at this stage strengthens the person's capability to assimilate the values. **3)** *Proportionate experience.* There is a need to achieve a fine equilibrium between goading the candidate to new progress and maintaining such a requirement within a reasonable framework, since otherwise anxiety may arise and the defence mechanisms be mobilized. An example illustrates this idea: It has been observed that all-permissiveness subjects a person to the power of his needs and instincts, while an imperious stance kills any initiative. There is a need for an individual approach to each candidate, because each person is of a different "psychological" age. **4)** *Support experience.* At the beginning of a professional undertaking every person is wont to learn varying activities and to seek psychological safety and satisfaction from other people; such an attitude and perception should change with the advent of maturity. The candidates should make use of the freedom to be mistaken. Yet, they too should be offered a freedom to change themselves so as not to repeat their mistakes. The candidates need support in order to learn from their mistakes to acknowledge that they may err. If candidates' endeavours do not achieve the stated objective, they should be called on to revise their attitudes and even their decisions. (qtd. Θερμός, *Ἡ Ἱερατική* 295-6)

Thermos expresses the idea that there are many psychological types among the candidates for priesthood. Inherent in this idea of a range of types is the mutual relationship between the Church authorities and the candidates. In fact, quite a spectrum of characters is hidden behind this mutual relationship. At the extremes of this spectrum are two characters: the "conformist" and the "rioter" (Θερμός, *Ἡ Ἱερατική* 296). Referring to the observations of Rulla, Thermos affirms that these two types of character represent the disharmonic vocation. Rulla et al. (*Entering* 135) explains the origin of this disharmony in the following way: "The unquenchable desire to satisfy personal needs leads these young men necessarily to long-term fiascos (which may also be caused by Church authorities' failures). Inasmuch as a fiasco threatens their inner safety, they react by following one of two behavioural schemes: they either manifest disobedience or conform to the circumstances" (qtd. Θερμός, *Ἡ Ἱερατική* 296-7). Thermos argues that both psychological reactions may be attributed to the conformists. The difference between them consists of the following: the rioter is disharmonic both psychologically and socially, whereas the conformist is disharmonic only psychologically (Θερμός, *Ἡ Ἱερατική* 296-9). With relation to society, the conformist does not manifest any roughness. The problem here is that the Church authorities or ecclesiastical mentors often encourage the conformists, mistakenly considering them to be "good persons", whereas the rioters are taken to be "bad persons", and therefore gain more attention. Thereby, considerable attention is devoted to the problems of rioters, while the problems of conformists are shelved (Θερμός, *Ἡ Ἱερατική* 296-9). In this context, Quinlan (52) says that "the capability of a young individual to get on with other candidates for the priesthood (inside the seminaries or theological colleges) is not necessarily a sign of vocation; this kind of smooth association does not preclude serious communication problems within the Church society in which this young person wishes to later minister as a priest" (qtd. Θερμός, *Ή Ίερατική* 300). Thermos (*Ή Ίερατική* 300-6) suggests that the Church should institute seminaries which are closer to the reality of Church life, because the peculiar way of life inside traditional seminaries, with their atmosphere favourable to the promoting of anyone except of strong-minded and resourceful among its students, may cause within some an illusion of vocation. This, however, is not necessarily the case, as a considerable number of true vocations may also be advanced (Θερμός, *Ή Ίερατική* 300-6).

Thermos states that the Church should also provide psychological guidance to those with a sense of vocation. In this respect, he highlights the following problems linked to such psychological guidance: the dialectic between quantity and quality, the dialectic between stress on the Church's mission and stress on the formation of a candidate's personality, and finally the question of freedom (Θερμός, *Ή Ίερατική* 300-6).

Thermos states that the dilemma posed by "quantity versus quality" has received various solutions in various places over the centuries. In light of this, he considers that many problematic persons with various psychological disorders have been attracted to the hieratic vocation at all times. Dunn (132) believes that "the Church authorities often proved to be relatively uninterested when dealing with neurotic behaviour, paying it little attention, or considering it not dangerous; the same position seemingly reigns supreme to-day as well" (qtd. Θερμός, *Ή Ίερατική* 300). What endangered the quality of pastoral ministry at times of quantitative dearth was that many lay persons expressed the will to moderate this insufficiency of priests. These laypersons were not closely connected to the Church and the Church authorities made fateful concessions with regard to their policy of checking the suitability of particular persons for the priesthood. Thermos (*Ή Ίερατική* 300-2) argues that the problem arising from this dilemma is one of self-consciousness in the Church authorities; in other words, when excessive attention is paid to the quantity of vocations, questions may be raised regarding the quality of the Church's conviction and life.

The dilemma—as to whether it is more important to prioritize the mission of the Church or the formation of a candidate's personality—is another enormous problem. When the former is encouraged, the latter is neglected; while stressing the formation of a candidate's personality may cause the mission of the Church to stagnate (Θερμός, *Ή Ίερατική* 303-4). Kennedy and Heckler (95-98) consider this dilemma to be false: "The authorities usually give priority to the Church organism. Thereby, the question is subject to modification: whether the promotion of psychological maturity will be on the ecclesiastical agenda or whether conformism to the institutional expectations at the expense of the successful formation of personality will take priority. In assisting the formation of mature rounded personalities, an institution contributes to the successful realization of its mission" (qtd. Θερμός, *Η Ἱερατική* 302-3). In this regard, Thermos expresses his conviction that "the pastoral activity of each pastor manifests whatever he has experienced as a parishioner; thus, if the pastor did not experience proper care when he was young, he too will not be able to display this proper care toward others either" (Θερμός, *Η Ἱερατική* 303).

McAllister (11-2) affirms that

> the negligence of ecclesiastical authorities in the issue of properly guiding the vocations may sometimes be explained by a lack of psychological education and experience, and therefore they repair to routine theological statements and are wont to keep, at all costs, the newly emerged vocation for the priesthood. This negligence is rooted in a situation, according to which they are not compelled to assist the candidates in managing their feelings, but only to intellectually assist the candidates with reasoning about those feelings. Such a standpoint makes the authorities neglect the candidate's self and his maturity, leaving him alone to desperately fight for his identity. (qtd. Θερμός, *Η Ἱερατική* 302-3)

The final issue to be carefully considered by the Church authorities is the problem of freedom. Certainly, lack of freedom is not always obvious and, what is more, it is mostly reflected only in an indirect and obscure way. To describe the essence of this problem, Thermos uses as a real-life example the state of affairs in the Roman Catholic Church before the II Vatican Synod[15] as described by Rulla (*Entering* 324-327):

> Offering guidance, the emphasis on the ideals of the Church authorities had priority. The ideals of the candidate for priesthood were not attended to and therefore the latter conformed himself to the Church authorities. It practically meant that the ideals of vocation were perceived as the performing of roles. These ideals were comprehended as something far from reality, as an idealized conception of a role, which "was performed" by the individuals, something that led to their depersonalization. Thereby attitudes developed in combination with roles, but the concealed disharmonies remained untouched. In the long run, "holy uniformity" prevailed for the candidates and autocracy for the authorities. (qtd. Θερμός, *Η Ἱερατική* 304)

This phenomenon directly concerns the "institution-centred" Church, and not the one that regards the individual's personality (person-centred) as being of paramount importance. This phenomenon of "institution-centred" Church means that the Church seeks to reproduce itself, its system, instead of opening itself toward freedom in God and toward estimation for the human personality (Θερμός, *Η Ἱερατική* 304-6). Evidently, the appeal to hold on to freedom is closely connected, according to Thermos (*Η Ἱερατική* 304-6), with the demand

---

15 Remarkably, this state of affairs may, according to Thermos, be met in an obscure form inside the modern Greek Orthodox Church as well (*Η Ιερατική* 301-5).

that every person be approached individually. Indifference toward the freedom and originality of others stifles the consciousness among ecclesiastical authorities of their responsibility toward the individual candidate, since thereby the candidate's conformism is preferred. D'Arcy (83-84) says: "The system assists the candidate's inclination to conform and strengthens it. Thereby a particular candidate begins to live with the values of others so that he experiences extreme disappointment when he realizes that this is the case. The seminaries are either families or depersonalized bureaucratic organizations" (qtd. Θερμός, *Ἡ Ἱερατική* 304). Kennedy and Heckler (43) stated in a burst of Roman Catholic self-criticism: "We are more interested in the candidate's obedience, his conformism to the system and a lack of problems than his real development" (qtd. Θερμός, *Ἡ Ἱερατική* 304). Furthermore, they warn that "the training of seminarians may quite often lead to their concealing their lack of psychological development rather than to their revealing and confessing it. The reason for such deviation is that the training predominantly encourages conformism. Moreover, it prevents candidates from acquiring the experiences bound to their age-development phase (social life, meeting people of the opposite gender)" (qtd. Θερμός, *Ἡ Ἱερατική* 304-5).

According to Thermos (*Ἡ Ἱερατική* 304-5), the Roman Catholics failed to improve this situation in their issuing of new pastoral resolutions during Vatican II. Liberal tendencies emerged in the proposed resolutions, with regard to the guiding of the vocations, tendencies which for some issues bordered on the loss of any idea of true measure. Rulla (*Entering*, 203-4) says:

> The subjectivity, the diversion of ecclesiastical ideals… the freedom "without discretion"… the "holy individualization" may, regardless of the good intentions of both sides, influence the capability of the candidate for the priesthood to hear God's voice, in other words, to perceive in a right way his (candidate's) mission. All these abovementioned factors may lead a candidate "to lose" himself, to assimilate the attitudes of vocation to the detriment of values, and also to justify his hidden unconscious conflicts. (qtd. Θερμός, *Ἡ Ἱερατική* 306)

Thermos believes that the Roman Catholic Church jettisoned the former proclivity to autocracy only to replace it with secularization. It happened either because of unconcerned quantity-hunting or because of intense feelings of guilt (Θερμός, *Ἡ Ἱερατική* 306-7). Whichever of these is true, the Orthodox must, according to Thermos (*Ἡ Ἱερατική* 306-7), draw the necessary conclusions from the experience of the Roman Catholics, and as a result follow "the golden mean" of Church self-consciousness. This means the wise combination of order and authority with the estimation of human personality. Such an attitude will lead the Orthodox to "the assimilation of true values and attitudes, devoted ministry, the capability to hear both God's voice and that of one's neighbour" (Θερμός, *Ἡ Ἱερατική* 307). Therefore, Kennedy (40-41) is right in averring: "The most important thing in assisting the development of vocation for the priesthood is that the authorities have to change within themselves, they have to obtain self-knowledge, to comprehend their own feelings as well as the motives of their own behaviour. We have to concentrate not on our ideas, but on the candidates for priesthood" (qtd. Θερμός, *Ἡ Ἱερατική* 306).

2.3.2. New generation of ecclesiastical mentors

What aims should the Church pursue in its involvement in the process of the development of vocation?

From the above it is needless to say that the chief aim of the Church, when it involves itself in the process of the development of vocation, is to assist a candidate for priesthood in achieving psychological maturity. The ultimate fulfillment of this aim depends, according to Thermos, on the emergence of a new kind of educators / mentors (*Ἡ Ἱερατική* 307). Contrary to Roman Catholic supporters of the same opinion, Thermos believes that in the Orthodox field the clergymen themselves may fulfill the duties of the new educators, after obtaining special training. The clear need for such educators comes across because of the objective demand to diagnose and cure the following problems among candidates for the priesthood:

> 1) *Problems of a spiritual nature:* doubts over faith and Christian moral principles.
> 2) *Problems connected with age development, which emerge at certain stages.* These kinds of problems should usually be overcome by the age of twenty-seven.
> 3) *Disharmonies within the sphere of unconscious:* disharmonies that are not easily detectable in external behavior and that are not classified as psychopathological.
> 4) *Mental disorders attributable to psychiatric diseases.* (Θερμός, *Ἡ Ἱερατική* 307)

Thermos points out that the first two types of problems may be independent of and not connected to the other two. In such a case, the first two categories of problems may be easily solved (Θερμός, *Ἡ Ἱερατική* 308). They are solved with time, when a particular candidate acquires new experiences, receives Holy Communion regularly; in other words, these are solved by the grace of God (Θερμός, *Ἡ Ἱερατική* 308). Yet, certainly, some problems which originate in the unconscious or even in psychopathological conflicts can also manifest themselves as "spiritual" or "age conflicts" (Θερμός, *Ἡ Ἱερατική* 308). In such a case, the situation is serious and the aforementioned means of assistance insufficient. Such a situation can deteriorate rapidly when responsible Church mentors witness the symptoms of psychopathology and do nothing, since the candidate who suffers from the psychopathology may take the non-intervention as a signal that there is nothing wrong with him (Θερμός, *Ἡ Ἱερατική* 308). In this respect, it is a must, according to Thermos, that each ecclesiastical mentor responsible for the training of the future priests acquires special skills which enable him to become a new, and up-to-date educator. Such new educators would be expected to be free of the problems described in the points **3** and **4** above so as to avoid the harmful impact of their projecting their unsolved problems on the collective or any of its particular members (Θερμός, *Ἡ Ἱερατική* 308-9). The educator's task is, according to Thermos, to work with the unconscious sphere. Thereby they should assist and supplement the activity of the authorities and the spiritual fathers (confessors), who work with individual's conscious sphere. If these educators are not clergymen, they should be, according to Thermos (*Ἡ Ἱερατική* 309-10), more like spiritual fathers than authorities, since the image of authority, i.e. a superior, subjugates the desire of a candidate to be sincere. Besides that, these educators should possess a kind of maturity which will not undermine the ideals of the church authorities, with subjective and extreme interpretations. They should not send contradictory messages and cause unpleasant feelings in another person during their interpersonal interactions with him (Θερμός, *Ἡ Ἱερατική* 309-10).

As a whole, the description of these educators and of their mission stresses the idea that there should be a combination of special knowledge with deep virtue, i.e., the combination of spiritual and psychological components. Thus, Thermos approaches the idea of cooperation between God and the individual in the formation of the vocation for the priesthood.

2.3.3. Divine grace and human freedom

Thermos (*Ἡ Ἱερατική* 311) acknowledges that the human component of hieratic vocation is interlaced with its divine component. "After the incarnation of the Son of God, all phenomena of spiritual life began to function within the framework of cooperation between God and the individual. Therefore complete knowledge of the way in which this cooperation functions cannot be acquired, since it continually recaptures the Chalcedonian mystery" (Θερμός, *Ἡ Ἱερατική* 311).

The dialectical character of cooperation between God and the individual is present also in the issue of vocation. Accordingly, the issue of vocation is a matter of "dialogue between divine and human freedom" (Θερμός, *Ἡ Ἱερατική* 311). What is this dialogue all about? Thermos is convinced that grace presupposes the existence of nature, and therefore grace shadows the process of development of the human nature. Kornarakis (*Ποιμαντικά*, 56) believes that the personality of the candidate functions as a natural "predisposition" toward divine grace which always founds everything on the predispositions of each human being (qtd. Θερμός, *Ἡ Ἱερατική* 312).

Certainly, according to Thermos, one must not reduce holiness to psychological maturity; and, what is more, the lack of the latter does not deprive any person of the possibility of attaining salvation (Θερμός, *Ἡ Ἱερατική* 315). However, psychological maturity produces favourable effects on the individual's predisposition toward divine grace and assists him in successfully embracing the aims of a hieratic vocation (Θερμός, *Ἡ Ἱερατική* 315). Unconscious disorders, as a visible symptom of psychological immaturity, hinder the process of overcoming the self and leads to the substitution of the psychological need for the ideals of vocation (Θερμός, *Ἡ Ἱερατική* 315). The lack of these disorders is a baseline condition for a particular candidate to be successfully guided by God (Θερμός, *Ἡ Ἱερατική* 315).

The fact that God is almighty does not imply that He will interfere with the laws He himself has implanted within the human being (Θερμός, *Ἡ Ἱερατική* 31). His respect for human freedom entails the everlasting impact that the psychosocial shortcomings of a candidate will have on his subsequent pastoral effectiveness (Θερμός, *Ἡ Ἱερατική* 315). Thermos acknowledges the relative value of marking the line of demarcation between the "harmonic" and "disharmonic" candidates because it is very difficult to ascertain whether a particular person is mature or not (Θερμός, *Ἡ Ἱερατική* 315). Therefore, Thermos believes that the measure of cooperation with divine grace will be a decisive factor in deciding what is going to prevail within a particular person: harmony or disharmony (Θερμός, *Ἡ Ἱερατική* 315). Divine grace chiefly works, according to Thermos, by repairing to the conscious part of human self so as to increase the effectiveness of pastoral activity and to make the pastor ever aware of his freedom which can make him more capable of moving toward harmony and stability (Θερμός, *Ἡ Ἱερατική* 315). The objective of ecclesiastical care with relation to vocation should be the same, "to actualize the capability of the individual to hear the inward voice of God who speaks to him by means of Holy Scripture as well as by various existential situations in life" (Θερμός, *Ἡ Ἱερατική* 315-6).

Cooperation between a candidate for priesthood (or clergyman) and divine grace should result in the overcoming of self (*αὐθυπέρβαση*) (Θερμός, *Ἡ Ἱερατική* 316). A person's capability for overcoming himself is an essential feature of human nature; this feature grants to him the gift of self-actualization. If a clergyman cultivates the element of overcoming himself within his life, he correspondingly manages to avoid the danger of slipping into ordinary professionalism, by which certain candidates or clergymen remain happy with the realization of their dreams and development of their talents, alone (Θερμός, *Ἡ Ἱερατική* 316). Thermos believes that, when the spiritual motive withers, there is a high probability that the particular person will be subject to psychological conflicts (Θερμός, *Ἡ Ἱερατική* 316); such psychological conflicts are very dangerous because they can even cause a candidate for the priesthood or a clergyman to abandon his vocation. Thus, the responsibility of the ecclesiastical authorities increases exponentially since it is they who often bring about the collapse of spiritual motives, either by not sufficiently cultivating spiritual motives among candidates for the priesthood and even clergymen or by undermining the effectiveness of these motives through the provision of poor personal example (Θερμός, *Η Ἱερατική* 316).

2.4. Conclusions

In conclusion, Thermos claims that the authorities of each Orthodox Church should take into account the human (psychological) component of a hieratic vocation, since it will have a profound effect on the effectiveness of both future and contemporary clergymen. It is obvious that Thermos attaches great importance to the human component of the hieratic vocation, and is guided in this by Freud's psychological research. Freud pointed out the immense importance of taking the unconscious sphere of the human psyche into consideration in order to understand human behaviour.

Thermos's initial thesis is based on the premise that an individual's psychological maturity coincides with maturity of vocation to the priesthood. He closely analyzes all stages of development passed through on the way to psychological maturity, establishing that a particular person reaches psychological maturity when he has put his values, attitudes and needs in proper order. This implies a superior position for values, and an ancillary position — for attitudes and needs. Evidently, Thermos is against the precipitous ordination of young candidates (under the age of twenty-seven), because there is a great probability that such individuals will not yet have overcome the psychological immaturity associated with the problems of their chronological age.

Thermos claims that the effectiveness of the pastoral ministry is closely associated with the wise guidance of candidates by the Church authorities. He calls on these authorities to be watchful so as to detect candidates unsuited for the priesthood; but the authorities should not be precipitate in hurriedly rejecting those who cast doubts on their own good match to the priesthood; too stringent requirements for the vocation may discourage potentially good candidates. Illusions should not be fostered concerning the quality of newly emerged vocations. According to Thermos, many individuals with a sense of vocation are immature when measured against psychological criteria, so that the Church authorities are responsible for assisting these young people to become psychologically mature. Mere theological education by the ecclesiastical mentors is not enough. There is an additional need for psychological training; and, if it is difficult to undertake, qualified specialists in psychology or psychotherapy should be consulted or even invited to the seminaries as advisers to the school administration.

It should be acknowledged that Thermos admits the artificiality of the line of demarcation he has traced between the human and divine component of vocation. Therefore, he does not claim that the destiny of the Church is dependent on how it will act toward his appeal to repair to the expertise of secular psychology in order to contribute to the successful development of the human component of vocation. He tries to keep the necessary balance between the measure of divine and human action. This point forces us to acknowledge that Thermos does not share the opinion of certain Roman Catholics who claim that there is a complementary relation between theology and psychology. This conclusion emerges chiefly on the basis of his statement that holiness is not attained by way of psychological maturity and that psychological immaturity does not prevent a human being from receiving salvation.

Why does Thermos deviate from certain nuances of Freud's way of structuring the human personality when he describes the development of the psychological component of a vocation for the priesthood? This deviation occurs at the point where he endows the psychoanalytic notion of 'ego' with great autonomous power. This autonomous power can be manifested when the crookedness of an unsuccessfully developed vocation is being rectified. In the context of psychoanalytic scientific theory, this autonomy is inexplicable.

3. Problems of clergy ineffectiveness and solutions advanced by Thermos

3.1. Confessor and his "unconscious"

Thermos (*Ὁμοιοπαθεῖς* 23-4) believes that the effectiveness of clergymen is considerably dependent on their awareness of the existence of the "unconscious" and on their attempt to apprehend the latent motives of their behaviour. Therefore, the effectiveness or ineffectiveness of clergymen actually depends on the correlation of two factors: the "unconscious" and "self-knowledge" (introspection). Thermos provides the following definition of the "unconscious": "The unconscious is a space of psychological life that is exempt from the control of our consciousness and will" (Θερμός, *Ὁμοιοπαθεῖς* 23). Thermos believes that we do not realize the effects of this psychological sphere on our thought and behaviour; and therefore there is a need for self-knowledge. Self-knowledge should begin, according to Thermos (*Ὁμοιοπαθεῖς* 23-4), with the issue of *motives*. Unfortunately, very little attention is usually paid to this essential element of self-knowledge. Thermos provides a kind of vector for making his reader understand the idea of introspecting for behavioural motives, by asking the following questions: "Why did I want to become a confessor?" or "why do I like to confess the faithful?" (Θερμός, *Ὁμοιοπαθεῖς* 23-4) Each priest should, in Thermos's opinion (*Ὁμοιοπαθεῖς* 24), answer these questions, the earlier the better, both for the confessor and the people confessed.

He believes that there is one point which should make every confessor mistrustful regarding the purity of his motives. This point concerns the definition of the work of confessor as "fatherhood". Certain "side-effects" may occur in this context. Thermos explains these by analogy with the way in which natural paternity usually becomes apparent (*Ὁμοιοπαθεῖς* 24). It is well known that parenting is often subject to "side-effects" caused by human imperfection. Paternal care often turns into paternal authority, and even worse into the abuse of authority (Θερμός, *Ὁμοιοπαθεῖς* 24). Thermos is convinced that by exerting power a person may achieve psychological satisfaction which compensates for psychological gaps or conflicts rooted in the experiences of childhood (Θερμός, *Ὁμοιοπαθεῖς* 24). Thus, fatherhood and the exertion of power often co-exist, regardless of intention, just as the sun co-exists with its spots (Θερμός, *Ὁμοιοπαθεῖς* 24).

The feeling of pleasure which accompanies this psychological compensation constitutes the unconscious motive, which causes clergymen to seek to exert spiritual fatherhood, according to Thermos (*Ὁμοιοπαθεῖς* 25). The causes of a confessor's probable ineffectiveness are briefly expounded by Thermos in the following statement:

> Inferiorities deeply rooted in the past, a disposition to controlling others, the experience of oppression during the childhood, uncertainty about one's own self

> and a feeling of insecurity are all reasons that may cause one to try to exert power in pastoral care. This proclivity for power over others results in the degeneration of the ministry, in the loss of its saving character, in the deprivation of another's responsibility and freedom, turning the ministry into a relationship whereby the confessor dominates another person. (Θερμός, *Ὁμοιοπαθεῖς* 25)

Clearly, the confessor's past may have a negative effect on his spiritual ministry. The unconscious here can be compared to a reservoir within which the personal past is gathered up and preserved (Θερμός, *Ὁμοιοπαθεῖς* 25). In being bound to the exertion of power, the paternal character of the confessor's ministry proves to be a favourable ground for turning pastoral care into a field within which the psychological lacunas of a confessor's past are compensated (Θερμός, *Ὁμοιοπαθεῖς* 25).

Thermos considers that "motives connected with the psychological compensation of inner lacunas distort the meaning of spiritual fatherhood, because fatherhood presupposes true childbirth and not adoption" (Θερμός, *Ὁμοιοπαθεῖς* 26). The mutual relationship between a particular confessor and his spiritual son or daughter is not determined by simply being appointed pastor, but by an inner organic relationship acquired through painful processes. To ground this idea, he quotes several citations from the New Testament: "For though you might have ten thousand instructors in Christ, yet you do not have many fathers; for in Christ Jesus I have begotten you through the gospel" (1 Cor 4.15). There is no pleasure but pain, care, concern, agony and delivery in childbirth. Yet one who gives birth "no longer remembers the anguish, for joy that a human being has been born into the world" (John 16.21), here, into the Kingdom of God .

Thermos (*Ὁμοιοπαθεῖς* 26) suggests several kinds of confessor behaviour that may interact with each other: the rigorous confessor, the flexible confessor and the dupable (naïve) confessor.

To begin with, the rigorous confessor attracts Thermos's attention, since there are people who confuse such rigour with the rigour apparent in certain holy Fathers. One must distinguish the first kind of rigour from the second. Therefore, Thermos attempts to analyze the probable motives certain confessors have for behaving in a rigorous way. Rigour is often manifested by the itemization of sins as well as by their denouncement (Θερμός, *Ὁμοιοπαθεῖς* 26). A rigorous confessor may appear as a defender of violated divine rights; in such cases, the confessor commits a great theological blunder against the Orthodox frame of reference (as God never takes offence) (Θερμός, *Ὁμοιοπαθεῖς* 26). Such rigour may be caused by "righteous anger", which is usually, according to Thermos (*Ὁμοιοπαθεῖς* 27), simply sacrilegious wrath. The reason for this wrath may be that a particular sin represents the latent spiritual attributes of the confessor as well (Θερμός, *Ὁμοιοπαθεῖς* 27); on the other hand, that wrath may also mean that one is struggling to manifest his quasi uncompromising attitude toward the sin confessed, and perception of it as frightful and unimaginable. Such a struggle indicates that the confessor involved is still unaware of the great truth that the human race bears within itself the seeds of all sins (Θερμός, *Ὁμοιοπαθείς* 27). Furthermore, rigour may also stem from a confessor's inner quasi experience of an avenging God. According to Thermos (*Ὁμοιοπαθείς* 27), this experience is a product of a confessor's neurotic mechanisms and his existential envy of people that feel more at ease with God than he. Finally, rigour may be rooted in ignorance of certain psychosomatic conditions of the confessing person, whereby the confessor demands that a parishioner correspond to a pattern of virtue that he has fabricated (Θερμός, *Ὁμοιοπαθείς* 27-8). The link between rigour and the unconscious is expressed indirectly in the following claim: "The more we [confessors] investigate the dimensions of sin within us, the better we know the human proclivity to sin as well as the fragility of each individual's first attempts to get rid of sin, and thereby we [confessors] prove to be realistic and down-to-earth" (Θερμός, *Ὁμοιοπαθείς* 28). According to Thermos (*Ὁμοιοπαθείς* 28), the further we are from the reality of life, the more unaware we are of the existence of the unconscious within us.

Thermos believes that the confessor should accept the parishioner in his actual spiritual and psychological condition, i.e., his mindset, feelings, habits, psychosomatic condition and, from this point, start to guide him (Θερμός, *Ὁμοιοπαθείς* 28). The precedents for such forbearing between confessor and the confessing person are seen by Thermos (*Ὁμοιοπαθείς* 28-9) in the incarnation of the logos, the descent of the High Priest into hell, and the utterances of Pentecost when every individual heard of the works of God in his own mother tongue. According to Thermos only a small part of contemporary pastoral guidance is practised in this way. Thermos (*Ὁμοιοπαθείς* 28-9) believes that pastoral guidance is probably now more demanding than ever before was, in particular with regard to qualitative changes. The modern individual demands individualized contact with the confessor, and needs to affirm his own particularities, because only in such circumstances is he ready to trust, and open and reform himself self (Θερμός, *Ὁμοιοπαθείς* 28). Thermos (*Ὁμοιοπαθείς* 28) is convinced that the majority of modern individuals are willing to come into contact with the confessor only if the latter is willing to moderate his self-evident matters.

The peculiarity of the rigorous confessor stands out in the issue of reprobating sins. This issue reveals both a lack of the confessor's trust in the person confessing and the confessor's doubt over the capability of the latter to assume responsibility in front of God (Θερμός, *Ὁμοιοπαθείς* 28). Moreover, by being treated coldly and superficially as another bore, the confessing person receives no alleviation of inner pain (Θερμός, *Ὁμοιοπαθείς* 28). In this context, the reader is introduced to the problem of ecclesiastical penances, which represent a kind of spiritual punishment applied when the human will needs healing. In relation to this problem, Thermos does not call for the abolition of ecclesiastical penances; he just emphasizes the fact that the rigorous use of penances could be taken as a suggestion that a particular confessor has never entered into contact with the psychological world of the confessing person (Θερμός, *Ὁμοιοπαθείς* 28). In such a case, "it is obvious that, because of our ignorance of his abilities, we, confessors, feel unsure as to the confessing person's capability to apply our admonitions and therefore we resort to the "mechanical" assistance of penances" (Θερμός, *Ὁμοιοπαθείς* 28). The question which arises, however, is: why do some confessors avoid establishing psychological contact with a particular confessing person? For Thermos, the answer to this question is important both locally and globally. By locally, he means that the quality of pastoral care in a particular parish depends on the quality of the inter-personal relationship between confessors and confessing persons (Θερμός, *Ὁμοιοπαθείς* 28). By globally, he means that the quality of the present day encounter between Orthodox pastoral care and the modern world, a world which demands an individualized approach to such care, depends on the quality of inter-personal relationships (Θερμός, *Ὁμοιοπαθείς* 28). In terms of answering this question, apart from the objective factor of physical tiredness a particular confessor may avoid psychological contact with a confessing person because he is afraid of another human personality, or frightened at the prospect of getting close to this person (Θερμός, *Ὁμοιοπαθείς*, 28). Therefore, some confessors seem to be more inclined to develop group activities within the Church, since these activities are devoid of the "danger" of getting close to other people (Θερμός, *Ὁμοιοπαθείς*, 28).

The case of a flexible confessor certainly deserves a better understanding, too. Although the apostle Paul urges Christians to "let your tolerance be evident to everyone" (Phil 4.5), it is necessary, in Thermos's opinion, to analyze the flexibility of a confessor in the light of possible psychological motives. Flexibility can stem from an inner disparagement of the divine law (Θερμός, *Ὁμοιοπαθείς* 29). Such confessors must check their hieratic vocation, because the lack of total devotion to the divine may mean that something else other than the desire to serve God caused them to take up this ministry (Θερμός, *Ὁμοιοπαθείς* 29). In any case, the more frequent reason for flexibility during the confession is consciousness of one's own guilt (Θερμός, *Ὁμοιοπαθείς* 29). Having not been solved through deep and sincere repentance, the problem of guilt does not allow the confessor to develop sensitivity and discernment concerning those confessing, and hinders him in being even-handed in establishing the limits of tolerance (Θερμός, *Ὁμοιοπαθείς* 30). Thermos explains such behaviour in the following way: "Disapproval of the deeds committed by those confessing compels the confessor to disapprove of his own deeds and this is quite painful" (Θερμός, *Ὁμοιοπαθείς* 30). In this case, one is dealing with the repression of a confessor's inner experiences which start to break through to consciousness, when a particular parishioner confesses similar experiences (Θερμός, *Ὁμοιοπαθείς* 30). Thus, those confessing become a confessor's mirror and any painful acknowledgement of certain sins by the spiritual son or daughter echoes within the confessor's soul (Θερμός, *Ὁμοιοπαθείς* 30). The guilty conscience is the diametric extremity of rigour. Here, the driving force is the confessor's sadistic super ego which manifests exactly the same sadism toward other persons (Θερμός, *Ὁμοιοπαθείς* 30).

Flexibility makes recourse to certain excuses that usually represent rationalizations of the confessor's personal amorality masquerading either as divine philanthropy or sinfulness common to the entire human race, or as an adaptation to the peculiarity of the present epoch (Θερμός, *Ὁμοιοπαθείς* 30). Thermos is convinced that flexibility stemming from a confessor's sinfulness, and not spiritual discernment, will always prolong the personal agony of a particular confessing person and leave him unsatisfied in his spiritual pursuits (Θερμός, *Ὁμοιοπαθείς* 30).

In some cases, it is true, flexibility and its excuses may be rooted in the secularization of a confessor's conscience, which makes apparent his inability to communicate truly and ecclesiastically with his parishioners. Thermos says:

> Our complexes whisper to us that we will become likeable through maximum flexibility; yet this point raises the question: Why do we want to become likeable? Are we likely to be considered potential spiritual fathers? May be within the depth of our soul there is jealousy toward other successful confessors and we would like to detach people from them? Or maybe the acknowledgement and appreciation of the believers is a necessary condition for our need to be "important", to obtain "deference" in society, since we are not at peace in the awareness that God loves us? In each of these cases confession covers mainly our own needs so that the other person becomes only a mere means. I believe that this is one of the most serious sins. (Θερμός, *Ὁμοιοπαθείς* 30-31)

Thermos (*Ὁμοιοπαθείς* 30-1) believes that there are also cases when flexibility stems from the general psychological decline of the confessor, brought about by the feeling of being stuck in a routine, disappointment with the ecclesiastical atmosphere, and with the priesthood, underestimation of self and discouragement rooted in family problems. He states that "the sensation of failure cannot provide a helpful stimulus for circumspection and creativity" (Θερμός, *Ὁμοιοπαθείς* 31). Responsibility for the consequences of such a case rests with the Church authorities, because in being lax in facing the problems of ecclesiastical life and organization, or inconsistent as to their own personal life, ecclesiastics with the right to give orders do "not strengthen (but rather weaken) the conscience of clergymen and increase inner conflicts within priests" (Θερμός, *Ὁμοιοπαθείς* 31). In this way, they goad priests into searching for relief in mundane things and create conflict within the priests' families; they provoke complaints and acrimonies, they cause disappointment and anger, and they "make the priests feel shame toward their environment" (Θερμός, *Ὁμοιοπαθείς* 31). Thermos believes that "notwithstanding the possible loss of scandalized people from the Church because of the improprieties of ecclesiastical authorities, the repercussions of these improprieties on the souls and spiritual life of priests are much more tragic and difficult to heal" (*Ὁμοιοπαθείς* 31).

Finally, the last kind of behaviour which may develop among priests is the dupable (naïve) confessor. This behaviour pattern does not emerge as a solution to the dilemma between rigour and flexibility, but represents profound weakness in a confessor's ability to voice strong opinion. Such a confessor accepts the facts and their interpretations uncritically, thereby becoming a kind of "rear ship" (instead of "leading one") for the believers, with the latter therefore being compelled to exert a kind of self-guidance (Θερμός, *Ὁμοιοπαθείς* 31-2). Sometimes, this weakness lies in a frail personality which lacks formation and courage. However, there are cases, according to Thermos (*Ὁμοιοπαθείς* 32), when the confessor suffers from this weakness because he ignores the existence of unconscious motives both in himself and in those confessing. In other words, he accepts confessions at face value, assenting to the interpretation advanced by a believer. Thermos asserts that there is a golden rule, according to which "we are only able to recognize in other people whatever we have already managed to recognize within ourselves" (*Ὁμοιοπαθείς* 32).

Thus, Thermos has presented several behavioural patterns to be found within a confessor, those of rigour, flexibility and naïvety. Each of them, except naïvety, is not actually pathological, but they could become so if a confessor does not take into account the probable impact of his unconscious upon his rigour and flexibility. Therefore, Thermos suggests that every confessor should analyze his own behavioural motives and thereby acquire the self-knowledge that will enable him to deal properly and effectively with his own problems and those of others. Thermos (*Ὁμοιοπαθείς* 39) believes that the purification of the sphere of the unconscious depends on a clergyman's walking toward sanctity and maintaining unrelenting vigilance over his soul.

It is therefore obvious that a confessor's ineffectiveness may be caused to a considerable extent by ignorance of the unconscious, although this is not necessarily so. Another important factor in a confessor's effectiveness is whether Church authorities consistently confront contemporary problems / experiences with the truth of Christian witness. Ineffectual practice in this respect may have devastating impact upon the effectiveness of priests. The only solution for all these problems is a life lived according to the divine commandments and self-knowledge (introspection) in both Church authorities and confessors. Thus one approaches the issue of the interplay between Church authority and clergy effectiveness.

3.2. Church leadership vis-a-vis the quality of ecclesiastical life

Thermos is convinced that there is a direct connection between the way the Church leadership functions and the quality of Church life. He outlines his ideas on this issue in the following three articles: 1. «*Ἐξουσία καί διακονία στήν*

Ἐκκλησία» [Power and ministry within the Church], 2. «*Ὁ τῶν ἀρχόντων τρόπος...*» [The Manner of authorities ...], 3. «*Ψυχολογικές παράμετροι κατά τήν ἄσκηση τῆς ἐκκλησιαστικῆς ἡγεσίας*» [Psychological parameters in the exertion of Church leadership].

Thermos elaborates his reasoning in the following three steps: 1) he clarifies the virtual meaning of the concept of authority within the New Testament; 2) he ascertains the way in which the Church authorities should fulfill their duty; 3) he points out the psychological framework within which each church leader, bishop, priest or theologian has to move. It will be immediately noted that in conducting his research, Thermos relies on both Patristic thought and psychoanalytic theory.

3.2.1. The concept of "authority" within the New Testament

Clarifying the virtual meaning of the concept of "authority" within the New Testament, Thermos makes two assertions: Firstly, that the institutional framework of Church, "law" and "order" is called on to protect the content of Church mission, i.e., the ministry of salvation, and when this institutional framework acquires more ambitions, the ministry of salvation becomes difficult to carry out. Secondly, that the transition from the framework (authority) to the content (ministry) is difficult in psychological terms (Θερμός, *Ὁμοιοπαθεῖς* 11-13).

Concerning the first assertion, Thermos points to the fact that the Church was organized, after Christ's ascension, in conformity with "law" and "order". This new mystical reality (Church) was not chaotic and unstructured, but had its own organizational form. Thermos points out that

> the Church has resorted to the law and order, on the one hand, with the purpose of expanding the limits of the Church, to streamline its organizing structures, and to curtail the egocentric ambitions, moral failings, and theological aberrations of its members, as well as the possible interference of the state in ecclesiastical life; on the other hand, by subjecting human individuality to a pattern of asceticism, this new reality demands that Christians look beyond appearances, i.e., the 'great' and 'first' is simultaneously 'servant' and 'slave'. By adopting such a perspective, Christians comprehend that they 'are not of this world' but 'alien to the world', a comprehension which serves as a shield against the temptation of secular authority. (Θερμός, *Ὁμοιοπαθεῖς* 13)

The transition from the attitudinal model of Christ concerning the statutory institutes of the Israelite religion, whereby He positioned Himself over the previous laws, to the structure of the Church, with its laws and order, is a praxis of philanthropy that has incomparably greater depth and saving power than the religious establishments of the Old Testament (Θερμός, *Ὁμοιοπαθεῖς* 13-4).

All these laws always had a relativistic meaning, and therefore the notion of "*oikonomia*"[16] has surrounded the life of the Church. Law and order are, according to Thermos, relativistic but not conventional. They are relativistic because they reflect a way of solving, in the Holy Spirit, issues concerning human nature and its institutions, whereby human nature introduces the notion of historicism as a decisive factor in the relativity of laws. Meanwhile, these laws are divested of any conventionality because they are issued by way of inspiration from the Holy Spirit, who is above all law, order, and negotiation (Θερμός, *Ὁμοιοπαθείς* 13).

It is important to understand that Jesus Christ himself granted authority to his disciples: "Behold, I give you the authority to trample on serpents and scorpions and over all the power of the enemy …" (Luke 10.19). Obviously, the idea of ecclesiastical authority was part of the evangelical world of the ancient Christian Church; but Christ's words granted ecclesiastical authority over the devil alone, even if largely to intervene in human matters (Θερμός, *Ὁμοιοπαθείς* 14). To illustrate the statement above Thermos explains that Christians accord respect to a clergyman, but this respect is actually directed to Christ and divine grace, whose minister a particular pastor is (Θερμός, *Ὁμοιοπαθείς* 14). However, if one considers the ecclesiastical penalties applied to priests and laypersons, it is important to understand that this is Church authority exerted over the devil, whose will a particular priest or layperson has freely followed. Although penances issued by the Church authority are never devoid of pedagogical function, this authority fundamentally represents "the true authority" both in relation to its source (Christ's words—"every authority has been given to me") and in relation to its vector (the devil) (Θερμός, *Ὁμοιοπαθείς* 15).

It is a fact that in Christian history the notions of law and authority were often understood lopsidedly at the expense of their spiritual content, i.e. that the Church ministers in the Holy Spirit, and ecclesiastical authority extended only over the devil and not the people. The poor understanding of the meaning of law, order, and authority within the Christian Church has been demonstrated within the Roman Catholic Church during previous centuries (Θερμός, *Ὁμοιοπαθείς* 15). In this part of Christianity, the organizing structure of the Church has been misinterpreted, according to Thermos (*Ὁμοιοπαθείς* 15), to the detriment of the evangelical spirit manifested in Christ's personality and life. The reaction to this misinterpretation was tragic for the whole of Western Chris-

16 "Oikonomia [the dispensation] is a provisional and judicious deviation, which is competently issued and originates in the Christian spirit, from strictly observing the canon in accordance with all its constitutive parts. Yet, this deviation does not mean any change in the dogmatic constitution of the Church, and provides tolerance for the salvation of human souls within (and even outside) the Church." Μπούμη, Παναγιώτου. *Ἡ ἐκκλησιαστικὴ «οἰκονομία» κατὰ τὸ Κανονικὸν δίκαιον* [The Ecclesiastical "Economy" according to the Canon Law]. Ἀθῆναι, 1971(Ἀνάτυπον ἐκ τοῦ περιοδικοῦ *Ἐκκλησία*), 7.

tendom, because it unleashed the advent of Protestantism, which represented the futile attempt of Western civilization to fault Rome. However well-intended the reformist movement was, church life moved in its propagation from one extreme—clericalism, to another—secularism (Θερμός, *Ὁμοιοπαθείς* 15).

Unfortunately, there is also a certain confusion between the true meaning of ecclesiastical law and authority and their secular analogues among some clergymen and laypersons in the Orthodox Church, although Orthodoxy castigates such confusion (Θερμός, *Ὁμοιοπαθείς* 15).

The function of the Holy Canons in Orthodox coenobitic monasticism and the preservation of truth in the Orthodox Church are two examples which Thermos cites in order to illustrate the intolerance of Orthodoxy toward such confusion. To begin with, the Holy Canons operate within the Orthodox coenobitic monasticism as follows: 1. "Functions and tasks are shared out on the basis of accomplishments or special needs of the monastic community; 2. The abbot (spiritual leader) is unanimously chosen; 3. Each member of the community owes obedience to the abbot; 4. Economic issues are decided by the council; 5. Either the community or the bishop has the power to deprive the abbot of authority, should the latter violate the basic precepts of monastic life" (Θερμός, *Ὁμοιοπαθείς* 15-6). Thereby "the Orthodox abbot / pastor perceives his duties: 1) as ministry, 2) for the community, and 3) on the commission from the Church" (Θερμός, *Ὁμοιοπαθείς* 15). Furthermore, the preservation of truth within the Orthodox Church is described by Thermos in the following way: 1. "the bishop is responsible for the observance of truth; 2. the synod exerts control over the authority of the bishop; 3. the ecumenical synod issues binding resolutions on the problems of faith, by cancelling or even declaring heretical the resolutions of local [national] synods; 4. The congregation (clergy and people) of the whole Church tests whether the particular synod is a true and binding ecumenical one or not" (Θερμός, *Ὁμοιοπαθείς* 15-6). The structure of Christian coenobitic monasticism and the preservation of the truth within the Church clearly show that ecclesiastical organization does not come down to the authority of a certain person over the entire Church but to the action of the Holy Spirit among all Christian believers (Θερμός, *Ὁμοιοπαθείς* 15).

Thus, law and order within the Church are only an institutional framework to protect the mystery of salvation (Θερμός, *Ὁμοιοπαθείς* 15). In this context, the authority embedded in certain ecclesiastical structures is conceptualized as a commission given by all believers to particular persons to offer the ministry of salvation toward the community (Θερμός, *Ὁμοιοπαθείς* 15). The distortion of this meaning of law and power always has severe repercussions for the quality of Church life, repercussions which one can see in the entire history of Christianity (Θερμός, *Ὁμοιοπαθείς* 15).

Yet, the reality is much more complex and quite removed from the content of certain principles of Orthodoxy discussed above. Therefore, Thermos claims that, in contemporary times, the exploratory mind can establish more and more deviations from the above conceptualization of authority and order in the Church. Moreover, at times, obedience to the Church turns into administrative subjugation (Θερμός, *Ὁμοιοπαθεῖς* 16). How does this aberration arise? Thermos says: "Subordinates treat superiors without any modicum of filial love, and even with fear. Superiors in turn remember their subordinates only when they need them, because they feel feeble and poor. Finally, it is only a secular interrelationship between the administration and its subjects that remains" (Θερμός, *Ὁμοιοπαθεῖς* 16). This raises another important issue concerning the psychological transition from the framework (authority) to the content (ministry). To speak of the concentration of powers and ministries within one person is fairly unusual for the Orthodox frame of reference. However, Thermos believes that certain notions concerning law and authority within the Orthodox Church have been divested of their initial content over the centuries. He sticks to the guiding precept of authority over the devil, not over the people, as given by Christ to His disciples (Θερμός, *Ὁμοιοπαθεῖς* 16). When this precept is broken, the holy space of the Church turns into a field in which human ambition and aggressiveness reign supreme. The very fact that the Church received the divine precept of mutual love and the repudiation of both sin and the devil as a guiding principle underlines the gravity of each believer's mission within and without the Church.

An important factor in successfully pursuing this mission is to overcome both spiritual and psychological deficiencies, because these deficiencies prevent the full development of personality (Θερμός, *Ὁμοιοπαθεῖς* 17-8). Examples of spiritual and psychological deficiency are the bipolar extremes of "clericalism / secularism". Clericalism is destructive because it alienates people psychologically and, subsequently, physically from the Church, since an arrogant priest sporting the illusion of spiritual enlightenment causes aversion. However, it is equally destructive for the unanimity of Church when certain laypersons endeavor to realize their egoistically based and latent ambition to exert authority within the Church (Θερμός, *Ὁμοιοπαθεῖς* 18). In this case, the failure to realize the ambition to dominate in worldly matters seeks an equivalent opportunity within the Church which is guided by a totally different interpretative vision concerning power, authority and order (Θερμός, *Ὁμοιοπαθεῖς* 18-9). Admittedly, the problem amounts to negating the overriding purpose of the Church which is to build a society of fully rounded personalities who are free and equal.

Interestingly, Thermos does not suggest any solution, as he is convinced that no institutional change can constitute a complete solution, "unless this solution is produced within the everlasting theological premises of the Church: the Cross, the resurrection of Christ, and the inspiration of the Holy Spirit" (*Ὁμοιοπαθεῖς* 21). "The clergymen and theologians have to immerse themselves in the depths of repentance in order to be able to move to a level of healthy Church belief" (Θερμός, *Ὁμοιοπαθεῖς* 21).

3.2.2. Experiencing the true pattern of Church leadership

Thermos refers to the ideas of St *Photius Constantinopolitanus*, which are a litmus test for the evaluation of ruling authorities, to help ascertain how Church authorities should fulfill their duty. Photius' ideas were expounded in his epistle to the newly baptized, ambitious Mikhail (former Boris) — the head of the Bulgarian State (Θερμός, *Ὁμοιοπαθείς* 70). The Grand Duke Mikhail requests autonomy for the Bulgarian Church from the Patriarch of Constantinople in order to achieve certain political objectives (Θερμός, *Ὁμοιοπαθείς* 70). The Patriarch Photius in turn sends the Grand Duke an answer outlining the duties of a governor, without considering the demand for ecclesiastical autonomy (Θερμός, *Ὁμοιοπαθείς* 70).

Thermos (*Ὁμοιοπαθείς* 70) argues that it is the problems of a Church leader even more than those of a state leader that reverberate in Photius' response. By Church leader, Thermos (*Ὁμοιοπαθείς* 70) means both a bishop, as head of eparchy, and a priest, as head of parish.

Proceeding from the epistle of St Photius, Thermos emphasizes his ideas concerning the way the conscience of a church leader should develop. These ideas can be classified as three kinds of commitment assumed by each Church leader, commitments which when met increase effectiveness, and when dishonoured lead to its opposite. These commitments are: responsibility toward one's own self, responsibility toward persons seeking spiritual guidance, and responsibility toward the entire Church.

First of all, the responsibility of the Church leader toward one's own self is clearly depicted in the case of Grand Duke Mikhail; notwithstanding his recent baptism and consequent lack of expertise in issues of Christian faith and life, Mikhail sought to expand his authority over the whole Bulgarian Church by securing its administrative autonomy from Constantinople. Any newly appointed Church leader who looks for the expansion or exertion of his authority in order to satisfy narcissistic desires demonstrates a similar lack of self-knowledge (Θερμός, *Ὁμοιοπαθείς* 70). Photius points out that the Grand Duke seems to have forgotten the well-known deontological precepts: rather than following imperial ambitions, the governor needs 1) "to immerse himself deeply in the faith" and 2) to crave visionary leadership (Θερμός, *Ὁμοιοπαθείς* 70).

Forging ahead toward the first goal should be accompanied by a willingness of clergymen to concentrate upon their "inner person"; such direction of a special focus on the "inner person" underscores the importance to a Church leader of being virtuous. To substantiate this statement, Thermos quotes St Photius:

> The more a person is distinguished by his authority, the more he should be distinguished as a virtuous person. Yet, if a particular leader does the opposite, he does three deleterious things: 1) he loses own self, 2) he induces those who look to him to share his vice, 3) he causes God to be blasphemed, because He has

> entrusted such authority to an unworthy individual. Therefore every person should avoid such behaviour and this, in particular, refers to the authorities. (PG 102.672c)

From the foregoing passage, it is evident that, in being virtuous, a Church leader actually meets the three kinds of commitment outlined above.

Yet, the invitation to cultivate moral virtues does not necessarily imply the deep personal immersion in the faith; it may simply suggest the prevention of certain serious problems that are at the heart of the difficulties of operating leadership. One the most serious problems connected with leadership is the jealousy that often emerges in relationships between colleagues. St Photius regards this passion as a perverseness:

> Jealousy is a dangerous disease in humans; but it is a far more serious disease when found in those in power. Such jealousy makes the one possessed by it see his colleagues as adversaries due to their virtue and to plot against them as if they were enemies, instead of viewing them as contributing to the prosperity of the community. Could something be more ruinous and thoughtless than this? (PG 102.673d)

This passage from St Photius leads one to the root of the problem. Jealousy is "illogical, if a leader perceives his colleagues as co-working for the same worthy ends" (Θερμός, *Ὁμοιοπαθεῖς* 72). However, jealousy is natural, if a leader / pastor is "serving not a common and sacred mission but selfish ends, even those of a psychological nature" (Θερμός, *Ὁμοιοπαθεῖς* 72). In this case, a pastor believes that he is serving his flock whereas he is unconsciously seeking to garner benefits for himself alone. Here the flock becomes, according to Thermos, a means for the pastor to "pasture himself" (Ezek 34.2). Certainly, the presence of successful colleagues seems to pose a threat to the psychological interests of such a pastor and therefore to arouse his jealousy. For most of the time, the pastor is unaware of the jealousy so that it is only through resentment and questioning his colleagues' competence for pastoral ministry that the jealousy becomes evident (Θερμός, *Ὁμοιοπαθεῖς* 72).

It is helpful for the idealized image of a Church leader to endure the stress caused by the successes of colleagues with gratitude (Θερμός, *Ὁμοιοπαθεῖς* 72), since such stress signals the necessity for a cure. By showing heartfelt gratitude a leader repairs the hiatus in his own virtues: "Repentance assists providence. Accordingly, if there is something that providence ignores and leaves stranded, it is the repentance that takes up, restores and saves it" (PG 102.673d).

On the other hand, Thermos (*Ὁμοιοπαθεῖς* 70-1) remarks that the problems of leadership are not always caused by the personality of the leader. In fact, sometimes it is the institutional framework found in the church, public corporation or army that has a strong impact on the effectiveness or ineffectiveness of the leadership. However, it is important in scrutinizing the probable reasons for a leader's ineffectiveness to consider his personality, because there is often an inclination to shift responsibility from the individual to the corporate level. Experience seems to show, according to Thermos (*Ὁμοιοπαθεῖς* 70), that usually a leader's incompetence and inappropriateness for a particular office is rooted in his seeking to work according to, and to implement, the agenda of an authoritarian institution. Such aspiration, however, does not help for visionary leadership to develop, because the well-known secular methods of reinforcing authority "lead to the formation of a mask and to the existential alienation of the leader" (Θερμός, *Ὁμοιοπαθεῖς* 70). The existence of mask implies that the leader is naked in the field of interpersonal communion and therefore dependent on other strong stimulus to obedience than love. Such stimulus is fear.

Admittedly, obedience arising from love is easier and preferable. But, if it is preferable, why do certain ecclesiastics resort to fear to achieve the obedience of their flock? Thermos believes that the reason that many leaders repair to fear is to be found in the depths of their inner need: a) "to bolster an inflated self-image, the psychoanalytic 'idealized ego', and b) to reduce the pain inflicted by their inadequacy" (*Ὁμοιοπαθεῖς* 71-2). By surrendering to the dynamics of an idealized ego, an individual invested with authority is precipitated into a gulf of arrogance, snobbery and haughtiness (Θερμός, *Ὁμοιοπαθεῖς* 71-2). These passions efface the society of fully rounded personalities and create optimal conditions for the spiritual exploitation and depersonalization of a human being. Over against this, only when the authorities maintain and cultivate love in their relationships with their subordinates or those they are spiritually guiding can the human personality and human relationships flourish and spiritual growth take place (Θερμός, *Ὁμοιοπαθεῖς* 72).

There is another reason why fear may be chosen over love. Thermos considers that certain Church leaders refer to God in a vein of fear because they are aware of their own uncertainty as to whether they sincerely love God. Such a leader may surreptitiously encourage his flock to feel and relate to God in a similar way to him (Θερμός, *Ὁμοιοπαθεῖς* 72). A psychological pattern with regard to relationships is already formed within such a leader; in the aftermath, this pattern is "automatically reproduced in the leader's relationship with others, and the leader may not even be aware of this" (Θερμός, *Ὁμοιοπαθεῖς* 72).

The second responsibility of each Church leader concerns the spiritual guidance of people within the Church. Here, as in the case of cleric's responsibility toward his own self, the requirement of a virtuous life is foundational as well. Thermos (*Ὁμοιοπαθεῖς* 73) considers that this is not about saintliness; rather, it is a powerful reminder of the social character of sin, since any sin humiliates the name of God because it is extremely difficult for subordinates and those being spiritually guided to resist the temptation of a Church leader steeped in sins. Unfortunately, clergymen unimaginably underestimate the repercussions of their sinfulness on laypersons. This underestimation may occur, according to Thermos (*Ὁμοιοπαθεῖς* 71-3), because clergy are often unaware of the speed with which this temptation devastates the Church. This temptation sometimes proves to be irresistible because it is unconscious, with the result that people may not even realize that the devastation within them is already immense. The improper behaviour of an ecclesiastical leader becomes law for a subordinate's psyche. In this context, St Photius claims: "The behaviour of authorities becomes a law for the subordinates" (PG 102.673c). What has the most damaging effects for any person is "the lawlessness that becomes a psychological law" (Θερμός, *Ὁμοιοπαθεῖς* 73). Yet, if lawlessness eventually inhabit certain spaces within the Church, the invited penalties for spiritual failures should nevertheless be limited, since these always represent a partial solution (Θερμός, *Ὁμοιοπαθεῖς* 73-4). Thermos states that the ability to ensure the reeducation of subordinates or those being spiritually guided is the mark of a true leader. Photius supports this claim:

> Castigation is common in an irascible person rather than a virtuous one. Since the former can hardly command the people in a wise manner, he strongly depends on penalties. Even the worst tyrant can castigate, whereas only the true leader is able to command wisely. It is always the uncorrupted virtue of a ruler that makes for more numerous and better subordinates. (PG 102.673a)

On the other hand, indulgence toward the established lawlessness may encourage and reinforce passions and prejudices in the people and thereby breed spiritual conformism (Θερμός, *Ὁμοιοπαθεῖς* 74-6). It seems therefore that the true leader must create a careful balance between the frequent recourse to penalties and the injudicious use of lenience.

In being a paragon of virtue and securing real, spiritual and psychological benefit for the flock, the Church leader promotes true communication in the ecclesiastical space. In the opinion of Thermos, St Photius believes that qualitative not quantitative results distinguish the true leader, making him a role model:

> There are some rulers who have claimed that it is a virtue to make from a small city a great one; in my opinion, however, it is a much greater virtue to turn a corrupt city into a worthy one. A small city becomes a great city naturally in the course of time, whereas to turn a corrupt city into a worthy one is only possible for a distinguished leader. By becoming zealous of such a leader, you will celebrate the real achievement in the growth of moral condition in your subordinates (PG 102.673b)

St Photius's statement is certainly instructive for many contemporary Church leaders, since a quantitative increase in believers / priests within parishes / bishoprics often dulls the vigilance of pastors / bishops with regard to improving the quality of ecclesiastical life (Θερμός, *Ὁμοιοπαθεῖς* 76).

An important issue concerning the second kind of commitment is the leader's choice of retinue. St Photius offers the following observation:

> A city bounded with crumbling walls loses its prestige despite its magnificent buildings, health-enhancing seasons, and plethora of goods. In the same vein, a potentate surrounded by corrupt administrators and advisers compromises his reputation. Having experienced the corruption of his retinue, the potentate's subjects assume him to be also corrupt (PG 102.673b)

Thermos asserts that the image of a leader is often much more influential in shaping the behaviour of his subordinates than his true ego. Although God eventually reveals the truth about the true ego of an ecclesiastical leader, the harm that in the meanwhile his corrupt retinue can produce in the faithful is difficult to estimate.

Why do many notable leaders pay no regard to their immediate environment? The unconscious criteria by which the leader chooses his immediate social circle is psychologically significant in this case. The choices made may reveal the leader's unconscious need to be surrounded by persons indulgent toward his counsels and overwhelmed with wonder, admiration, and respect for him (Θερμός, *Ὁμοιοπαθεῖς* 77).

Ultimately, the Church leader has to meet his commitment toward the whole Church. Thus, the expansion of the Church is dependent upon the morality of its leader. Photius says:

> When someone governs his own self, undoubtedly he can also govern his subordinates indeed. Because when his subordinates see that their leader governs his passions and, moreover, controls his desire for pleasure, they ardently and readily submit themselves to him. If, however, he is a slave of pleasures and passions, they feel repulsion and will not obey a slave. (PG 102.676b)

Based on this passage, Thermos (*Ὁμοιοπαθεῖς* 78-9) states that, if a leader is virtuous, people respect him and this respect generates eagerness and obedience. In contrast, a leader's pathology makes him ridiculous in his subordinates' eyes (Θερμός, *Ὁμοιοπαθεῖς* 78-9). The leader whose reputation has been compromised is unable to recognize this, because he is spiritually blinded by his passion[17].

---

17 Alluding to St Photius, Kornarakis asserts that the process *of becoming* obscured with relation to the mind, *of being* plunged into the darkness of passion, does not just impact the moral aspect of a personality. "When a particular person experiences a sin, the whole of his inner world participates in this, and each part of the soul seeks, along with others, to attain whatever this experience promises them" (Κορναράκη, *Τὸ Ψυχολογικόν* 38). St Photius designates this integral character of experiencing sin, resorting to the term "*ἔρως παραβάσεως*" (the love for transgression). When an individual experiences sin, he is in state of blindness due to the power of love for transgression: "… as when they sin, they are in the state of blindness due to the power of love for transgression". (PG 101.132d) "The love for transgression divests the human person of the inner integration. This way the process of becoming spiritually blind is set in motion." (Κορναράκη, *Τὸ Ψυχολογικόν* 38)

The abuse of power may, according to Thermos, lead to insensibility of conscience (Θερμός, *Ὁμοιοπαθείς* 78-9). This insensibility may make spiritual leaders either indulgent or intolerant. In quoting St Photius, Thermos (*Ὁμοιοπαθείς* 79) states that sheer indulgence and injudicious intolerance make pastoral care ineffective:

> You will be the best judge for others, when you detect everything you did and give account for every deed, having as a judge your own conscience, and then find the proper ways to remedy your sins. Otherwise, how can you not feel ashamed in rebuking others for the sins that you commit as well? What do you think they will feel toward you if they are punished by you who treats himself indulgently on the matter of the same sins? (PG 102.677b)

This passage delineates the critical situation when the message of secular and ecclesiastical authority falls into disrepute among right-thinking people and the faithful. Thermos believes that an adequate reason for either of these authorities gradually being curtailed is that at the present time power is not viewed as a means to promote justice but as an instrument to achieve personal or corporate objectives. He suggests that the spiritual and moral edification of the faithful has gradually moved from reality to virtuality, because clergymen show no great concern to practise the Christian creed within their own lives.

Thermos also discusses the choice of improper individuals for ecclesiastical leadership. Wrong choices can decimate the Church more seriously than a plague, because adverse feelings against such individuals can be directed at God, who ostensibly allowed such impropriety. St Photius says:

> Those who are rich with virtues should be, first of all, appointed as rulers; yet, if there are no such persons, the rulers should be chosen among the most just people, because, if someone among the rulers transgresses the law, the hatred and anger of the crowd are directed at the one who has appointed this ruler. (PG 102.676-7a)

This emphasis on the morality of the leader does not mean derogating the importance of the intellectual capacities necessary for a leader, since the success of a mission often greatly depends on wisdom, intelligence and counsel. "It happened that the hands of many persons could not succeed in matters where pene-

---

One finds the same idea by the famous Methodist theologian, Robert Cummings Neville, who puts it as follows: "… in the condition of depravity, one's love is turned to a kind of bondage. Like being caught up in sexual lust (St Paul's favorite image) in which one can hardly feel other things and one's desire becomes blinded to its harmonious disposition regarding diverse objects of love, depravity of the heart consists in fixations and obsessions. A depraved heart may still be capable of loving, even organizing a love life. But it is susceptible always to fixation and obsession". Robert Cummings Neville. *A Theology Primer*. New York: S U of New York, 1991. 86. Print.

trative deliberation immediately could. Therefore you should prefer the wise counsel to the hands of many" (PG 102.673d).

Thermos is convinced that in this statement Photius is expressing the "deep Orthodox concern for strategy", a factor with which the contemporary Church still concerns itself (*Ὁμοιοπαθείς* 80). In this respect, the psychological and spiritual resources of the ecclesiastics are frequently consumed in an inefficient and ineffective manner. Thermos (*Ὁμοιοπαθείς* 80) believes the same concern to be relevant to spiritual guidance. Thus, pastoral counsel often solely consists of the suggestion to further intensify one's spiritual life through prayer and asceticism with no attempt being made to understand any psychological factors which may have contributed to a transgression.

A further factor relevant to the problem of appropriate leadership is unity between the leader and the citizens / flock. Knowing that the main task of a leader is to maintain unity, St Photius offers the following advice:

> Turning the mutual controversies between citizens against the enemies, transform them (these controversies) into the fight for the benefit of the homeland. Tyrants trouble the crowds by means of seditions, because in the common corruption and discord there is safety for tyranny. The ruler and potentate, however, maintain unity among citizens because their authority is premised on the salvation of citizens. (PG 102.677d)

According to Thermos (*Ὁμοιοπαθείς* 80), maintaining unity is proof of a church leader (especially, a bishop). This is the foundational criterion for determining a true bishop (Θερμός, *Ὁμοιοπαθείς* 80). The most unscrupulous guides do not emerge by accident. Rather, in attempting to strengthen and perpetuate tyranny, they resort to discord and conflict. By spreading discord among people, a political leader betrays his people as much as a bishop is "a wolf in sheep's clothing" when he purposefully causes discord among God's people (Θερμός, *Ὁμοιοπαθείς* 80). On the other hand, the true leader is concerned with maintaining unity since the energy of a unified Christian group is a strong defence against external threats.

St Photius continues: "Being generous, protect the citizen, as if they are your own nerves and limbs of authority, because, if these break apart, the danger is that your authority will perish as well" (PG 102.689c).

It is therefore to the leader's own benefit that his citizens / flock feel secure, because, by scattering their trust and security, he undermines his own position. Thermos claims that indifference to unity itself is strange, because, according to Apostle Paul, "we, being many, are one body in Christ, and individually members of one another" (Rom 12.5) and, therefore, we must live accordingly since "no one ever hated his own flesh, but nourishes and cherishes it, just as the Lord does the Church" (Eph 5.29).

3.2.3. Escaping the psychological pitfalls of Church leadership

According to Kernberg's psychological research[18], progress in Church leadership depends on equipping ecclesiastical leaders with the necessary knowledge of the psychological pitfalls inherent in Church leadership. These pitfalls exist at the individual and collective psychological levels. The individual psychological level refers to pathological characters among Church leaders, whereas the collective psychological level refers to the laws which characterize the behaviour of a group as a whole (Θερμός, *Ὁμοιοπαθεῖς* 44).

Thermos (*Ὁμοιοπαθεῖς* 43) here focuses on three general ideas: the impact of the leader on the group, the influence of the latter on the former and finally the impact of the group on its members. He begins with the following premise: "The mutual influence between a leader and his subordinate has an effect both on their psychological condition and their effectiveness" (Θερμός, *Ὁμοιοπαθεῖς* 43).

An observer may experience a leader's psychological difficulties and make safe assumptions about his inner person by observing the problematic behaviour of that leader's subordinates. In contradistinction when the disorders in the psychological function of a group are imputed exclusively to the leader — it may be that the condition of the group is in actual fact being revealed. Both cases differ from each other in relation to the origin of the psychopathological disturbance: in one case, it seems to originate within the leader, while, in the other, within the group. However, according to Thermos, psychopathological disturbance has in most cases its roots in both the group and the individual. Consequently, making an accurate diagnosis is difficult. Notwithstanding this complexity, Thermos believes that it is necessary to consider each case separately.

3.2.3.1 Psychological disturbance at the individual level

Thermos outlines the following types of pathological leadership:
1) "Schizoid personality: The leader is distant, cold, and difficult to get on with, averse to emotional contact, isolated 'in his own world'" (Θερμός, *Ὁμοιοπαθεῖς* 44). (It is presupposed that all these features are real characteristics of the personality and do not consist of intentional behaviour or an unconscious defensive process).
2) "Obsessive-compulsive personality: Such a leader exhibits punctuality, fastidiousness, hesitance, and scholasticism" (Θερμός, *Ὁμοιοπαθεῖς* 44); the moderate presence of these features favours organization and efficiency in work, while

18 Thermos borrows several psychoanalytic ideas from two texts by the American psychiatrist and psychoanalyst, Otto Kernberg. The first text is "Regression in Organizational Leadership", and the second one — "Leadership and Organizational Functioning: Organizational Regression" (*Ὁμοιοπαθεῖς* 43-4).

when intensely present "they obstruct productivity and cause the leader to tyrannize his subordinates" (Θερμός, *Ὁμοιοπαθείς* 44).
3) "Paranoid personality: The leader is suspicious, feels himself threatened, attributing evil motives to others, and stands by his attributions never revising his constructions" (Θερμός, *Ὁμοιοπαθείς* 44).
4) "Narcissistic personality: this is the most dangerous personality type for the Christian mission and its ministers" (Θερμός, *Ὁμοιοπαθείς* 44). The narcissistic personality is characterized by the inner necessity to be the centre of attention. This has either been the "leader's stable psychological condition from the outset or has developed gradually to compensate for inferiority and anxiety arising from a lack of basic skills" (Θερμός, *Ὁμοιοπαθείς* 44). This type is met among those of medium talent; it also embodies the specific psychological standard of perceiving one's own dignity which is necessary for the normal functioning of self-confidence in each individual; finally, it too represents the attempt to maintain inner psychological quasi-balance and self-respect (Θερμός, *Ὁμοιοπαθείς* 44). Thus, the egocentric and immature personality fed by the praise of others is the archetype for this type of personality. (Θερμός, *Ὁμοιοπαθείς* 44)

According to Thermos, all these types can be found among Church leaders. Thus, when an impressionable adolescent hungry for psychological contact encounters a cold and distant spiritual leader, the leader will either display a specific natural character formed by social circumstances or a psychologically unbalanced schizoid personality (Θερμός, *Ὁμοιοπαθείς* 45).

Furthermore, a fastidious bishop can indicate a character permeated by a fervent zeal for the further development of spiritual life and improvement of intra-ecclesiastical relations or can indicate psychological alienation in the form of an obsessive-compulsive personality disorder (Θερμός, *Ὁμοιοπαθείς* 45). It is extremely difficult to decide whether such personality attributes arise from pathological causes or are the healthy manifestations of a dedicated Christian. Thermos offers little to aid the making of such a decision. He suggests only *approximate* types of pathological character, since these tend to cluster together so that the emergence of atypical groups is highly probable.

Despite this, Thermos suggests that the narcissistic personality is the most prevalent type among Church leaders. Of course, Thermos can only make reference to the Greek ecclesiastical environment, since he is not familiar with the other Churches and the characteristics of their intra-ecclesiastical relations. With regard to the Greek Church, Thermos is of the opinion that the excessive and arbitrary use of authority is peculiar to the Greek Church in some locations. Since the emergence of psychopathological characteristics among ecclesiastical leaders is also influenced by the way in which ecclesiastical authority is exerted, one can understand why some psychopathological persons at the individual level would want to be part of certain structures within the ecclesiastical institution. These structures may both invest psychopathology with collective authority and debar any intra-ecclesiastical attempt to disempower such authority (Θερμός, *Ὁμοιοπαθείς* 45). In relation to other Orthodox Churches, it seems appropriate here to draw attention to the narcissistic personality within other Churches. The Russian theologian Very Reverend Eumenius says:

> Unfortunately, we are compelled to acknowledge that contemporary spiritual guidance sometimes consists of a direct, rough intrusion by the pastor into the inner world of the parishioner; this intrusion is accompanied by the reorganization (and often even by the breaking) of the parishioner's inner psychological structure in order to make him just like "his confessor". Sometimes this behaviour is a result of the priest's self-conceit and haughtiness. Yet, we should also consider that the clergy's attempt to shape his parishioners to his own subjective religious experience is a result of his not knowing other approaches, or other ways of guiding God's people. (284)

Taking Kernberg's writings as a basis, Thermos states that a narcissistic leader is incapable of carrying out the most important functions of leadership, which are: a) "to understand the problems of one's subordinates, and b) to assist those subordinates in solving their problems" (*Ὁμοιοπαθείς* 45). The ministry of such a leader is psychologically based on the need for external confirmation and honour, which, when absent, leave his psychological world without any motivation (Θερμός, *Ὁμοιοπαθείς* 45). In this case, the leader is unable to act as an ecclesiastical guide: a) "sustaining and fortifying his subordinates, b) supporting them in their problems, c) relieving them in periods of dryness, d) leading them to independence and autonomy in their work" (Θερμός, *Ὁμοιοπαθείς* 45). Such a leader is a very bad fellow-traveller. The problem consists in the reversal of roles: instead of inspiring, supporting, understanding, sympathizing, and spiritually regenerating his subordinates or associates, the leader is only concerned with deriving narcissistic satisfaction from others' praise, flattery, and admiration (Θερμός, *Ὁμοιοπαθείς* 45). A bitter conflict emerges when this reversion of roles does not function: the leader is not treated according to his expectations, while his subordinates / flock feel that they are subject to a spurious rather than an authentic spiritual guide (Θερμός, *Ὁμοιοπαθείς* 46-8). Thermos (*Ὁμοιοπαθείς* 46-8) states that similar situations may occur in the relationships between a bishop and a priest, a priest and his flock, a teacher and his disciple. Significantly, these occurrences reveal that the ecclesiastical establishment lacks the insight to recognize such persons and prevent them being placed in ecclesiastical positions (Θερμός, *Ὁμοιοπαθείς* 45-6). Thermos quotes St Basil the Great in support of the statement that the greater the narcissism, the deeper the ignorance of the true nature of ecclesiastical mission:

> Let the one who is distinguished by his authority not be extolled by his office, lest he should break away from the blessing of humbleness or "lest being puffed up with pride he fall into the same condemnation as the devil" (1 Tim 3.6). Yet, let him be persuaded that to rule over the majority means to serve them. Just as the

> one who serves the wounded, removing the pus from their wounds and administering healing medicines appropriate to the experienced injury, does not have a motive for haughtiness, but rather a motive for humbleness, agony and struggle, so even more so does the one who is entrusted to heal the feeblenesses of community. Being the servant of each one and ultimately accountable for his care of these, he should reflect and struggle on with his task. Thereby the word of the Lord will be fulfilled: "Whoever desires to become great among you shall be your servant and whoever of you desires to be the first shall be the slave of all" (Mark 10.43-44). (PG 31.992a)

Beside these psychopathological types which are destructive of ecclesiastical authority and life, Thermos (*Ὁμοιοπαθείς* 52-6) turns his attention to other subtle ambiguous psychological conditions: aggressiveness, loneliness and self-perceived charisma.

Aggressiveness is a subtle and ambiguous psychological condition because it may sometimes seem to be fully justified and even necessary, while at other times it may be ruinous not only for the person manifesting it but also for the Church as a whole. A leader's natural aggression, in the sense of a hostile mental attitude and destructive behaviour, as reaction to injustice and ingratitude of the members of the group would seem reasonable. However, when a hostile mental attitude and destructive behaviour are used to cope with arbitrary shifts of authority within the hierarchical world of the group, and are followed by revenge and a disproportionate application of punishment, discord and confusion result for both the leader and the group. Force and coercion as a means of persuasion bring about discord and confusion because an ecclesiastical leader is primarily a pedagogue / role model whose words and actions must be as peaceful as possible, even in the face of injustice and ingratitude (Θερμός, *Ὁμοιοπαθείς* 52). Thermos frames the dealing with aggressiveness in canonical and patristic terms. The Ninth Canon of IV Ecumenical synod and 118 Canon of Carthaginian synod prescribe that bishops from adjacent eparchies alone must pass judgment on clergymen who mistreat their own bishop, since the latter may provoke controversy, and lack clear thought, during the course of a trial due to his probable thirst for revenge (Θερμός, *Ὁμοιοπαθείς* 53). In patristic terms, St John Chrysostom states that Christian ministers promote the consolidation of the Church only when they are not subject to the duress of human passion and worldly interests, and are not inclined to behave improperly on account of bonds of friendship or impulses of hatred (PG 62.525).

The practical aspects of a leader's life may cause loneliness. Usually, election to a position of leadership reduces the circle of persons with whom the leader can share his problems, anxieties and "queries" (Θερμός, *Ὁμοιοπαθείς* 53-4). Furthermore, a position of leadership obligates one to behave in accordance with a certain professional image, and therefore impulsiveness or other unsuitable psychological traits may be suppressed, and not overcome, in order to preserve image. Leaders are expected to be able to take quick and effective decisions in critical situations; an expectation harmful to the individual incapable of this, since deep anxiety over personal failure may heighten feelings of loneliness. Thermos (*Ὁμοιοπαθεῖς* 54) is convinced that these demands are harder for bishops, priests and theologians in the provinces. Thermos considers that Church authorities should and can do more to reduce the effect of loneliness on the psychological state and effectiveness of ecclesiastics. Negligence in this matter may lead to the psychological alienation of ecclesiastical leaders. Such alienation is often manifested in the behaviour patterns of leadership within the Church. These are represented by two extremes: servility and autarchy. The former represents the vector upwards, when a subordinate communicates with his superior; the latter, the reverse. These two patterns also imply an inability to communicate with colleagues of the same rank, an inability which leads to the eventual abolition of the Orthodox synodic exertion of authority within the Church (Θερμός, *Ὁμοιοπαθεῖς* 54).

Since leadership and a hierarchical structure will never cease to exist within the church, Thermos suggests that loneliness and the gradual abolition of the Orthodox synodic exertion of authority can only be dealt with by changing the personal attitude of every ecclesiastic and increasing the opportunities for communication and dialogue between clergymen (Θερμός, *Ὁμοιοπαθεῖς* 55).

A person who perceives himself as charismatic is, in Thermos's opinion (*Ὁμοιοπαθεῖς* 56), a great danger to Church leaders, because such a person may substitute his will for ecclesiastical law. This self-perception may enter the consciousness of a leader *at the beginning* of his ministry; it too may *gradually* percolate into his ministry; and, finally, the emergence of such self-perception may be "assisted" *by the leader's environment* (Θερμός, *Ὁμοιοπαθεῖς* 56). The emergence of this lawlessness takes place predominantly within a leader himself, but it is the life of the entire group that is irrevocably damaged, since each group member begins to experience inwardly the relativity of ecclesiastical law so that the tendency toward lawlessness becomes almost unrestrained and difficult to halt by exterior measures (Θερμός, *Ὁμοιοπαθεῖς* 56). Thereof, since the collective violation of law often originates in the careless attitude of a leader toward this law, the enforcement of the law seems to be effective only if it is implemented by the particular leader. In this context, Thermos emphasizes the importance of the following words by St John Chrysostom:

> Absolute authority is unbearable … [The Scripture] ordains and decrees that [bishop of Old Covenant] should have [his] head not being bare but covered, with the purpose of making [the bishop] learn that he too has a head [his subaltern relation to someone else]. For the same reason, during ecclesiastical ordination to the priesthood the Gospel of Christ is laid on the head of the one being ordained to symbolize to him the acceptance of the true crown of Gospel and to remind him that, much as his investment as the head of parish is true, it is nevertheless also expected of him to act in accordance with the laws of this Gospel so that in holding everyone under his authority, he too should be held under the authority of

> these laws, and in admonishing others with his pastoral word, he must be admonished by the word of the divine law as well. (PG 56.404)

Thus, St John Chrysostom envisioned the world of exemplary ecclesiastical authority in two dimensions: 1) humbleness of mind combined with self-awareness of standing as Christ's missionary and 2) moral life combined with a sense of responsibility for the effectiveness of pastoral word.

3.2.3.2. Psychological disturbance at the collective level

Relying on psychological expertise, Thermos draws on Kernberg's research in outlining a theory of the pathology of the group and its impact on a leader. Kernberg designates this by means of a psychoanalytic term — "regression" (qtd. Θερμός, *Ὁμοιοπαθείς* 47). By this, he means that a group has reverted to earlier, more immature patterns of behaviour. When these early patterns are re-established, the group begins to function in a way that is harmful to the psychological condition of each member and that undermines the individual's productivity (Θερμός, *Ὁμοιοπαθείς* 47). Thermos (*Ὁμοιοπαθείς* 47) describes two pathologies of group function: 1) a dependent pattern of behaviour and 2) a polemical pattern of behaviour.

1) "*Dependent pattern of behaviour*". The group cleaves to the leader and has increasingly unrealistic expectations of him. When disappointment inevitably sets in the group looks for another new leader and re-establishes the same unrealistic expectations (Θερμός, *Ὁμοιοπαθείς* 47).

2) "*Polemical pattern of behaviour*". The members of the group appear to be united when they share a "common enemy" (Θερμός, *Ὁμοιοπαθείς* 47). If the common enemy disappears, emerging conflicts within the group affect each member and eventually lead to a split in the group (Θερμός, *Ὁμοιοπαθείς* 47). The entities that then emerge tend to be either submissive or rebellious, the former usually identifying itself with the leader, while the latter resolutely resists him (Θερμός, *Ὁμοιοπαθείς* 47).

When both collective patterns of behaviour are found in the ecclesiastical community, individual members damage relationships by substituting: passion for love, servility for freedom, and partisanship for unity.

Proceeding from the principle of mutual interaction between a leader and a group, we are able to foresee the necessary consequences of collective behaviour for the leader (Θερμός, *Ὁμοιοπαθείς* 48). An immature and dependent flock "will fatally expose the priest to the danger of overrating his capabilities and excessively interfering in the freedom of people" (Θερμός, *Ὁμοιοπαθείς* 48). It is possible, however, that the priest will directly challenge such collective behaviour (Θερμός, *Ὁμοιοπαθείς* 48). These problematic ecclesiastical patterns of behaviour should always be analyzed from the perspective of the two-way interaction between group and leader as outlined above.

Thermos (*Ὁμοιοπαθείς* 48-9) then analyzes the reasons that a polemical pattern of behaviour can be found within certain ecclesiastical groups. He expresses the opinion that this pattern is rooted in the thirst for power; as a matter of fact, power is often interpreted, as St Isidori Pelusiotæ puts it, "not as a source of responsibility but as a confirmation of imperial authority" (PG 78.1485b).

It may be dangerous for an ecclesiastical leader to be ministering to a group subject to the polemical pattern of behaviour, because the leader may provoke pretentious sectarianism by taking sides instead of maintaining group unity and restoring peace between adverse tendencies within the group (Θερμός, *Ὁμοιοπαθείς* 49). Because his responsibility is great, the leader must not let his judgment, which should be objective, impartial and autonomous, be too strongly influenced by external factors arising from narrow sectarianism (Θερμός, *Ὁμοιοπαθείς* 49). Yet, sometimes the leader may "polemically identify himself with a particular group, because he is simply wrong or has been insufficiently informed by subordinates / colleagues" (Θερμός, *Ὁμοιοπαθείς* 49). The group may intentionally or even unconsciously provide inaccurate information in order to impose its own agenda through gaining the support of a misinformed and misled leader (Θερμός, *Ὁμοιοπαθείς* 49).

Thermos (*Ὁμοιοπαθείς* 49) points out that the principle of mutual influence has the effect of mutually binding the sides involved: the problems of a morbidly functioning group can be resolved by finding a new leader and supporting the drive for change; the problem of an unpopular leader can be resolved by activating the positive elements in group members which enhance their unity and productivity and by eliminating disorganization in the leader's own personal life. Thermos claims:

> The solutions should not be pictured as simple. If there is a problem of autocracy and arbitrariness, the solution does not lie in establishing "democracy". Kernberg warns that there are dictatorships that pertain to groups. If certain persons around a leader have a share in his arbitrariness, this very sharing, nevertheless, does not promote democracy. (Θερμός, *Ὁμοιοπαθείς* 49)

To show how much autocracy reduces effectiveness, Thermos quotes a testimony from St Cyril Fileotis:

> If someone with fear of God and with humbleness orders his brother to do something, this order, when told in a manner pleasing to God, will cause this brother to obey however unpopular the order might be. If, however, an individual, who does not have the fear of God, wishes to issue commands with the sole purpose of demonstrating his authority over his brother, then God, who sees the hidden content of the commander's heart, causes the brother not to hear and, consequently, to abandon the command. There is an enormous difference between an order issued out of the fear of God and one enforced through authority. The former is humble and with entreaty, while the latter is full of anger and confusion, which are from the devil. (98)

Finally, the impact of the group upon its members is an important issue which should be considered. This refers to the group as an entity with its own psychology, which exercises real power over each of its individual member's psychological world. Thermos (*Ὁμοιοπαθείς* 50-1) asserts that, when this "psychology of the group" begins to operate, the convictions and reactions of each individual member undergo a palpable change, in both a positive and negative direction. Thermos says:

> 1) being placed among a group of trouble-makers and reactionaries, a forbearing and organized pupil takes on the same characteristics; 2) if placed in a group of undignified, servile collaborators of the bishop, a rounded and serious priest either loses his opinion and falls silent, or behaves in a reactionary way; 3) in attending a synod presided over by the primate, a bishop with visions and self-criticism will either remain silent or identify himself with the majority; or even approve the declarations of self-justification and self-praise made by the ecclesiastics. Thus a previously self-critical and idealistic bishop appears to take issue with those criticizing the Church; and in doing so follows the group and not the demands of his own reason which require him to test and prove the ecclesiastical behaviour which sparked external criticism. (Θερμός, *Ὁμοιοπαθείς* 50-1)

Obviously, when an ecclesiastical group abolishes the freedom of each of its members, then the repercussions for the life and witness of this group have an impact on the way in which the clergy ministers; clergy with limited freedom are likely to inhibit their creativity and to render the mission of Church less and less effective.

In looking for solutions to this problem, Thermos states that effective approaches to the dysfunctions in the mechanism of collective ecclesiastical life, as constituted by leader, group, and each member of the group, require spiritual struggle at the individual and collective levels of ecclesiastical groups. Besides this spiritual approach, he suggests setting the stage for more detailed discussion of this problem within theological schools. However, the process of learning how collective ecclesiastical life functions should continue at all stages of professional life, from the stage of seminarian to that of patriarch.

3.3. Conclusions

To conclude, Thermos claims that the effectiveness of Orthodox ecclesiastics depends on the following: 1) the extent to which each ecclesiastic is aware of his unconscious, 2) the psychological practice of self-knowledge (or introspection), 3) and the spiritual practice of repentance. It is important to learn to be aware of the existence of this psychological sphere within the human soul because it is critical to efficient pastoral care. Another point which Thermos stresses is that there is a direct relationship between the ways in which the Church leadership operates and the quality of Church life. This is an important issue since an inwardly qualitative Church life can ensure the effectiveness of the Christian mission within the world. Therefore, Thermos calls on the current Orthodox Church authorities to be more responsible in considering the issue of preparing future Orthodox spiritual leaders. New criteria should be established for identifying effective / ineffective candidates who aspire to ecclesiastical authority. Those ecclesiastics who have such aspirations must have a clear understanding that Christian authority consists primarily in responsibility and ministry. This can be done only within an atmosphere in which authority is continually experienced as ministry, not distinction. Orthodoxy has a future only when spiritual struggle is undertaken at both the personal and collective level, and when an excellent collective organization mirrors an analogous organization at the personal level of each individual of faith.

4. Admissible limits of interaction between Orthodox pastoral theology and psychoanalysis

4.1. Thrashing out the conceptual apparatus

Herbart (81-123) and Wolkoff (140-50) have argued that, for a logically consistent re-construction of demonstrative reasoning, there is a need to understand clearly and exactly the elements of this reasoning. For the purpose of demonstrating something, one needs to understand distinctly what exactly is being said and deduced; this seems possible only when the meaning of terms and propositions making up the arguments are defined and put forward as concepts.

Therefore, it is important to ascertain what Thermos understands by Orthodox pastoral theology and psychoanalysis, to verify Thermos's hypothetical paradigm of the interaction between Orthodox pastoral theology and psychoanalysis accurately. By doing so, it should be possible to establish whether his understanding and presentation of the core of these two disciplines are proper and adequate. In addition, proper understanding and adequate presentation may demonstrate the extent to which this hypothetical paradigm is theoretically sound and is an example which can be followed.

4.1.1. The concept of psychoanalysis

To investigate the way that Thermos understands psychoanalysis, we need to answer a number of questions. First of all, does Thermos cover both the scientific and philosophical strands within psychoanalysis? This question is important because scientific and philosophical inquiry yield the different results (Herbart, 1993; Rosenberg, 2012). Matsukas (*Δογματική* 37-9) affirms that scientific knowledge originates in the cognition of the physical world; this knowledge represents an intellectual dissection of this reality. In other words, there is a *gnoseological* relationship between the human mind and the object that the mind scrutinizes (Herbart 29-69; Rosenberg 1-18). It is important to understand that the mind that maintains this *gnoseological* relationship with the physical world needs, according to Matsukas (*Δογματική* 38), a means / tool for acquiring knowledge; "this tool is the method" (Ματσούκα, *Δογματική* 38). On the other hand, philosophical knowledge outlines a mental reality participating in a philosophical truth which is broader than physical reality (the world) (Herbart 29-69; Ματσούκα, *Γένεσις* 107-110; Rosenberg 1-35). "For the ancient Greek intellectuals, philosophical truth is the essence of immovable being (*τὸ ὄν*), whereas, for the contemporary philosophy of existentialism, this truth is the dynamic live motion of existence" (Ματσούκα, *Γένεσις* 107-110). When ancient Greek philosophy was at its peak, the correlation between philosophy and science represented the correlation between theory and practice (Ματσούκα, *Ἐπιστήμη* 55-95). Science examined the apparent phenomena of this world, each examination providing fragments of knowledge, which then had to be grouped into intelligible units (Herbart 29-69; Rosenberg 3-18). This work of systematization of established knowledge was performed by philosophy (Ματσούκα, *Ἐπιστήμη* 55-95). Therefore, the task of philosophy was an interpretative one — to make intelligible whatever new information the exploratory mind extracted from the world (Herbart 29-69; Rosenberg 3-30). The systematization of knowledge provided by the sciences helped philosophy in the establishment of the principles of the universe, which could be secured by the unification of knowledge (Ματσούκα, *Ἐπιστήμη* 55-95). Thus, there is a ratio between objective scientific and subjective philosophical knowledge. In this context, it is important to emphasize that the essence of objective knowledge has never been contested by Orthodox theology, since this knowledge concerns the function of the physical world only. In relation to philosophical knowledge, this is understood to be a subjective interpretation of knowledge drawn from physical reality (its origin, meaning, etc.), and Orthodoxy has always subjected it to examination through divine revelation and truth (Ματσούκα, *Ἐπιστήμη* 55-95).

Furthermore, does Thermos distinguish between the scientific and philosophical strands within psychoanalysis? In his recent work—*Ἄνθρωπος στόν ὁρίζοντα* (2011)—there are several passages that demonstrate that Thermos is aware of a necessary distinction between psychoanalytic scientific knowledge and Freud's philosophical interpretation of the individual, culture, and religion. Thermos says that psychoanalysis appeared as an attempt to decipher the *symptom*, as a need to give it some sense (Θερμός, *Ποιμαίνοντες* 86-90; *Ἄνθρωπος* 129). In another passage, he claims that, being devoted to the spirit of the epoch of modernism, psychoanalysis perceived the psyche autonomously, without metaphysical reference (Θερμός, *Ποιμαίνοντες* 163). Thermos expresses the idea that psychoanalysis itself aimed at rationally controlling the unconscious; yet, in aspiring to dominate this sphere of the human psyche rationally, psychoanalysis virtually undermined the omnipotence of rationalism by showing the depths to which this rationalism is subjected (Θερμός, *Ποιμαίνοντες*; *Ἄνθρωπος*).

It is not difficult at all to see a direct relationship between the *symptom* and science. The symptom is a sign that somewhere things have gone wrong and, if possible, in observing the symptoms, we can identify the underlying cause (Bendaly, 1973).[19] By assuming that a symptom was not simply perverted and pathological, but sensible and expedient, psychoanalysis embarked on the task of interpreting the psychology of the sufferer (Bendaly, 1973). In so doing, psychoanalysis has demonstrated the importance of symbols and their proper interpretation for understanding the unconscious and the healing of the human psyche (Bendaly, 1973). In stressing the importance of the individual's capability of thinking in symbols, Freud stirred up great resistance in the academic and scien-

---

19 From now on, the author's own translation from the following French texts

tific world. He made the following statement: "There is a fixed correlation between the element of any dream and its translation (interpretation) as a symbol. This element itself is a symbol of the unconscious thinking in a dream" (Ricœur, *De l'Interprétation* 166). Consequently, Thermos is right when he states that psychoanalysis undermined, to some extent, the omnipotence of rationalism.

Thermos (*Ἄνθρωπος* 27-51; 167-191) points out that scientific materialism, the disregard of the metaphysical and a commitment to rationalism underpinned the interpretation and practice of philosophy and science during the epoch in which Freud lived. These interpretations profoundly influenced the premises of Freud's theory by bringing about two effects on Freud's creation: one positive and the other negative.

What effects are we talking about? What is the quintessence of these effects?

These effects are Freud's scientific discoveries concerning the individual's psychological life and his resultant philosophical interpretation of these discoveries. The positive effect consists in the investigation of the unconscious, the discovery that the unconscious is a manifestation of the instincts, the idea that the energy of the instinctive urges determines the dynamics of human psychological life, the discovery that the structure of the psyche, an individual's character and social and cultural phenomena, can be explained through this psychodynamic of instincts, the idea that the facts and impressions of the early phases of childhood determine the chief characteristics of the psyche of the individual (Манн 372).

The negative effect comes from Freud's tendency to raise his scientific method of investigation of affectivity to a universal principle which interprets the individual. This is a kind of totalitarian doctrine and Freud therefore has deviated from the rules by which science is guided. The Antiochian theologian Bendaly (1973) argues that the issues raised by psychoanalysis point to the limited nature of this approach. "Freud himself asserted that, having worked out a 'system', Adler slipped into philosophy and this was, according to Freud, against the crux of psychoanalysis" (Hanry 152).

Freud's theories were conditioned by his a priori assumptions. The first assumption stems from scientism,[20] while the other four are of a biological, psychological, pathological and fatalistic character (Bendaly, 1973). The first a priori assumption postulates that the human intellect (lat. "*ratio*") is the only criterion of truth, the only proper means for understanding reality (Freud, *L'Avenir* 32-45). The biological assumption consists of the idea that human behaviour is completely explainable in terms of biological processes, and that these processes are physical and chemical in nature (Bendaly, 1973). However, Freud could not confine his discoveries to this ideological framework. In his work, "L'Esquisse"

20 Scientism is a "complete belief in scientific methods, or in the truth of scientific knowledge." Hornby, A. S. "Scientism." Def. 2. *Oxford Advanced Learner's Dictionary*. 8th ed. 2010. Print.

(1895), Freud departs, to some extent, from this biological model, and places the concepts of the repulse and censorship of an impulse, i.e., the unconscious urge, in the inter-human context, in the interpersonal situation. According to Ricœur (*De l'Interprétation* 94, 377), though, Freud never openly excluded the possibility that the last word in psychoanalytic interpretation will pertain to biology. Freud says:

> The source of impulse means the organic process, which takes place in a certain organ or part of the body and the excitation of this process is presented in the psychic life as an impulse. We do not know whether this process is actually of chemical character or it corresponds to releasing other powers, e.g., a mechanical one. To investigate the sources of impulses is out of the reach of psychology, though the stemming of impulse from the organic source is definitively an obligatory condition for the impulses. We know the impulse in the psychic life is only the beginning of the impulse. (*Métapsychologie* 19-20)

The psychological assumption is closely connected with Freud's conception of the "psychodynamic apparatus" (Bendaly 1: 49-59). Proceeding from this concept, Freud defined the other as an "object" of instinctive "powers" and stated that the physical nature of these "powers" is manifested through attraction and repulsion (Bendaly 1: 49-59). The further development of this idea obliged Freud to exclude the objective existence of God, since the emergence of "another person on the horizon of psyche is a work of fantasy, a perversion of instinct, which is able to leave the prey and to chase the shadow, something peculiar to the individual" (Bendaly 1: 49-50). Therefore, to ascertain the probability of whether another person actually really exists was not important for Freud (Bendaly, 1973). The only rational task was, for Freud, to ascertain how this fantasy arises, i.e., to ascertain what obscure psychological alchemy lies behind the mirage (Bendaly, 1973). In this respect, Freud profited from his scientist [scientism] and biological assumptions when he embarked on developing his theory of religion as an "illusion" (Bendaly 1: 50). Let Freud himself speak, though: "To a considerable extent, the mythological conception of the world, which inspires even the most contemporary religions, is nothing more than psychology that is projected on the world. And so, we should translate 'metaphysics' as 'metapsychology'" (Freud, *Psychopathologie* 276-277).

The pathological assumptions posit that, since it is a product of psychological processes and therefore does not correspond to reality, religion should be subsumed under the rubric of pathological phenomena (Bendaly 1: 50-60). If an individual practises a religious way of life, his psyche functions, according to Freud, in the delirium mode. In his book *Moïse et le Monothéisme*, Freud says: "Religion is nothing more than a neurosis of mankind … Its enormous power may be explained in the same way as the neurotic obsession of our several patients …" (*Moïse* 76).

His fatalistic assumption closes this discussion of Freud's presuppositions, which determined, to a considerable extent, his psychoanalytic theory (Bendaly 1: 50-60). In religion, Freud sees the "invention of human desire, which seeks to find complete satisfaction in the religious life; yet, this quest is unrealizable, according to Freud, since human desire is doomed to insurmountable disappointment" (Bendaly 1: 50-1). The empirical dissatisfaction of man is the supreme reality of existence, which is nothing more than a cruel necessity indifferent to human need (Bendaly 1: 50-60). In other words, this is *anankē* (from the Greek word "*ἀνάγκη*" – deep necessity) (Bendaly 1: 50-60). In this sense, there is room to speak of Freud's fatalistic assumption. In one of his letters to Jones, he says: "As a fatalist and atheist, I can only resign myself to the horror of death" (Freud, *Lettre* 160).

These a priori assumptions are the most vulnerable link in the scientific concept of Freud's psychoanalysis, as they witness to his scientific bias and his slippage into philosophy (Bendaly, 1973). Thus, Freud's positivistic dogmatism and philosophical preferences have had a negative impact on the scientific image of psychoanalysis (Bendaly, 1973). Therefore one of the many critics of Freud's ideas, David, claims that "we have to distinguish between psychoanalytic knowledge and the *Weltanschauung* that psychoanalysis has inherited from Freud" (David 16-17).

Many scholars are therefore unanimous in their opinion that psychoanalytic knowledge itself is useful and trustworthy, whereas Freud's philosophy is limited by his personal *Weltanschauung* and the positivistic premises of his epoch. Yet, what does this psychoanalytic knowledge stand for exactly? Bendaly affirms that "this knowledge comes down to the idea of the *genetic* priority of the instinct principle and the *ontological* priority of the spiritual principle within human beings" (Bendaly 1:306). Of course, the second part of Bendaly's statement (1973) is a component not of Freud's scientific reductionism, which actually claimed the absolute priority of the instinct principle, but rather of his rich ideas and practical experience, which were not taken into account when he elaborated his psychoanalytic theory. The point is that, in some of his works, Freud himself acknowledged that the instinct principle has the ability to overcome itself infinitely (Bendaly, 1973). Ricœur says:

> Freud has also bumped into this imaginary principle that is not vestigial and is bearer of a new sense: not with relation to the religion, but to the art ... The very phantasm of the hawk within Leonardo's work sets in motion the transfiguration of the vestiges of the past; all the more such a masterpiece, as the *Gioconda*, is a creation, in which the past could, according to Freud's acknowledgement, be 'disavowed and overcome'. (*De l'Interprétation* 517)

According to Ricœur (*De l'Interprétation* 517), Freud could not appreciate the idea that the same phantasm can bear two opposite vectors: the regressive vector pointing at enslavement by the past, and another progressive vector signalizing the presence of a detector of meaning. It seems that, in being in thrall to his scientific bias and philosophical preferences, Freud was not able to invest the human ego with real autonomous power, though it would be wrong to say that he did not realize the necessity of this autonomy (Bendaly, 1973). At the end of his life, Freud discovered the opposition between *Eros* and *Thanatos*, which shook his previous idea of the principle of constant economic balance within psychic life, and on which the idea of the complete dependence of the *ego* on the *id* was based (Ricœur, *De l'Interprétation* 186). Yet, it is an established fact that Freud could not scientifically ground the idea that the *ego* has the ability to progress, which was necessary for overcoming the "*passéisme*" (Ricœur, *De l'Interprétation* 474-476).

As for the concept of sublimation, we can say that, when this concept is understood only in relation to the regressive vector, i.e., as a kind of supplementary process which is actually used by an economy of desire, one abrogates the notion of morality (Bendaly, 1973). "Only sublimation as a symbolic process with the potential to manifest itself regressively as well as progressively can save the notion of morality from being reduced to the '*superego*', religion from being reduced to a neurotic compulsion, and both of these from being reduced to the vestiges of infantile phenomena linked to the child's relationship to his parents" (Bendaly 1: 381).

Now to return to Thermos. The first part of this research has established that Thermos does not understand the position of *ego* in the same way as Freud did. Thermos presents *ego* as having great autonomous power. He also states that he does not reduce moral conscience to the *superego*, but clearly delineates these two from each other. And therefore, we can state that, in building his hypothetical paradigm of the interaction between Orthodox pastoral theology and psychoanalysis, Thermos did not use Freud's model of the individual, but rather a psychoanalytic knowledge of the same. This latter is nothing more than a transfigured psychoanalysis which is adopted by way of scientific and philosophical criticism; a psychoanalysis that is devoid of Freud's scientific dogmatism and philosophical personal prejudices; a psychoanalysis that does not pretend to be an anthropological system, but is rather a simple method of investigating the human psyche. How did Thermos actually succeed in acquiring this transfigured psychoanalysis? The answer is at the beginning of this book, where it was established that Thermos did not limit himself only to the use of psychoanalysis but also resorted to other trends in psychology: to pastoral psychology, social psychology and the psychology of religion, the psychology of the human "ego", the psychology of the family, and the psychology of professional orientation (Θερμός, *Ἡ Ἱερατική* 11).

This exposition of the notion of psychoanalysis does not claim to be systematic or exhaustive, of course. This was never the objective. It is more important to establish that Thermos has managed to manœuvre between true psychoanalytic knowledge and Freud's scientific dogmatism along with philosophical personal prejudices. The final answer is that Thermos has utilized a genuine and acceptable scientific concept of psychoanalysis.

4.1.2. The concept of Orthodox pastoral theology

Thermos's work provides constructive guidelines by which Orthodox pastoral theology can be defined. Theology should not be an abstract discipline, but should be closely linked to pastoral care. Furthermore, the practice of both theology and pastoral care should be anchored in the priest's true existence within Christ, the whole Truth (Θερμός, *Ὁμοιοπαθεῖς* 31, 55). Therefore, Orthodox pastoral theology can be defined as: *true spiritual knowledge of God and the individual, by which pastoral care, in the person of each particular priest, contributes to the mission of Church, which is to save every person for the Kingdom of God.*

Since Orthodox pastoral theology maintains that it is in possession of true spiritual knowledge about the individual, it is important to address fully Thermos's reconstruction of the Orthodox model of the individual, because this will clarify whether there is any common ground between Orthodox pastoral theology and psychoanalysis.

Thermos asserts that Orthodox anthropological knowledge is rooted in the Judeo-Christian model of the individual. In the Old Testament, there is a tendency to represent the human soul in terms of thinking, feeling and desiring (Θερμός, *Πρός μία θεολογική* 97-99). Thermos (*Πρός μία θεολογική* 97-98) points out that the Old Testament did not refer to these operations in terms of abstract notions. What really mattered for the religious mind of the Old Testament is not the *notion* of "substance" but the *reality* of the "flesh", which clearly indicates the whole psychosomatic individual (Θερμός, *Πρός μία θεολογική* 97-99); an Israelite of the Old Testament does not care about the *notion* of "feeling", but about the *reality* of "heart", which loves, hates, and feels (Θερμός, *Πρός μία θεολογική* 98). In other words, Hebraic (Old Testament) anthropology does not treat psychological operations as separate entities; this anthropology defines the human being as a whole which performs a particular psychological operation in a particular moment (thinking, remembering, feeling, desiring, etc.) (Θερμός, *Πρός μία θεολογική* 98). Elsewhere in the Old Testament, a Hebraic writer enunciates that God has "inspired" the human being "with an active soul"[21] (Wisdom of Solomon 15.11). According to Thermos (*Τά ὀφφίκια* 125-126), two Hebraic words predominate[22] as terms for the modern idea of "soul":

---

21 «τὸν ἐμπνεύσαντα αὐτῷ ψυχὴν ἐνεργοῦσαν» (Σοφία Σαλωμῶνος 15.11).

22 There is also a much more rare third term *Leb* "לב" = "heart" (*καρδιά*) (Θερμός, *Τὰ ὀφφίκια*). Špidlik expresses a somehow different opinion to the foregoing one: "In the Bi-

(*Nefesh*) "נפשׁ" and (*Ruah*) "*רוּח*". The former is translated in the Septuagint as "soul" (*ψυχή*), while the latter is termed "spirit" (*πνεύμα*) (Θερμός, *Τά όφφίκια* 125-126). While both these terms at once seem to indicate a psychological dimension within the human being, they also overlap in meaning to some extent. Bratsiotu (*Ἀνθρωπολογία* 125-159) points out that the word *Ruah* represented the relation of the individual to God, so that *Ruah* was perceived as something naturally directed to divinity. *Nefesh* (and the word *Leb*) mostly refer to an individual's earthly life at the psychosomatic level (Μπρατσιώτου, *Ἀνθρωπολογία* 125-159). Importantly, what is said about the "spirit" is that it does not die — "then the dust shall return to the earth as it was; and the spirit shall return to God who gave it" (Eccl 12.7), while the "soul" is said to die.[23] Wherever the "soul" within the Hebraic text is considered immortal, it is identified with the "spirit" (Μπρατσιώτου, *Ἀνθρωπολογία* 95-99). Thermos (*Τά όφφίκια; Πρός μία θεολογική*), too, indicates that, within the Old Testament, the Hebraic word *Nefesh* (soul), unlike *Ruah* (spirit), often overlaps in meaning with the "flesh" and "breath", therefore pointing to the entire psychosomatic human being. Furthermore, on an equal footing, the word "soul" gained currency within the Hebraic vocabulary in referring to animals, without, however, being confined to their biological life alone — "*יורע צריק נפשׁ בהמתו*" [24] ("A righteous man regards the life of his beast" (Prov 12.10). Not so with the "spirit", it is said about animals that "their horses are flesh and not spirit" (Is 31, 3)[25]. Finally, pointing out Adamo's findings (32), Thermos (*Πρός μία θεολογική* 99) indicates that the word "spirit" is used in relation to God in 35% of cases, while the word "soul" only in 3% of cases.

---

ble, the word 'heart' applies about ten times to the physical organ, while it is *used more than a thousand times* in a metaphorical sense to signify the seat of various psychological functions. It is the heart that thinks and reflects, that conceives projects and takes resolutions, that makes decisions and assumes responsibility. It is the heart, and not the soul, that plays the central role in the interior life. Seat of the moral life, the heart is also that of the religious life" (362). Tomaš Špidlik. "The heart in Russian spirituality." *Orientalia Christiana Analecta*, 195 (1973): 361-374. Print

23 «καὶ τῇ νεάνιδι οὐ ποιήσετε οὐδέν· οὐκ ἔστιν τῇ νεάνιδι ἁμάρτημα θανάτου, ὅτι ὡς εἴ τις ἐπαναστῇ ἄνθρωπος ἐπὶ τὸν πλησίον καὶ **φονεύσῃ αὐτοῦ ψυχήν**, οὕτως τὸ πρᾶγμα τοῦτο» (Δευτερονόμιον 22.26); «καὶ ἄνθρωπος, ὃς ἐὰν μιανθῇ καὶ μὴ ἀφαγνισθῇ, **ἐξολεθρευθήσεται ἡ ψυχὴ** ἐκείνη ἐκ μέσου τῆς συναγωγῆς ...» (Ἀριθμοὶ 19.20); «**ἤγγισεν δὲ εἰς θάνατον ἡ ψυχὴ αὐτοῦ**, ἡ δὲ ζωὴ αὐτοῦ ἐν ᾅδῃ» (Ἰώβ 33.22).

24 It seemed more relevant to bring the respective passage from the Hebraic text as no English version keeps the proper biblical term "נפשׁ" = the Nefesh. The latter is rendered in English by the words needs or life. (Biblia Hebraica, 1984, 1290) Cf. the appropriate verse from the Septuagint: «*δίκαιος* ***οἰκτίρει ψυχὰς κτηνῶν*** *αὐτοῦ, τὰ δὲ σπλάγχνα τῶν ἀσεβῶν ἀνελεήμονα*» (Παροιμίαι 12.10).

25 «Αἰγύπτιον ἄνθρωπον καὶ οὐ θεόν, **ἵππων σάρκας** καὶ οὐκ ἔστιν βοήθεια» (Ἠσαΐας 31.3).

These various strands of meaning for the Hebraic word *Nefesh* cover the possibilities of interpreting this word both in the contemporary sense of soul and in the sense of psychological operations which can be attributed to animals and humans alike (Θερμός, *Πρός μία θεολογική* 99). However, with the advent of Hellenism, it became more appropriate for the Judeo-Christian tradition to call "soul" the object which was termed *Ruah* (spirit) in the Old Testament, while psychological operations came across in the New Testament as the Hebraic *Nefesh* (soul) (Θερμός, *Πρός μία θεολογική* 99). Accordingly, the apostle Peter told Jesus: "I will even lay down my life [*ψυχήν μου*] for you" [26] (John 13.37). Here, life corresponds to the Greek word "*psyche*", which means nothing more than the Hebraic *Nefesh* that is common to humans and animals. This life is Apostle Peter's psychological operations. Yet, when Christ introduces the discourse "psyche — soma" (body — soul), he uses "*psyche*" in terms of the Hebraic word *Ruah* (spirit), since, according to Him, only God can destroy both body and soul in hell (Matt 10.28), while people can only destroy the body.

In this context, Thermos claims that, both in the New Testament and the Apostolic Fathers, the words "soul" and "spirit" are often used in such a way that they might be taken to point to slightly different semantic dimensions. To put it in perspective, the apostle Paul prays "may the very God of peace sanctify you wholly; and may your spirit and soul and body be preserved without blemish to the coming of our Lord Jesus Christ" (1 Thess 5.23). Thermos (*Πρός μία θεολογική*) emphasizes the idea that certain Christian exegetes interpreted the word "spirit" in the sense of Holy Spirit, an interpretation which could only be based on a misunderstanding because one therefore comes to think that the apostle prays for the Holy Spirit to be impeccably preserved within the believers, making Him equal with soul and body. On the other hand, others referred to the familiar trinity-schema to make Paul's words intelligible. Not so with Thermos; he enunciates the following idea:

> This passage owes its terms to the nomenclature of the Old Testament, according to which the "soul" expresses the psychological operations and the "spirit" expresses the element that we used to call "soul", i.e., the human being's core implanted by God (Gen 2.7) or as certain Church Fathers interpret it: the "spirit" is the higher psychological operation of the *nous*, whereas the "soul" is the inferior operations of affect and desire.[27] (Θερμός, *Πρός μία θεολογική* 100)

Thus, Thermos (*Πρός μία θεολογική* 100) maintains that, within the Holy Scripture, there are lines of distinction between the human soul and psychological operations. With the advent of Hellenism, Biblical language, with its multi-

---

26 "τὴν **ψυχήν** μου ὑπὲρ σοῦ θήσω" (Ἰωάννην 13, 37).

27 St Gregory of Nyssa says: "In accordance with the Apostle's words to the Ephesians … the nutrient part [of human being] is called the body, the sensuous part is rendered by the word soul, and the mental one — by the spirit." (PG 44, 145d)

layered meanings and ideas, borrowed linguistic and conceptual terminology from the new, Greek-educated converts, while simultaneously preserving its own theology (Θερμός, *Πρός μία θεολογική* 100).

These newly acquired terms covered two key areas: 1) the theological and 2) the anthropological. Theological terms referred to substance (*οὐσία*), energies (*ἐνέργειες*) and person (*πρόσωπο*), and stood for the fundamental ontological triad necessary for enunciating the mystery of God and the individual. Anthropological terms referred to the Platonic tripartite distinction of soul as reason (*λογιστικόν*), zeal (*θυμοειδές*) and desire (*ἐπιθυμητικόν*) (we seldom meet references to the memory (*μνημονευτικόν*) and the imagination (*φανταστικόν*) (Θερμός, *Πρός μία θεολογική* 100).

Several patristic passages are quoted to support Thermos's position on this subject; for example, St Basil the Great says: "The soul is cognized from its energies alone" (PG 31.216a). St Maximus the Confessor adds: "The concept of natural energy is a condition of essence, and characterizes naturally all those in whom it emerges according to their essence" (PG 91.1037c).

These Church Fathers identify, in Thermos's opinion (*Πρός μία θεολογική*), the soul of the human being with his substance (*οὐσία*) or nature, while human psychological energies correspond to the energies of human nature. Another Father, St John of Damascus, adds: "The energy is a drastic and essential motion of nature / substance … and this is the hypostasis which is acting and disposing of the energy" (PG 94.1048a). In this way, the ontological triad is, according to Thermos, completed.

In stating this anthropological fundamental, Thermos asks:

> What relationship is there between the soul, on the one hand, and the reason, zeal and desire, on the other hand? This relationship is of the same nature as the relationship between the sun and his rays. The sun is that substance from which the rays emanate; we perceive the possibilities of the sun only through the rays, i.e., the possibilities to heat, to give light, to breathe life into something. There is no other way to know of the characteristics of the sun. (Θερμός, *Πρός μία θεολογική* 101-2)

This paradigm of the relationship between the sun and its rays appears very often in the patristic tradition, because it had proved expedient for presenting the distinction between the substance and energies of God. It is equally true that this paradigm is very relevant for comprehending the human psyche, because the human being is created in the image of God. Thus, the psychological operations emanate from human nature just as the rays of the sun emanate from the latter (Θερμός, *Τά ὀφφίκια*; *Πρός μία θεολογική* 100-1). By canvassing the concept of psychological operations (functions), we are considering not an abstract phenomenon, but the concrete characteristics of human nature: namely, its energies. St Gregory Palamas states: "the soul is not simply the provident powers, but it has powers" (ΕΠΕ 2.682).

Further, Thermos analyzes the notion of (*πρόσωπο*) person. This stands for "the way of existence of nature (or substance)" (Ζηζιούλα 946). The importance of the individual consists in his freedom; in other words, in his possession of the highest energy of self-government (*αὐτεξούσιον*)[28], which also provides other energies of nature with moral content (Θερμός, *Τά ὀφφίκια*; *Πρός μία θεολογική*). St John of Damascus says: "Just like it is natural for any sensitive being to desire, so self-government is natural for any reasonable entity. It is a matter of fact that each reasonable being possesses self-government, and this represents the image of God"[29] (PG 95.112a). The highest energy of self-government gives power to these energies to follow the divine commandments or to resist them. When it (*αὐτεξούσιον*) is used to resist the divine commandments, the psychological energies / operations as a unit commit, according to Thermos, different sins which have a negative impact on the condition of each discrete psychological energy (operation) (Θερμός, *Πρός μία θεολογική* 101-102). Thermos quotes St John of Damascus who says:

> The sins of the reason (*λογιστικόν*) are unfaithfulness, heresy, foolishness, blasphemy, ingratitude; the sins of the zeal are mercilessness, hatred, grudges, jealousy, homicide; and finally the sins of the sphere of desire are gluttony, prostitution, adultery, drunkenness, avarice, lewdness, vanity, and sensualism. (Φιλοκαλία 303-304)

After establishing the exact meaning of the terms (nature, energy and person) as taken by the Orthodox tradition from the ancient Greek sciences and philoso-

---

28 In 2011, A. A. Darovskih [Даровских, Андрей Александрович] submitted a PhD dissertation under the title— The Concept of Synergy within Gregory of Nyssa's Anthropology <rus> [Учение о синергии в антропологии Григория Нисского]— to the Philosophical Faculty of the Sankt-Petersburg University in Russia. The author argued that the idea of self-government played a substantial role in Gregory Nyssa's developments of early Christian anthropology. Within this research, the author stated that Gregory Nyssa's developments of early Christian anthropology represent the "golden mean" between two conflicting concepts of the freedom of human will as broached by Augustine and Pelagius. And while Augustine's global thought suggests the idea of divine predestination, diminishing thus the importance of human self-government, Pelagius in turn overstates the importance of this, making salvation possible to anyone without divine help, i.e. a matter of each individual's will. Apart from that, Gregory Nyssa favors the idea that human freedom cannot "create something ex nihilo" but "is only able to restructure whatever exists" (Darovskih 122). For him freedom is not so much to be looked for in the notion of will, as suggested by Augustine, but in the existence of a real choice within a system of outward motions, impulses or motives [an allusion to the energy of self-government that is not to be confused with human will—P.C.]. This subtleness of Gregory Nyssa's thought may also lie behind the ideas about self-government as discussed above by Thermos.

29 «Ὥσπερ οὖν ἡ φυσικὴ ὄρεξις πάσῃ λογικῇ φύσει ἔγκειται ... πᾶν γὰρ λογικὸν αὐτεξούσιον, καὶ τοῦτό ἐστι τὸ κατ'εἰκόνα Θεοῦ. » (PG 95.112a)

phy[30], Thermos expounds the Orthodox understanding of the relationship between the human soul and body. He says that the human soul is the principal feature which distinguishes each individual (Θερμός, *Τά όφφίκια*; *Πρός μία θεολογική*). This feature is planted by God in every human being on his very conception. From this moment on, a close lifelong coupling of soul and body begins which is only interrupted by death, and for a certain duration of time at that (Θερμός, *Τά όφφίκια*; *Πρός μία θεολογική*). Thermos argues that this close relationship between body and soul produces a gradual revelation, and not an immediate emergence of psychological operations. This gradual emergence is unavoidable since a necessary condition to its taking place is the maturing of the body. St Gregory of Nyssa states: "The soul is a begotten living intellectual substance, which from itself communicates vital power as well as the ability to perceive the tangible world to the organic perceiving body until the compound nature which receives and perceives this tangible world exists" (PG 46.29b).

Thermos (*Τά όφφίκια*; *Πρός μία θεολογική*) points out that, between a child and a mature adult, there is a difference in relation to their intellectual capacity to think; between an embryo and a baby, there is a difference in relation to each one's emotional perception. He agrees, therefore, with the following statement by St Gregory of Nyssa:

> In relation to the growth of an individual, the power of soul grows gradually in an analogous measure to the corporeal growth. Firstly, the psychological power emerges, manifesting itself through the nourishing and augmentative operation in the development of embryos inside the womb; afterwards, this psychological power communicates the pleasure of feelings to those who are born; finally, after the plant (body) has grown, it conceptualizes the logical power as a kind of apogee; but then again, this power is not immediately but gradually formed exactly as is the growth of a plant. (PG 46.128a)

Thermos believes that this passage has a huge importance since it introduces a term analogous to the ones of contemporary physics, which is "Unified Field Theory" (*Πρός μία θεολογική* 103). Here, it is all about one and the same developmental line for (1) the somatic growth of embryo, (2) the further development of its senses, and (3) the appearance of thinking (Θερμός, *Πρός μία θεολογική*). In other words, Thermos claims that this passage by Gregory of Nyssa "unifies

---

30 This statement needs more clarifications and could invite debates additional to those encouraged in Vladimir Bibichin's *Energeia* (2010) [В. В. Бибихин. *Энергия*. Москва: Институт философии, теологии и истории св. Фомы, 2010]. This modern Russian philosopher claims that a huge misunderstanding about Aristotle's concept of energy still occurs between many Western and Eastern thinkers. Bibichin argues that the basic distinction that Aristotle makes between *energy as actuality* and *energy as possibility* is often taken lopsidedly to mean that energy as actuality is dependent on the fortune of energy as possibility, a lopsidedness that puts forward the Aristotelian concept of energy as motion at the expense of the one as immobility [stillness].

the somatic and psychic operations as a fact of the one and the same ontological order, as energies of the one and single, but two-compound (psychosomatic) human nature" (Θερμός, *Πρός μία θεολογική* 103).

The unification at the level of energies is completed with the unification on the level of substance (nature) (Θερμός, *Πρός μία θεολογική* 103). St Gregory of Neocesaria says: "To the extent that the body is substance (nature), the soul also should be considered substance. It is impossible that the vitalized one is substance (nature), while the one vitalizing to be not" (PG 10.1141a). Proceeding from these patristic passages, Thermos asserts that "the nature and substance of the human being are jointly the couple 'soul-body'" (Θερμός, *Πρός μία θεολογική* 103). As to the hypostasis, St John of Damascus says: "the substance (nature) becomes energy in the hypostasis" (PG 94.613a).

Yet, Thermos is swift to preempt any misunderstanding of this interpretation of the human being. He considers that the body and the soul are two different entities, two distinctive components within an individual (Θερμός, *Πρός μία θεολογική* 109). What is important about these two components within an individual is that "they cannot be gnoseologically separated" (Θερμός, *Πρός μία θεολογική* 109). It is impossible "to learn something about one, if we intellectually separate it from the other" (Θερμός, *Πρός μία θεολογική* 109). The body as substance of an individual does not dispose of its own (somatic) operations (energies), neither does the soul as a substance (nature) of an individual dispose of its respective psychological operations (energies), but the couple 'soul – body' as one substance (nature) of the human being dispose of and emanate operations (energies), some of which are characterized as "psychological" and others as "somatic" (Θερμός, *Πρός μία θεολογική* 110). How are they differentiated? The "somatic" operations, as distinct from the "psychological" ones, are perceptible and measurable (Θερμός, *Πρός μία θεολογική* 110). Thermos (*Πρός μία θεολογική* 110) believes that, in relation to the individual, with his one but mixed nature, the characteristic reference to a "psychological" and "somatic" operation is a convention which refers only to the form of the operation and not to its provenance. He refers to St John of Damascus's following words:

> The energy is a drastic motion of the one who acts; the energy of nature / substance, as such, is a drastic motion of nature / substance, be it the logical motion of the reason or the vital, nourishing, augmentative, reproductive function and the motion of lust, which are the motions of the body; and here should be added the function of fantasy, memory, zeal, desire and urge, which are at the head of the stimulating operation and of other similar operations. (PG 95.109b)

Thus, Thermos (*Πρός μία θεολογική* 110-2) stresses that the natural energy of the human being is ontologically one, but has many peculiarities concerning its contents, which can be psychological and somatic. Why is this important? It means, in Thermos's opinion (*Πρός μία θεολογική*), that, from the theological standpoint, the psychological disorders of thinking, desire, will, behaviour, memory (and many others) do not differ ontologically from somatic disorders. They may have different clinical symptoms, and the method of cure may also differ (Θερμός, *Πρός μία θεολογική* 110-2); however, in essence, both sets of disorders remain disorders of the energies of human nature. What unifies them? Thermos (*Πρός μία θεολογική*) asserts that, after the fall, the universal corruption (depravity) of human nature unified these somatic and psychic disorders. The fall brought about two kinds of suffering for human nature: the propensity to sin and corruption in the psychosomatic entity (nature) (Θερμός, *Πρός μία θεολογική*). Thermos quotes St Maximus the Confessor, who says:

> First of all, the will of choice (*προαίρεσις*) was corrupted because of Adam's trespass; then, the will corrupted human nature, bereaving it of the grace of impassibility, and thus sin was committed. The first sin is reproachful. It is the estrangement of the will from good to evil. On the other hand, the second sin, caused by the first one, is a non-reproachful change of human nature from imperishable to perishable. In point of fact, the first man and woman committed two sins when they transgressed God's commandment: one reproachful and the other, caused by the reproachful sin, non-reproachful. Thus, the sin of will has voluntarily rejected the good, while the sin of nature has rejected immortality under compulsion, because of the will. (PG 90.405c)

Thermos therefore formulates three ideas in relation to the model of the human being as used in Orthodox pastoral theology: the first consists of the assertion that the Judeo-Christian model of the human being has an unchangeable nucleus that pertains to theological knowledge (or truth), revealed by God Himself, and the second states that this nucleus was shaped and elaborated over a long period. This means that one can never set about changing the nucleus, without the risk of falling into heresy, whereas one can effect some additions to the shape of this nucleus, moving, thereby, in the course of the Orthodox tradition. Such additions come to the fore when one remembers the adoption of knowledge from within science and philosophy. Finally, he conceives of the somatic and psychic operations (energies) of human nature as being ontologically unified. This means that, within human nature, these two different entities have one psychosomatic energy. In other words, the somatic and psychic operations are morphologically two, but ontologically one.

There are other Orthodox theologians, like Bendaly, Matsukas, and Staniloae, who share these ideas as expounded by Thermos. With regard to the first idea concerning the nucleus of the Judeo-Christian model of the human being, Bendaly affirms:

> To the Hebrew way of thinking, the human being is worthy, in the whole of his entity, in whatever concrete, material component of which he consists, to enter into the Kingdom of God. An individual is transfigured from his head to his feet, to the smallest cell ... The body and the passions have one high vocation; they are

> destined to inherit one supernatural destiny... Judeo-Christian asceticism is a sublimation of desires[31], and not their eradication; it is a transfiguration of the flesh, and not its extermination. (Bendaly 1: 305)

Therefore, the Judeo-Christian perception of the human being as being worthy to enter the Kingdom of God jointly in body and soul is worth setting on the base of Orthodox anthropology, since this preserves the authentic theology and anthropology of the Old and New Testaments.

In regard to the second idea, the adoption of knowledge from within science and philosophy, something allegedly effected by the patristic tradition, it should be said that this is an established fact in the history of Christianity. Matsukas points to the adoption of secular knowledge in certain works of St Basil the Great, such as the *Hexaimeron* (*Ἑξαήμερον*). In discussing the behaviour and role of the four elements of nature (water, fire, earth and air), St Basil uses Heraclites's viewpoint, according to which the counteraction of these natural elements calls forth harmony and equilibrium within nature (Ματσούκα, *Ἐπιστήμη* 85). St Basil remarks that antagonism between water and fire should continue infinitely, and neither of these elements should disappear, since otherwise the whole of nature would disintegrate in a flash. "Neither the mutual counteraction should cease, nor the total disappearance of one of the two (water or fire) should occur, otherwise it will be given cause for everything to disintegrate" (PG 29.65c). Another adoption is evident, according to Matsuka, in St Basil's writing of the inability of human reason to penetrate the mysterious structure of things and to mark out "*vividly*" (*ἐναργῶς*) their hidden causes. St Basil says: "Nothing is without cause, and nothing happens accidentally. Everything harbours in itself an inexpressible wisdom. What word is able to express it? How can human reason investigate everything in every detail and perceive the properties, distinguish *vividly* the mutual differences and imagine completely the hidden causes?" (ΕΠΕ 202)

According to Matsuka (*Ἐπιστήμη* 92), St Basil has borrowed the term "vividness" from the philosophy of the Skeptics, and has retained the same semantic content at that. The philosophy of the Skeptics shakes the self-sufficiency of any dogmatic knowledge, pointing to the limited nature of an individual's cognition (Ματσούκα, *Ἐπιστήμη* 92-93). St Basil uses this term in order to express the idea of the limited nature of human perception (Ματσούκα, *Ἐπιστήμη* 92-93); although the world is created, it is nevertheless much deeper and more complicated than any individual could imagine (Ματσούκα, *Ἐπιστήμη* 92-93).

Within the works of St Basil the Great, who is called the "Father and teacher of the Church"[32], there are other passages that could be presented in support of

---

31 For instance, one can point to the prayer of St Isaac the Syrian: "Lord, give us to love You with the force of our passions." (Bendaly 1: 305-306)

the fact that the patristic tradition drew on and used secular knowledge (Ματσούκα, *Ἐπιστήμη*). However, I will limit myself to the above-mentioned testimonies in order to avoid going into excessive detail. Of primary importance is the fact that Thermos's statement concerning secular knowledge being actively used within the patristic tradition to shape the rudimentary Judeo-Christian model of the human being is convincing.

The third idea delineated by Thermos, i.e., that the somatic and psychological operations are morphologically two, but ontologically one, finds support in writings by Staniloae, the Romanian theologian, who states:

> The individual self is rational and sensitive; yet, at the same time, the individual is above all and beyond everything. He is not dominated by reason and sensitivity, i.e., the operations by which he perceives and dominates the sensible rationality of the body and the world ... The individual's inner self (soul) is eventually of an immaterial order ...The body complements this spiritual hypostasis so essentially that without the body an individual could not be a being who has consciousness of his own self, in which ... is included the consciousness of the world as well. (7-13)

In conclusion, Thermos provides an acceptable concept of psychoanalysis and of an authentic Orthodox understanding of the human being. With relation to psychoanalysis, he rallies support for this by accentuating the significance of a transfigured psychoanalytic knowledge and by indirectly deprecating the dogmatism and philosophical bias of Freud. Evidently, Thermos could succeed in this due to his drawing on other trends within psychology in which naturalism is perceived through the transcendental premises (as in the case of the psychology of religion). Moreover, Thermos adheres to an authentic Orthodox model of the human being (with its harmonic combination of naturalism and spirituality), and this without doubt has had an effect on his interpretation of psychoanalysis. Therefore, one can fairly assert that the conceptual apparatus used by Thermos to delineate his hypothetical paradigm of the interaction between Orthodox pastoral theology and psychoanalysis is unimpeachable.

4.2. The "pros and cons" regarding the interaction

The interaction between Orthodox pastoral theology and psychoanalysis has many different aspects which could be perceived as either favourable or unfavourable to the realization of Thermos's paradigm. Thermos appears to be aware of the complexity inherent in this issue. He asserts that there is both a real basis

---

32 Luc Brisson offers the following definition for the term "Father of the Church": "This expression is applied to the individuals who exhibit such characteristics as doctrinal orthodoxy, holy life, and approbation on the side of the Church, and belonging to antiquity". Brisson, Luc. «Le Christianisme face à la philosophie.» *Philosophie grecque*. 2 ed. Monique Canto-Sperber (Ed.). Paris: Presses Universitaires de France, 1998.701-743 (703).

for this interaction and objective difficulties that make it undesirable and even hazardous to Church theology and the practice of pastoral care.

4.2.1. The theoretical foundations of interaction

There are, according to Thermos, three strong arguments for establishing an interaction between Orthodox pastoral theology and psychoanalysis: 1) *the issue of psychopathology*, 2) *the issue of hermeneutics*, and 3) *the issue of interpreting the Orthodox faith in terms of contemporary gnoseology*. All these arguments are closely associated with three facets of the Orthodox model of the human being: 1) the fact of two corruptions within human nature, 2) the idea of the free human being, and 3) the latitude available in the elaboration of theological language.

4.2.1.1. The issue of psychopathology

To begin with, the problem of human psychopathology is one of the strongest arguments for promoting the interaction between Orthodox pastoral theology and psychoanalysis. After the fall of Adam and Eve, two things occurred within the human being: "because of Adam's will of choice (*προαίρεσις*) human nature (1) suffered transformation from incorruption to corruption, and (2) [Adam and Eve] lost the grace of impassibility (*ἀπάθεια*)" (Tollefsen 149). The will of choice (or "human intention"— Tollefsen 170) was damaged and consequently gravitates toward sin. The vocation of the Church is by the ministry of its pastors to transform the damaged human will and direct it toward God in order to open up further opportunities to partake of Christ and to receive the grace of salvation with which an individual is perpetually graced through the Holy Sacraments (Tollefsen 170). The corruption of human nature is a reality for which the individual does not bear responsibility (Tollefsen 149); this corruption, however, causes great suffering throughout life (different diseases and final death). It therefore requires, according to Thermos (*Πρός μία θεολογική*), the beneficial effects of the interventions of the psychological sciences.

There are certain misunderstandings which prevent the opponents of Thermos's view from accepting the advisability of such interventions. These misunderstandings revolve around a confusion between the moral and psychological [ontological] levels within the human being, i.e., confusion between the will of choice and the will of nature (Θερμός, *Πρός μία θεολογική*). The essence of this confusion arises from the idea that an individual is free and acts through the psychological operations of reason, zeal and desire; therefore, any problem (disorder) with these psychological operations should be dealt with by the means traditionally provided through pastoral care (Θερμός, *Πρός μία θεολογική*). Hence, certain clerics, according to Thermos, make either of two declarations: 1) "any psychopathology is due to organic causes and so, ought to be cured only by means of medicines; 2) any psychopathology stems from the corruption of the will of choice (i.e., the impact of sin) and therefore, it pertains to the Church's competence, and should only be treated through pastoral care" (*Πρός μία θεολογική* 113-114).

The first declaration actually implies the "illegality" of psychotherapy (Θερμός, *Πρός μία θεολογική* 113). The second, more seriously, precludes the possibility of any believer being able to resort to psychiatry and psychotherapy, in full awareness that he is following a course of action compatible with the principles of faith. Thus, the Orthodox Church is faced with a gnoseological challenge. This partial or complete denial of the psychological sciences appears to originate in the core Orthodox understanding of the human condition after the fall, understanding which rather represents a superficial knowledge of the crux of Orthodox pastoral theology and anthropology (Θερμός, *Πρός μία θεολογική* 113).

How does Thermos face this serious challenge to Orthodox theology? He accepts that all these misunderstandings are not the product of an evil intention, which is set on introducing confusion into pastoral care and theology, but rather are the result of the complex issues inherent in psychopathology (Θερμός, *Πρός μία θεολογική*). Thermos points out that the moral problems of human will (intention) and the psychological problems of psycho-disorder coexist in the majority of cases. The freedom of a person is reduced by any psychological disorder but by no means eliminated (Θερμός, *Πρός μία θεολογική*). Thermos offers the following examples:

> There are schizophrenic sick men as well as schizophrenic believers. There are both unbelievers and very devout men who are equally obsessive-compulsive or hysterical. There are depressed unbelievers and depressed struggling Christians. There are homosexuals who are proud of their identity, and there are others who shed tears and struggle spiritually. (*Πρός μία θεολογική* 113-114)

Thermos clarifies the above with the following illustration: "A psychopathological state has a dual nature just as does sunlight: as waves, the state retains its continuity with the world of sin and virtue. Yet, as particles, the state possesses relative independence" (Θερμός, *Πρός μία θεολογική* 129).

It is, accordingly, true that the freedom of the human being is expressed through the higher energies of his human nature, i.e., the psychological operations: reason, zeal and desire. As a matter of fact, the first sin was committed by the devil, i.e., an entity without a biological body. "Malice can be manifested without bodily mediation, as in the case of the demons" (PG 3.728d). The concept of the fundamental freedom of the higher energies of human nature appears to be important because it allows Thermos to stress the idea that some Saints suffered, by divine dispensation, from somatic diseases, but *never psychological ones* (Θερμός, *Πρός μία θεολογική* 115).

In other words, Thermos stresses that he does not rule out the significance of the moral dimension in psychopathology, although there are many cases in which responsibility is limited. He puts this idea as follows:

> The hatred of a paranoiac man is directed against his fantasized persecutors. This is different to the hatred of a person for those who are an obstacle to his wicked desires or his narcissistic purposes. Both these persons can kill under the influence of hatred; yet, within the paranoiac man, the disorder of psychological operation is primary ... The sorrow of a depressed man presents a primary disorder of feeling and is obviously different from the sorrow caused by despondency or from physiological sorrow caused by the experience of failure or injury. The sorrow of the second kind pertains to the spiritual order and stems from spiritual carelessness and selfishness... The disorder of a teenager's behaviour should often be interpreted through the patterns by which the aggressiveness is handled within the family but not by "malice", which may be insignificant in relation to the problem. (*Πρός μία θεολογική* 112-113)

Thus, in Thermos's opinion (*Πρός μία θεολογική*), apart from the laws of virtue and sin, there is another group of laws, those of psychopathological processes, which reduce freedom and impede the course of divine action.

In the case of psychopathology, according to Thermos (*Πρός μία θεολογική*), the confusion between the "deliberate choice (*προαίρεσις*) and the natural activity (*ἐνέργεια*)" is caused not only by the complexity of matter (existence of an interwoven connection between two corruptions) (Tollefsen 149, 170), but also by an ignorance of the crux of our faith. Some ecclesiastics claim that psychopathological problems should only be dealt with through pastoral care, with the exception of organically mediated disturbances. This is contrary to the Orthodox understanding of the human being. How has such a misconception arisen? Chiefly by following either of two wrong tracks, that is, by splitting the one and single human nature, or by setting the energy of human nature under the absolute authority of the person[33] (Θερμός, *Πρός μία θεολογική*).

---

33 It was mentioned above, where Thermos's concept of the Orthodox model of man was discussed, that "this is the hypostasis which is acting and disposing of the energy" (St John of Damascus —PG 94.1048). Therefore, it is unclear whether this statement by St John of Damascus relates only to the relationship between divine substance and hypostases and, correspondingly, to the relationship between human hypostasis and his natural energy before the fall, or also to the human condition after the fall. If the latter assumption is true, then it is not quite clear why the opinion that setting the energy of human nature under the absolute authority of the person should, according to Thermos, be perceived as a misunderstanding of Orthodox anthropology. On the other hand, if this statement by St John of Damascus only refers to the human condition before the fall, then why should one not presuppose the possibility that Saints could suffer from psychopathological disturbances [see Thermos's underlined statement on the previous page —P.C.]. Finally, it seems reasonable to assume the third idea that enactment and disposition of natural energy by human hypostasis [person] underwent huge changes toward a partial, but never absolute, alienation of

As to the first wrong track, one conceptualizes two natures within the human being: (1) the psychological and (2) the somatic. This is unacceptable to Orthodoxy because, in establishing the location of human freedom, the higher psychological operations (reason, desire and zeal) are invoked. This generates other problems, since human reason, zeal or desire have, however primitive and inferior, analogues within certain animals which can manifest desire in the form of instincts, zeal in the form of feelings, and certain kinds of primitive thinking (Θερμός, *Πρός μία θεολογική*). The Metropolitan John (Zizioulas) says:

> The special identity of the human being in comparison with animals is not concentrated in the reason, because the inferior animals also have a kind of reason and consciousness, even if vastly inferior … No animal can resist the inherent reason of its nature. An individual can, and in this demonstrates his chief feature is not reason, but freedom. (100-101)

Therefore, Thermos asserts that the boundary between an individual and an animal coincides with the line between self-government (*αὐτεξούσιον*), which an animals does not possess, and the other psychological and somatic energies of human nature, common to animals as well (Θερμός, *Πρός μία θεολογική* 116). Thermos (*Πρός μία θεολογική* 116) suggests that, even if conscious interference in the psychological operations can dampen / reduce these, nobody can ameliorate / modify his reasoning, feelings and desires, to the desired extent. This, according to Thermos (*Πρός μία θεολογική* 116), is because psychological operations are the products of an individual's nature and, consequently, are subject to the weakness of this nature. Therefore, one cannot commission any individual with modifying his character[34] (Θερμός, *Πρός μία θεολογική* 116). And a great deal of truth can be elaborated from this statement (about modifying the character) because the corruption of human nature did not leave even the highest energy of human nature, that of self-government, intact, neither in the daily struggle with "another law" (Rom 6.19) nor in the more exceptional aspects of psychological disorder, in which the limited nature of freedom is deeper and more complex (Θερμός, *Πρός μία θεολογική* 116).

This splitting of the one and single human nature also becomes obvious when clerics affirm that psychological diseases can only be dealt with by pharmaceutical means (because of probable organic reasons). In response, Thermos (*Πρός μία θεολογική* 116-9) quotes the universally known prayer — "because of my many sins my body and my soul are sick alike". The faithful nevertheless

---

primordial relationship of authority between person and energy of human nature after the fall.

34 On the complexity of building the human character, see more insightful thoughts by the German philosopher Johan Friedrich Herbart. Gerhard Müßener (Hrsg.). *Didaktische Texte zu Unterricht und Erziehung in Wissenschaft und Schule. Johann Friedrich Herbart.* Wuppertal: Deimling, 1991. 114-9. Deimling – Arbeitsmittel für Studium und Lehre.

resort to the assistance of physicians; in other words, they accept that the somatic energies are affected by the sinfulness of human nature (corruption). When disease occurs, it is physicians rather than the spiritual fathers that are consulted. In like manner, in prescribing psychoactive pharmaceuticals, a psychiatrist intervenes in the disordered processes of the biochemical energies within human nature (Θερμός, *Πρός μία θεολογική*). And why should the process of psychotherapy or a psychotherapist not be permitted to intervene in disorders within the emotional energies of human nature? Thermos deems that, "if our reservation regarding psychotherapy concern not the personality of a psychotherapist (something understandable), but the psychotherapeutic process itself, we thereby imply two natures within the human being" (*Πρός μία θεολογική* 117). The teaching of Gnosticism, according to Thermos, was marred by the same erroneous theory of the human being. Yet, St Gregory Palamas claims: "Neither me (the body) can do anything without soul, nor can the soul do anything without me" (PG 150.1361a). And further, St Gregory continues: "We are proceeding from the understanding of the nature of the human being, as revealed to us in the Holy Scriptures, i.e., an individual is neither soul nor body, but he is both of them jointly" (PG 150.1361c). Consequently, it is wrong, according to St Gregory Palamas, to divide ontologically the pair soul-body, because the being who results from this division is not a human being (qtd. Θερμός, *Πρός μία θεολογική* 117).

In regard to the second wrong track, the opponents of the rapprochement between Orthodoxy and the psychological sciences slip into the same anthropological mistake as the supporters of monothelitism (Θερμός, *Πρός μία θεολογική*). Claiming that psychopathology requires spiritual struggle and pastoral care, supporters of this viewpoint confound self-government with psychological operations (both of them liable to the voluntary modifications, but to very different degrees) (Θερμός, *Πρός μία θεολογική*). Such thinkers are also deceived by the huge difference between psychological and somatic operations. As a result they divide somatic and psychological disorders to the extent that psychological operations appear as disorders, on which the spiritual life (the pious human intention) can have an effect (Θερμός, *Πρός μία θεολογική*).

Thermos (*Πρός μία θεολογική* 119) points out that, if one advances the person to the detriment of the psychosomatic nature, and attributes to the former the absolute power to dominate human nature, he promulgates abstract moralizing and not Orthodox anthropological knowledge about the human being. By doing so, one is repeating the errors of monothelitic heresy. The supporters of this movement could not understand that energy stems from nature and not from the person. The monothelitic Patriarch Pyrros made, according to Thermos (*Πρός μία θεολογική* 119), an attempt to convince his contemporaries that energy proceeds from the person alone, so that Christ's will disposed only of the will of choice and not of the will of nature. Patriarch Pyrros said: "It is impossible for two wills to coexist, without being in contradiction, in a single person" (PG 91.292a). According to Pyrros, each human "motion'" is "passion" (PG 91.352a-b). St Maximus the Confessor corrected him, however, by stating that "each human motion is energy, i.e., natural quality, which can sometimes become a passion, because of the will of choice" (PG 91.352a-b).

Prior to the age of monothelitism, Apollinarius fell into the same trap of moralizing (Θερμός, *Πρός μία θεολογική* 120). He affirmed that Christ assumed only the body and soul without the mind / intellect (*νοῦς*—highest intellectual energy of the soul), because the *νοῦς* "is impassioned" (Θερμός, *Πρός μία θεολογική* 120). However, within the ancient Christian patristic thought it is an established truth that "only whatever is assumed by God is saved, as whatever is not assumed is not cured either" (PG 37.181c). According to St Gregory the Theologian, "Deity combined only with the flesh is not a human being, and, in an equivalent manner, Deity combined only with the soul or even with both soul and flesh, but without the *νοῦς*, is not a human being, either" (PG 37.184b).

Thermos (*Πρός μία θεολογική* 120) believes that Orthodox Christology confirms the basic anthropological fundamental that there is a crucial distinction between the energies of [human] nature and person; if the person is unique and therefore unrepeatable, the energies recur within a common, but individually shared, human nature; only within this framework does the exchanged formula—"whatever is not assumed is not cured either" make sense. The energies of human nature are assumed by Christ because they ontologically belong to human nature which he received and cured, whereas the personhood does exist in a unique and free manner, so that its cure cannot occur apart from its own individual freedom. Thermos concludes his reasoning with the following statement:

> The human being that is deduced from the afore-mentioned sacred Church standpoint is not a human being but a cripple. There is a confusion between the will of choice and the will of nature. There is a hidden pell-mell of monoenergism and Apollinarism. It seems that it is a natural law that any ontological confusion ends up in moralizing: ethics hurries to fill the ontological vacuum. (*Πρός μία θεολογική* 120)

My discussion here has focused on the conviction that Orthodox theology has serious and strongly founded reasons to cooperate with the psychological sciences of psychiatry and psychotherapy. If the latter, as a practical branch of psychoanalysis, does not attempt to heal outside its own areas of competence and expertise, but helps the individual to overcome the problems of the energies of human nature (his psychological operations, and the concomitant attainment of more freedom), it can be useful for the believers. If, however, psychotherapy turns to shaping the will of choice, it becomes a kind of universal quasi-panacea.

4.2.1.2 The issue of hermeneutics

Another strong argument for encouraging interaction between Orthodox pastoral theology and psychoanalysis can be found in the issues raised by hermeneutics. Here, it is important to clarify three items: 1) What is the essence of Orthodox hermeneutics? 2) What kind of problems is Orthodox hermeneutics currently experiencing? 3) How could psychoanalysis be used to deal with these problems?

Firstly, Thermos states that the essence of Orthodox hermeneutics consists in the idea that each Christian, as subject, interprets God's word, as object, by means of his own word, as instrument, and therefore, each Christian's own word must be true for rightly interpreting the Word of God (Θερμός, *Ποιμαίνοντες* 51-57). In saying that an individual's word should be true, Thermos is referring to its inner consistency. He says:

> Emancipation from 'self-evident matters' is a necessary condition for the preparedness of an individual for revelation, i.e., for his opening to hermeneutics (interpretation). With this emancipation, the individual's word becomes spontaneous, vivacious, veritable, since it is not diffracted and altered by the various fragments of his individual selfishness (or imperfection). Inasmuch as the concrete person is one, his word is also one. Whatever he does, i.e., the way he leads his life, the way he acts, interprets or worships, his actions are permanently accompanied by his word. He does all these things by means of his word and not by means of another's word. If this inner word of his existence is not true, it is not capable of interpreting the Word of God correctly. (Θερμός, *Ποιμαίνοντες* 51)

Thus, the condition for the truth of hermeneutics is, according to Thermos (*Ποιμαίνοντες* 52), the truth of its subject (individual), as a rational being. Yet, in such a case, the interpretation turns its subject into its object as well, since it also testifies of the subject, i.e. the interpreter (Θερμός, *Ποιμαίνοντες* 52). Moreover, hermeneutics interprets its subject and reveals him. Thermos (*Ποιμαίνοντες* 52) claims that the interpretations of God suggested by the Saints inform us not only about God, but also about those Saints. From a Saint's interpretation, "we learn more about different facets of his personality" (Θερμός, *Ποιμαίνοντες* 52).

Hence, Thermos affirms:

> The criterion of Orthodox hermeneutics does not coincide with the certainty of a pious reasoning, but it has to do with 'the examination of the self' and 'the knowledge of the spirit'. It is about a never-ending ritual, during which the believer is simultaneously the interpreter and the one who is interpreted; he is the one who officiates during the ritual and the Lord's table, likewise Jesus Christ: in a different way, but with a similar ethos, i.e., the ethos of the mediated creation. (*Ποιμαίνοντες* 54)

To clarify his understanding of Orthodox hermeneutics, Thermos compares it to Roman Catholic hermeneutics. He takes as an example the divine liturgy. The Roman Catholic mass of the "word" and "chalice", as opposed to the Orthodox liturgy of the "neophytes" and "faithful", presents the word and praxis mediated as objective (detached) things (Θερμός, *Ποιμαίνοντες* 53-4). The Orthodox liturgy of the "neophytes" and "faithful" presents the subjects (the believers) who are actually mediated, and for this reason the word and praxis (as their word and praxis) are also mediated. Thermos says:

> The word becomes praxis and the praxis has the word; the praxis refers itself to the words (reasons) of human beings and all the created things. The Orthodox priest is ordained 'to officiate the word of the truth' of God (the prayer of ordination) and then he brings to Him the offerings as 'verbal worship'. If we do not feel this unity within our hearts, i.e., the interpretative officiating of existence that is pregnant with and gives life to the personal truth, the latter becomes detached from Christ and the human being; as for the hermeneutics, they end in a technocratic act used by everyone as they wish. (*Ποιμαίνοντες* 55)

To understand why Thermos considers it so necessary to stress the existential truth of the person who wants to interpret the Word of God correctly one needs certain clarification here. The Greek theologian the Very Reverend John Romanidis suggests an interesting concept in his book "*Τό προπατορικόν ἁμάρτημα*" (The Original Sin)[35], a concept which can clarify the difference between Orthodox and Roman Catholic hermeneutics. Romanidis argues that, from very early times, Western theological thought interpreted original sin in the sense of a juridical transgression which caused suffering of human nature and death as a form of divine punishment for Adam's disregard of the law of God. In such a manner, there is apparently no reference to corruption of nature, but only to the will of choice, in the Roman Catholic theological line of thought. Therefore, according to this thought, human being needs a divine saviour-sacrifice who makes the redemptive, propitiatory offering to God on behalf of mankind. In addition, believers need a proper education, something carried out through the Church's interpretation of God's Word.

Not so with the Orthodox theological thought. This interprets death not as a punishment used by God against the transgressors, but as a natural result of their self-determination (Tollefsen 149); they tried to become gods without the almighty God and failed in attaining their goal, because an individual's existence is ontologically dependent on God. Thus, education is required by the corrupted human intention, whereas the split caused by death to the one and same human nature needs nothing more than healing. This healing was completed in the onto-

35 Cf. for additional references: Papageorgiou, Panayiotis (Very Reverend). "Chrysostom and Augustine on the Sin of Adam and Its Consequences." *St Vladimir's Theological Quarterly* 39.4, (1995): 361-379. Print.

logical gift of incorruption to the human nature offered by the person of the divine logos who, because of His great love for man, assumed that human nature[36] with all its shortcomings, and made it incorrupt in the act of His own rising from the dead (Tollefsen 155-8). The incorruption can be inherited by each believer in the communion with Christ within the church, His body. Here Christians are given the Word of God, but this Word should be assumed with the intention of practising it, as a sign that an individual freely (the will of choice) opens the door of his heart to the Lord, who is only able to grant incorruption to human beings by making them participate in His transfigured and deified humanity, i.e., the church. Within the church, the Holy Spirit works out the deification of believers through divine uncreated grace. Being a natural energy of divine nature, divine uncreated grace nevertheless is disposed of and directed by each divine person, according to St John of Damascus (PG 94.1048). This means that, in sending us His grace, God entirely is present within His grace[37]. On the other hand, in partaking of divine grace, Christians charismatically partake in it through a natural relationship. So, by means of real participation in the divine energies, Christians partake charismatically of God. Hence, the education of the human will of choice accompanies the ontological work of healing the human nature, i.e., the interpretation of God's Word should keep abreast with the practice of this word within an individual's soul, since it is the acquisition of divine grace that grants incorruption to our human nature. Thus, it is clear why Orthodox hermeneutics is not only an objective interpretation of God's Word, but also an inner self-interpretation carried out by the individual.

Thermos claims:

> This soul's way of functioning, which reminds us of a prism, seems to be a key element for understanding the mystery of the human being. Christ cannot be perceived as a kind of "object" of investigation, because He is not actually outside, but inside the individual, 'His Kingdom is within us' (Luke 16.21); and His Word has already judged each human person; His truth has met each man, and the individual's interpretation brings either liberation or conflict as a result of that meeting. (*Ποιμαίνοντες* 54)

---

36 The will of choice within Christ was a characteristic of a person and not of nature, and alien to the gravitation toward sin, since Christ's person is the divine logos Himself. Therefore St Maximus the Confessor says that "Christ acts humanely beyond the human" (*ὑπὲρ ἄνθρωπον ἐνήργει τὰ ἀνθρώπου* — *Ambiguum* 5, PG 91.1049b) (qtd. Tollefsen 152-6).

37 "grace […] effects the ineffable union itself. By grace *God entirely* comes to dwell in (περιχωρεῖ) all the worthy, and all the saints in turn dwell entirely (περιχωροῦσιν) in *God entirely*, receiving *God entirely* […]" (PG 150.1229d; PG 91.1076c-d). Transl. by R. E. Sinkewicz. This Orthodox conceptualization of *theognosia / theoptia* differs from the Western theological line of reasoning expressed in Aquinas' following words — "*Deus cognoscatur totus, sed non totaliter*" (The whole of God is cognized, but *not entirely*) [My translation]. Cf. T.-D. Humbrecht: *Théologie négative et noms divins chez Saint Thomas d'Aquin*, Paris 2005. 70, 329, 454, 741, 742.

Thus the essence of Orthodox hermeneutics consists of three elements: (1) the existential truth of the *human person* (2) who develops an interpretative *relation* with the Word of God by means of his own word (3) in order to express a true opinion about any issue in the *personal or social spheres of life* (Θερμός, *Ποιμαίνοντες*). These elements only work authentically when the individual maintains a consistent spiritual life, and places values above needs and attitudes, i.e., self-offering to the truth of revelation. This enables an individual to express an Orthodox opinion on any given issue (Θερμός, *Ποιμαίνοντες*).

What kinds of problems does Orthodox hermeneutics actually experience?

According to Thermos, any problems related to hermeneutics are caused by the incorrect functioning of any of its three elements: i.e., the existential untruth of the human person, the improper function of his word and the individualistic, as opposed to the subjective,[38] interpretation of social and personal issues.

According to Thermos (*Ποιμαίνοντες*), existential untruth in a human being, apart from being caused by the lack of a spiritual life, arises from the psychological phenomenon of false self. In such a case, the individual mobilizes his psychological defence mechanisms against his body, feelings, desires or urges (Θερμός, *Ποιμαίνοντες*). Therefore, such a person undermines the integrity of his personality by denying some of its components (Θερμός, *Ποιμαίνοντες*). For Thermos (*Ποιμαίνοντες*), such a person may have the right conceptions, but unhealthy attitudes. He says:

> A particular reader of the Holy Scriptures or of the Church Fathers may accept intellectually that he constitutes a personality, but approaches the texts by denying the integrity of his personality, i.e., by being partially present or even by denying some facets of a particular Father's personality. Some operations of his human nature may not, according to this person, meet with the message of God or of the Fathers and he does not want to be faced with some facets of the personalities of the Fathers. (Θερμός, *Προλεγόμενα* 27)

Why does such an attitude exist? Thermos believes that the interpretation of any text should end in the interpretation of self. He says:

> Within every one of us, there is an understanding that precedes every new text we are going to interpret; further, by means of this pre-understanding, we are able to penetrate into the meaning of the text that we have to interpret. Inasmuch as the meaning becomes clearer, it affects our pre-understanding in such a way that it makes the latter broader, modifies it and corrects it, if there is such a need. We

38 There is a difference between individualistic and subjective interpretation: being individualistic, the former is also subjective since it is rooted in the indescribable peculiarity of each human person, while the latter is not individualistic. Here, the point is that individualistic interpretation comes from the personality where interpretation is dominated by the individual needs and attitudes, whereas subjective interpretation comes from the personality where individual needs and attitudes are enthralled to the objective truth of divine revelation.

> could say that the interpretation of a text becomes simultaneously an interpretation of our self. (Θερμός, *Προλεγόμενα* 27)

Thermos (*Προλεγόμενα* 27) believes that such interpretation is rejected many times by the faithful. They want neither to reveal their inner selves nor to change themselves through the Fathers; they prefer the private world of their "self-evident matters" (Θερμός, *Προλεγόμενα* 27). They delude themselves by believing that they allegedly interpret the Fathers, instead of leaving themselves to be interpreted by the Fathers (Θερμός, *Προλεγόμενα* 27).

Thus, this psychological situation of alienating some facets of human existence (i.e., the body, feelings, desires or urges) can have a negative effect on a person's interpretation of the truth (be it the Word of God or the interpretative word of the Fathers). Here, it seems suitable to bring a very insightful remark made by Bendaly who stated:

> An individual has to seriously take into consideration his instinctive components in order to promote an authentic sublimation which would constitute the true overcoming of instinct (we overcome only whatever we pass through by assuming it) and not one of imaginary evasion. The latter actually is equal with a latent and streamlined triumph of instinct. B. Pascal was right in averring that 'the human being is neither an angel nor an animal, so that he who pretends to be an angel makes himself out in actual fact to be an animal'. (Bendaly 1: 306)

For Thermos (*Προλεγόμενα*), the phenomenon of the falsehood of the word is the second problem that may occur in hermeneutics. This problem involves the inability of an interpreter to develop a relationship with the text. According to Thermos (*Προλεγόμενα*), derogation of the personality, a lack of dialogue and a fear of otherness bring about the inability to form an authentic relationship with the Word of God or the interpretative word of the holy Fathers.

Why does Thermos place such emphasis on the word? He considers, as does Ch. Yannaras, the following to be true:

> The word is a precondition for every direct or indirect relationship of apprehension. Therefore it is also a precondition for the expansion of the borders of relationship as well as for the formation of a human person's otherness. The word is a starting point for the maintenance of a relationship, and the materialization of a relationship of comprehension with other persons. (qtd. Θερμός, *Προλεγόμενα* 29)

It is important to establish that St Basil the Great shares this view of the nature of the human word. He says:

> God has created and given us the word in order that everyone of us may open the thoughts of his heart to his nearest, and due to our common nature, as if out of some treasuries, to pass over the latent thoughts of the heart to his brother. And the reason is obvious here, i.e., if we lived with the incorporeal soul, we would

> have communicated with each other by means of the thoughts. Since our soul is behind the screen of the body, the former needs words and names for conveying whatever is in its depths. Thus, when the thought expresses itself through the voice, the former is transmitted from the speaker to the listener, traversing the air by the word, as by a ferry. And if the word finds complete serenity and quiet, as if in the serene dock, it settles in another person's consciousness. Yet, if the hubbub of listeners, like a violent wind, blows in the opposite direction, the word is wrecked, dissipating in the air… (Μέγα Βασιλείου, 6.215)

The first reason for problems arising in hermeneutics is the derogation of the personality. This requires some explanation. Derogation of the personality stems from the aforementioned false self. The text is not used with the intention of learning something new, of changing one's self-perception and life, but only to consolidate the status-quo (Θερμός, *Προλεγόμενα*).

The second reason is a lack of dialogue. This interpretative situation is not, according to Thermos (*Προλεγόμενα* 28), a linguistic deformity that has an effect on the clarity of understanding but a condition of the possibility to understand. The hermeneutic experience can make us participate in the text, only because there is not automatic agreement between the text and the interpreter (Θερμός, *Προλεγόμενα* 29-30). The starting point of interpretation seems to be a position. Yet, in reality, it is, as Thermos shows, a correspondence. The meaning of the interpretation is determined, in the same way as every correspondence, by the question (Θερμός, *Προλεγόμενα* 29-30). Thus, the dialectic of question-answer interlocution always precedes the dialectic of interpretation (Θερμός, *Προλεγόμενα* 30). This interlocution determines the understanding. Therefore, if the reader does not put questions to the text, he does not get an answer, and thereby no new understanding is created (of course, under the conditions described inside the text) (Θερμός, *Προλεγόμενα* 30). Thermos asserts that "assimilation is not a simple reproduction or repetition of the traditional text, but the creation of new understanding" (*Προλεγόμενα* 30), and he brings one significant remark from Florovsky: "The regaining of the way the holy fathers thought is a fundamental precondition for the renaissance of theology. Naturally, this is by no means a simple archaeological restoration or simple repetition or even a return … A theologian follows the Fathers when he creates, not when he simply imitates or repeats them" (26).

The final reason for an inability to develop a relationship with the text is the fear of otherness. Thermos (*Προλεγόμενα* 30) claims that everyone who reads the texts of the holy Fathers feels that their word is deep. This is because they were acting as persons who realized their otherness, but at the same time they had a thirst for communication with and a relationship to others (Θερμός, *Προλεγόμενα* 29). Thermos writes an interesting description of the dynamics of this adventure of personal meeting:

> The more genuine the conversation, the less its guidance is up to the volition of the conversationalists. A genuine conversation is never the one we intended to make from the beginning. It would be, generally, more right to say that we fall into conversation or we get involved in it … Nobody knows at the beginning how this conversation will end … The language of the conversation makes something appear, and this something continues to exist afterwards. (*Προλεγόμενα* 29)

He believes that any difference between the interpreter and the text is not an obstacle to interpretation, but rather a necessary condition for the success of interpretation, regardless of whether the difference is cultural, social or on any other dimension (*Προλεγόμενα* 30-1).

Thus, one comes to the third problem that may occur in Orthodox hermeneutics, i.e., an individualist interpretation of social or personal issues.

According to Thermos (*Προλεγόμενα*), there are two extreme trends. The first trend comes down to the criticism of the holy Fathers from a position of haughtiness and of a "progressive" mind. This kind of person pretends to know better how the Fathers had to act in their time, interpreting them according to modern "self-evident matters". The second trend represents the attempt to "solidify" hermeneutically the holy Fathers as having positions that are independent of the concrete chronological momentum of contemporaneous society (*Προλεγόμενα* 32).

In relation to these two trends, Thermos says: "These people approach the word of the Fathers, as if the Fathers fell from nowhere, i.e., they do not ask themselves who is interpreting and why he is interpreting this way and not another" (Θερμός, *Προλεγόμενα* 32). Obviously, Thermos endeavours to make a link between the Fathers' otherness and their simultaneous openness toward the world. He affirms that language was the means used by the Fathers to make the world understand the truth and whoever accepted it was transfigured, and became a new creation (*Προλεγόμενα* 32). Moreover, language was not simply a means, but a link to truth and knowledge on the one hand, and to reality on the other (Θερμός, *Προλεγόμενα* 32). Hence, Thermos (*Προλεγόμενα* 32) develops the idea that language is a social and historical phenomenon determined by the mind-set of each epoch. According to Thermos (*Προλεγόμενα* 32), hermeneutics should not become a key factor in the perpetuation and reproduction of the Church, but rather be a key factor in the endless incarnation of the Church Word in the language of each epoch, something that constitutes the ineluctable condition for the Church's own inner health.

Thermos's ideas seem open to challenge by Orthodox theological circles. One is tempted to doubt his position and to ask: who will check the Orthodoxy of these newly emerged interpreters, even if they *claim*, regardless of how, that they participate in the truth (Life in Christ) or *prove* their claim through miracles? The faithful have been given many warnings by Christ, the apostles, and the Church Fathers about pseudo-prophets and pseudo-teachers, so why should pseudo-interpreters not emerge? No clear answers to these unsettling thoughts are to be found within Thermos's works. Needless to say, it is important for the faithful to be given proper answers to these questions. One only needs to recall the history of the Church. It is well-known that many people were enthralled for almost a hundred years by the erroneous interpretation of the Scripture by Arius's "brilliant" mind. How many believers were lost to the Church because of the "spiritual" interpretation of the Gnostics? These questions continue to arise up until the present, and therefore only intensify our apprehension concerning an uncontrolled stream of interpreters within the Orthodox Church. Who can guarantee the faithful, laymen or clergy, that newly created understanding, as well as truth incarnated in the language of the modern epoch, are virtually true?

The guarantee is the Church, along with its Ecumenical Synods, in which the faithful have obtained the criteria for distinguishing truth from falsehood. Thermos himself actually acknowledges that the Ecumenical Synod is the Church's highest organ of power with the authority to express opinions on every problematical issue. However, this organ's rulings have to be accepted by the whole Church (believers, either clergy or laymen). Only in such a case is the expressed truth acknowledged as formulated in the Holy Spirit.[39] Therefore, there is a question to be answered here: is the truth formulated during the seven Synods something we are permitted to ignore when dealing with every newly created understanding, as well as when we incarnate the word of the Church in the language of modern civilization? Fortunately, Thermos gives a clear answer that can be viewed as a tool which could help to dissipate the unsettling thoughts outlined above. He states that "the new creation of understanding should be made under the conditions that are described within all the works of the Fathers; this former should not be a troublesome innovation" (Θερμός, *Προλεγόμενα* 29). This can be interpreted as follows: every interpreter has to move within the framework of ecclesiastical truth, i.e., he must proceed from authentic Christian theology and anthropology which have been determined within Church Tradition.

How can psychoanalysis be used to solve these problems? Thermos believes that it is necessary for an individual, firstly, to have within himself psychological truth on which theological truth can be built. He says: "Truth within the psychological world of a person leads to truth within his theological (spiritual) world (if, surely, the will of choice agrees); the psychological personal truth of a human person is an ally of theological truth of the Church" (Θερμός,

39 The limited nature of this research, and also the intention to delimit the issue to its psychological aspects, causes me to avoid discussing this subject. However, the following books by the contemporary Greek theologian P. Boumis are to be recommended: Μπούμη, Παναγιώτου. *Τὸ ἀλάθητο τῆς Ὀρθοδοξίας* [The Infallibility of Orthodoxy]. Ἀθήνα, 1996. Print; ———. *Τὸ κύρος καὶ ἡ ἰσχύς τῶν ἱερῶν κανόνων* [The Force and the Authority of Holy Canons]. Ἀθήνα, 2000. Print.

Αναζητώντας 71). Thermos (*Αναζητώντας*) claims that heresy is characterized by a kind of intellectual and existential "self-sufficiency" [autonomy], since it contests the truth, denying apprenticeship within the catholicity of the Church.

This intellectual and existential "self-sufficiency" is well known in the psychoanalytic tradition. It can be attributed to the false self. According to Thermos (*Πρός μία θεολογική* 123), the tragic nature of the human being consists in the fact that, when every person, undertakes the work of choosing between good and evil (around the fifth to seventh year of life), his emotional world has already covered more than half of his life[40]. Hence, every one of us has to deal with the accumulated weight of his nature. The pathological phenomenon of the false self stems from that period of life. Thermos resorts to the investigations made by the famous psychoanalyst Winnicott to show that psychoanalysis may be useful for investigating the early stages of a person's life. The essence of the false self is based on the idea that, when a mother incapable of dealing with a child's impulsiveness makes him compliant with her needs, the child receives the signal that his feelings, and the way he senses, interprets, and responds to the world is unacceptable, and thus he begins to concentrate on his intellect (Θερμός, *Αναζητώντας; Πρός μία θεολογική*). Therefore, the pair 'psyche-intellect' substitute for the pair 'psyche-body' (Θερμός, *Αναζητώντας; Πρός μία θεολογική*). This begins a process which cripples the human being by hampering his development as a person. To be a person means, for Thermos (*Αναζητώντας*; *Πρός μία θεολογική*), being positioned toward others as an integral being with body, feelings and soul. Thermos (*Αναζητώντας*; *Πρός μία θεολογική*) stresses that there is not any objection toward the intention to change the contents of these feelings and desires, but if the child's feelings and desires are rejected just because they bother us, this is very wrong as it leads to the alienation of the person. An alienated person develops "self-sufficiency" [autonomy] within himself self, since it is propagated as a solution to the anxiety caused by permanent feelings of insufficiency and dependence upon adults (the parents) who are psychologically inadequate to meet the needs of the child (Θερμός, *Αναζητώντας*; *Πρός μία θεολογική*). This "self-sufficiency" [autonomy] is an enemy to the individual's existence as a person, since the individual's existence as a person flourishes within the framework of accepting the limits of his nature, while the false self cannot accept these limits for the simple reason that the individual lives integrally not within the pair "psyche-body", but within the pair "psyche-intellect" (Θερμός, *Αναζητώντας*; *Πρός μία θεολογική*). The first case produces humbleness and acceptance of otherness, while the second is pregnant with arrogance and intolerance (Θερμός, *Αναζητώντας*; *Πρός μία θεολογική*).

---

40 Thermos is alluding to the fact that after birth babies represent a sponge which imbibes all the emotional atmosphere of their familial milieu, depositing, without being aware of it, both the positive and negative emotions of parents, siblings etc. in the deepness of their soul.

Since the problem of hermeneutics has first of all to do with the question of whether or not a particular person has achieved integrity, i.e., the true self, why could the psychoanalytic method of investigating the history of human desire not be used? Thermos considers that there is no principle which restricts this path. If the given assistance is offered with a conscious distinction drawn between transfigured psychoanalytic knowledge and Freud's psychoanalytic theoretical conception, there is a pragmatic benefit for the Church in undertaking this.

4.2.1.3. The issue of interpreting the Orthodox credo in terms of contemporary gnoseology

For Thermos, the third strong argument for encouraging interaction between Orthodox pastoral theology and psychoanalysis is the issue of interpreting the Orthodox faith in terms of contemporary gnoseology. The issues discussed above have prepared the ground for dealing with this issue. The holy Fathers were very flexible in dealing with scientific and philosophical knowledge accumulated outside the Church. They always proceeded from the truth of revelation, but the language they used to shape this truth evolved over time. Taking this into consideration, Thermos asks if there is any obstacle to the contemporary Orthodox Church using psychoanalytic language and knowledge to shape the truth of revelation (the theological knowledge) into language and gnoseology appropriate to the contemporary epoch. It seems that in principle such an obstacle does not exist, especially if such knowledge is sifted through theological and anthropological truth, and revelatory knowledge. However, we must take into consideration the fact that the holy Fathers resorted to secular knowledge and language for a particular reason. At the time, the Church (actually, the truth) was dealing with a number of heresies. The Church Fathers undertook to elaborate a theological language because there was a real necessity to clarify what the church believed in contrast to the heretics. Returning to Thermos's suggestion that psychoanalytic knowledge be employed within the church, we could ask if contemporary Orthodoxy has need of such language and gnoseology. Thermos answers in the positive, based on two issues he has explored and considered over many years: (1) the condition of the concept of hieratic vocation (*κλίση*) in the premodern patristic tradition, and (2) the subtleness of modern psychological language. With relation to the first, it is important to emphasize that the concept of hieratic vocation (*κλίση*) remained rudimentary within the works of the early Fathers; and even when they advanced certain opinions on this matter, they dealt only with the negative aspects (pathology) of the vocation and not its healthy development. Why such a limitation? Thermos also appears perplexed concerning this limited approach when he asks: "Is it about the echo of the Biblical vocation (*κλήση*) of the prophets and apostles? Is this an immanent component of the Fathers' ecclesiastical self-consciousness? Is it caused by a lack of development in the concepts of individual rights and individual desires, both of which emerged during the modern epoch"? (Θερμός, *Ἱερατική* 324) In his doctoral dissertation, Thermos does not answer these questions, since they need to be dealt with separately. He only establishes the fact that the pre-modern patristic tradition could not answer questions concerning the psychological development of hieratic vocation, and it would therefore appear to be necessary and desirable to conduct an analysis of the phenomenon of individual initiative for priesthood on the basis of the psychoanalytic model of the human being.

As for the subtleness of modern psychological language, Thermos explains what he means in the following words:

> Psychiatric language's realism and pragmatic fastidiousness in its choice of words can contribute to the expurgation of the obscurities that scourge our theological language and are rooted in our inner confusion. On the other hand, psychiatry's reasonableness, consistent methodology and extrapolation of psychological pretensions may have an effect on the unrealistic zest of our "spiritual" conclusions. Furthermore, the investigation of unconscious motives could cleanse the hieratic and monastic vocations of tendencies with relation to the preaching of theological attitudes. And, generally, in this way theology could be assisted in becoming more realistic and in re-establishing pastoral care. (*Ποιμαίνοντες* 27)

The fact that Thermos repairs to psychoanalytic language in his dissertation does not mean that he has determined which psychoanalytic terms should be assumed in the language of Orthodox pastoral theology. His dissertation is an attempt to construct and mediate interaction between theological and scientific knowledge. This represents no more than an experiment that must be further elaborated and analyzed. However, he does indicate that acknowledgement by psychoanalysis of the individual's power to love (as a critical feature of human nature), and the concepts of personhood, relationship and forgiveness, could form a meeting point for Orthodox pastoral theology and a psychoanalytic model of the human being. The individual's power to love, and the concepts of personhood, relationship and forgiveness, are regarded as four basic commonalities between Orthodox pastoral theology and psychoanalysis.

Firstly, Thermos endeavours to substantiate his statement that psychoanalysis acknowledges the essential role of the power of love within the human being so that, when this power goes awry, an individual precipitates within himself a pathological process. Thermos affirms that it is incorrect to state that Freud only understood love in terms of sexuality, since Freud allegedly made some statements which are close to Thermos's given standpoint.

Bendaly (1973) states that within Freud's global concepts there are acceptable ideas about Eros. For Bendaly (1973), this psychoanalytic concept of Eros completely overcomes the idea of carnal knowledge and reconciles sexuality in its corporeal reality. He points out that "Freud wanted to maintain at any cost not the materialist and reductive concept of symbol but, against any avatar of Gnosticism, the carnal consistence of symbol, its rooting within the body and history…" (Bendaly 1: 302).

Beirnaert (205), a psychoanalyst from the school of Lacan, says

> It is necessary to say that for Freud sexuality is simultaneously everywhere and nowhere. Everywhere in the sense that the position taken by an individual toward the phallic does signify sense, desire and the law, and commands all others facets of the individual, at all levels. Nowhere in the sense that sexuality is not identified with a precise behaviour, and that it is impossible in any case to reach saturation in the unification of sexes [or sexual intercourse] … (qtd. Bendaly 1: 302)

Thus, Thermos does not stand alone in asserting that Freud's understanding of sexuality is far broader than originally believed; the misperception arose out of confusion between Freud's psychoanalytic theory and the heritage of his dynamic thought.

Thermos believes that the meeting point for Orthodox pastoral theology and psychoanalysis coincides in the two disciplines' common conviction that an inability to love gives rise to psychopathology (Θερμός, *Θεολογία* 11-12).

The Freudian psychoanalyst Winnicott (162-3) has demonstrated that "the baby's 'primary egoism', which corresponds with the experience of good maternity, is the foundation for posterior generosity without resentment" (qtd. Θερμός, *Θεολογία* 11-12). Bendaly (1973) deems that, within Freud's global thought (the treasure trove of his ideas), there is room for the transformation of narcissistic libido into the altruistic Eros, and the libido may, thereby, become an inferior symbol of the spiritual concept of agape. Zilboorg states that "Freud openly expressed his wish that his Eros be used in the meaning of agape, as used within St Paul's epistles" (281).

A second commonality between Orthodox pastoral theology and psychoanalysis is, according to Thermos, the idea of personhood. Thermos does not claim similarity of content. However, he believes that "it was a great thing that, starting with the energy model of the human being, i.e., that energy produces symptoms unless it is defused, Freud gradually understood the importance of interpersonal relations" (Θερμός, *Θεολογία* 11). Thermos goes on to point out that Winnicot and Klein had introduced the theory of relations of the object into psychoanalysis. Within this context, the object refers, for Thermos, to each person who is psychologically important to the subject. Thermos (*Θεολογία* 12) believes the newly-emerged term "self" to be of critical importance to anthropology. And the term could, according to Thermos, be the first element in the idea of "person" (*Θεολογία* 12).

Thermos points out that the concept of self includes the ideas of self-consciousness and of clear boundaries between the individual and others. He claims that it is important for the individual to be a subject (chief player) of his own history. Thermos acknowledges the problems that arise out of the emphasis on the autonomy of the subject, since this idea is alien to theology. However, he also deems that the acceptance of the boundaries of self are an important matter, as any theological discussion of the social must preclude diffused boundaries for the self (Θερμός, *Θεολογία* 12).

In departing from the researches of Ricœur, we could say that Freud was aware of the idea of personhood as a manifestation of interpersonal relations. Freud had actually unleashed a war against the previous biological / chemical understanding of the human being, with his development of the notions of censorship, condensation[41], de-guise, etc., all of which implied the existence of a sense of self within the individual (Bendaly, 1973). However, Freud failed to develop an acceptable model of the individual, since, according to Ricœur, he endeavoured to describe "all the relations of sense in the language of a mental hydraulics. Thereby, Freud continues to inscribe his discoveries in the terms of the very framework he was nevertheless destroying" (*La Psychanalyse* 98).

I am by no means attempting here to throw doubt on Thermos's argument that psychoanalysis has endeavoured to contribute to the idea of personhood; rather, it should be emphasized that the concepts within psychoanalysis are very complex. Acceptable ideas of personhood are not to be found within Freud's psychoanalytic theory; however, it would not be true to make the same statement in relation to Freud's overall conceptual framework. Therefore, one can agree with Bendaly that "beyond the positivist apparatus imposed on Freud by his epoch and beyond his clinical approach to the facts, one is able to find in Freud's conception of symbolism an open space for creation and freedom" (i.e., for the personhood) (1: 300).

The third commonality between Freudian psychoanalysis and theology is the idea of relationship. In Thermos's opinion (*Θεολογία* 12-13), relationship is connected to the discovery of the primary dual relationship of baby-mother. Psychoanalysis states that the dual relationship of baby-mother must be overcome to such an extent that the child gradually develops the ability for triadic relationships, in which he opens himself up to loving others. If this does not take place, then the child will develop narcissistic love within himself, become unbearable to society, and become subject to psychopathological processes (Θερμός, *Θεολογία* 12-13).

The fourth and final commonality between Freudian psychoanalysis and theology concerns forgiveness. For Thermos, there is considerable convergence between confession and psychotherapy. He is certainly aware also that there is a large difference as to their aims. In the case of forgiveness, the person reconciles

---

41 Condensation is "the process by which a single symbol or word is associated with the emotional content of several, not necessarily related, ideas, feelings, memories, or impulses, especially as expressed in dreams." "Condensation." *American Heritage Dicitonary.* Web 10.04.2013. http://www.answers.com/topic/condensation#ixzz2Q3F4XmIh.

himself self with the catholicity of Church, the angels and with God, while in the second case, there is a simple positive impact on psychological health (Θερμός, *Θεολογία* 12-13). Yet, the meeting point is the significance that both approaches attach to forgiveness. Due recognition should be paid to the fact that psychotherapeutic theory maintains that a person cannot find inner peace unless he really forgives his parents (Θερμός, *Θεολογία* 13). Thermos believes that psychoanalysis can assist Orthodox pastoral care a great deal in developing the criteria of genuine forgiveness.

Another idea not mentioned by Thermos, which could also constitute a meeting point between Orthodox pastoral theology and psychoanalysis is the human proclivity to think in symbols. I have already established that Freud caused great resentment within the scholarly community because he attached great importance to the symbolic way of thinking.

Thus, on the basis of Thermos's research, one might state that there are three main arguments for encouraging interaction between Orthodox pastoral theology and psychoanalysis. However, these arguments do not seem to be equally strong, since there are certain weaknesses not fully dealt with by Thermos, i.e., in relation to the issue of Orthodox hermeneutics.

4.2.2. The difficulties with the interaction

According to Thermos, there are two main difficulties with regard to any interaction between Orthodox pastoral theology and psychoanalysis: 1) the degeneration of contemporary psychotherapeutic techniques and 2) religious fundamentalism.

4.2.2.1. Degeneration of contemporary psychotherapeutic techniques

The first difficulty is the degeneration of contemporary psychotherapeutic techniques. Scientific techniques to relieve human suffering (those of nature) became a would-be panacea for existential problems. Thermos speaks of the social and cultural conjuncture that resulted in an environment favourable to the degeneration of psychotherapies. Further, he describes the ways in which this degeneration has been refracted in psychotherapeutic practice.

With reference to the social and cultural conjuncture, Thermos claims that modern developments in the Western world have led to different "psychotherapeutic" endeavours which simply aim to support the client in his choices, whatever those choices happen to be (*Δύο πολιτισμικοί* 1). For instance, if a homosexual should want to cohabit with a partner and adopt a child, some psychologists or psychiatrists will support this choice and justify it "scientifically", stating that such a path can be undertaken without compunction, since the child will not be damaged in his psychological development. According to Thermos, these psychologists or psychiatrists are quick to offer psychotherapy to homosexual couples. "All these things are natural consequences of contemporary developments when the new term "client" reflected changed attitudes; the client, you know, is always right" (Θερμός, *Δύο πολιτισμικοί* 1-2).

Thermos states that all these psychotherapeutic trends have the concept of right as a common characteristic, and the mind-set of relativity of this concept of right. There is not a "consummate theory of the individual underlying these trends and even in the cases where there is such a theory, it is a completely empirical and tragically incomplete caricature of a theory stemming from the 'here and now' image of the Western individual of megalopolises. This image is isolated and generalized" (Θερμός, *Δύο πολιτισμικοί* 2).

As Thermos shows, these therapeutic trends retain whatever is in their interest. From modernism, they loot "the notion of individuality and self-determinism, ignoring the strong tradition of collective convictions and of emphasis on the sublimation of urges" (*Δύο πολιτισμικοί* 2). From postmodernism, they borrow "the annihilation of token normative systems and the triumph of subjectivity, forgetting the new possibilities of self-criticism, which stem from the post-modernistic sensitiveness toward the traps of cultural prejudice" (Θερμός, *Δύο πολιτισμικοί* 2). Pointing to the wide range of written sources, Thermos contends that this phenomenon is the natural deterministic evolution of American society (where the phenomenon chiefly developed) (Θερμός, *Δύο πολιτισμικοί* 3).

Thermos (*Δύο πολιτισμικοί* 3) cites May, who affirms that, in the USA since Freud's epoch, people have looked to the psychotherapeutic schools for psychological and emotional guidance; they might attend Church and partake of sacraments, but, "for some, confession lost its transforming power of reconciliation and absolution; it often seemed that psychology promised more prospects for completeness, health, adequacy and happiness" (qtd. Θερμός, *Δύο πολιτισμικοί* 3). Social and individual tribulations were referred to psychology and psychotherapy; these promised, according to Becker, "more stable joy, elation, festivity of life, perfect love and freedom" (qtd. Θερμός, *Δύο πολιτισμικοί* 3). Therefore, it was a natural and logical evolution for psychology to become a kind of fetish, a system of faith (qtd. Θερμός, *Δύο πολιτισμικοί* 3-4). Thermos considers that happiness also became "a fetish, inasmuch as euphoria and pleasure are presented almost as moral commands" (*Δύο πολιτισμικοί* 3-4).

All this reasoning is valuable, but it does not help us to understand what actually instigated the Western Christian loss of confidence in the Church and the filling of the resultant vacuum with psychotherapeutic techniques. Who is to blame for the Church's loss of real spiritual influence? Who is responsible for the dominance gained by psychotherapy?

Research carried out by Orthodox theologians and scholars indicates that the responsibility for these developments can be attributed to *Zeitgeist*, Western Christian theology and psychotherapy.

The spirit of the time has led the faithful to perceive psychotherapeutic techniques as a kind of panacea. Since we are mainly discussing American society here, it seems necessary to focus chiefly on the peculiarity of historical circumstances which played a primary role in the formation of the American State system during the Civil War (1861-1865). The influence of the Protestant religious movement was enormous in terms of a religious awakening and also reverberated in the movement for the abolition of slavery. The call for the abolition of slavery made the Protestant movement famous and influential inside the Northern States and later the Southern ones (The Columbia Encyclopedia 8:1608). Thus the Protestant movement from the outset paid attention to and had influence on social issues within the USA. Therefore, to the American people the development of mutual relationships between Protestant theological, anthropological, soteriological views and psychotherapeutic techniques seemed promising.

Furthermore, contemporary Protestant pastoral practice gives, according to Kornarakis (*Ἐγχειρίδιον* 3: 17*)*, a wide berth to the rich soteriological possibilities of the sacrament of confession not because of the Protestant dogmatic doctrine, but due to the drastic reduction of its (confession) popularity among the faithful. These resort to private consultation mostly with the purpose to find quick and effective pragmatic solutions to personal emotional problems (Κορναράκη, *Ἐγχειρίδιον* 3: 17). Entrenched in Protestant precincts, this tendency to quickly appease emotional problems has caused pastors to attach great importance to psychological progress and to various trends in the anthropological and social sciences[42], to the detriment of age-old Christian tradition which provides intense and deep relief in the act of confession (Κορναράκη, *Εγχειρίδιον* 3: 18). Yet, apart from the progressive loss of popularity of confession among the faithful due to the apparent efficiency of the newly emerged psychological sciences, there was an underlying theological reality which instigated the Western Christian loss of confidence in the Protestant Church.

Tselengidis, a well-known contemporary Orthodox theologian, presents a concise summary of Luther's theological teachings, i.e., the principal of Protestant movement. According to Tselengidis (*Ἡ σωτηριολογία* 25-240), Luther taught that humanity underwent an ontological change after the fall. Its highest characteristics — reason and will — were corrupted to such an extent

42 The emergence of psychoanalytic dialogue, as a therapeutic and "redemptive" systematic activity, especially encouraged many pastors in Protestant communities to seek emotional insight based on psychoanalytic techniques (Κορναράκη, *Ἐγχειρίδιον* 3: 18-9). Strong evidence for this development can be found in the work of well-known Protestant pastors. At the beginning of the psychoanalytic boom, the well-known Protestant pastor Oskar Pfister adopted the psychoanalysis of Freud completely and used it to guide believers. Cf. His sensational book: *Das Christentum und die Angst*. Zurich. 1944. It is important here to mention that Pfister appeared to have conflicting views — now he was disputing with Freud, pointing at the limited nature of his psychoanalysis and now he was unreservedly siding with Freud's way of thinking for unknown reasons. (Bendaly 1: 66, 1: 268-269)

that each human being became unable to do anything for his salvation; as a consequence, salvation is only the work of God and His grace (Lutherisches Kirchenamt, *Unser Glaube* 60). This salvation was completed in the person of Jesus Christ, who is at once human being and God. It is notable, in Tselengidis's opinion (*Ἡ σωτηριολογία* 25-240), that an individual's nature is so corrupted, under the authority of sin, that even after baptism the corruption of nature remains within him . Yet, once the individual believes and is baptized, he becomes justified in the eyes of God, and therefore he attains the divine grace that fulfills this salvation. Good deeds are the fruit of the Holy Spirit, but the individual actually does not agree as to whether he will or will not do these deeds (Τσελεγγίδη, *Ἡ σωτηριολογία* 25-240). They are done by divine grace and attributed to this individual only because of his faith in atonement. Salvation is a dynamic process that starts here on earth, but deification, i.e., the joining with divine nature / substance (according to Protestant doctrine) will happen only at the second coming because each individual is still ontologically sinful and so he cannot[43] be deified here on earth (Τσελεγγίδη, *Ἡ σωτηριολογία* 25-240).

What is unacceptable here for Tselengidis? He contends that, though Luther endeavoured to reject the scholastic theories of the Roman Catholic Church, he failed nevertheless to reach an authentic Christian theology, anthropology and soteriology. According to Tselengidis, Luther's anthropological mistake consists in an erroneous understanding of the individual as a being whose highest charac-

43 Relevant to this issue are the discussions summed up by Burns in the following: "More recently, there are important new interpretations of Martin Luther's writings that reveal themes of deifications in his theology as well. Scholars of the so-called Finnish School of Luther interpretation convincingly argue that, when read without the lens of neo-Kantianism, Luther's theology is clearly that of a "real-ontic" relation between God and humanity by which we are justified through deification (Mannermaa [1980] 2005; Kärkkäinen 2002; Braaten and Jenson 1998). But these themes are only now being uncovered in the context of dialogue with the Eastern Orthodox churches, for which the ideas are ancient and continuous; Orthodox theology serves as the template through which deification is read, wherever it is found in Christian thought. Also, although the Finnish School is convincing in its claim that Luther has been misread, this does not change the fact that subsequent Lutheranisms and other forms of Protestantism that evolved did develop a wide gap between God and the world" (127). Burns, Charlene P. E. "Altruism in Nature as Manifestation of Divine *Energeia*." *Zygon* 41.1 (2006): 125-137. *EBSCO Host.* Web. 27.06.2012. Gavrilyuk is swift to apprise his reader of Barth's awareness of the presence of the notion—"deification"—in the vocabulary of Lutheran theology, so that the discovery of the Finnish school should appear less revolutionary than one would like to think. Apart from this viewpoint, "with all that Luther had recourse to the concept of deification; however, later Lutheran confessions found very little place for this notion. It is still a subject of debate in Luther scholarship just how essential these notions are for Luther's account of justification and whether Luther's philosophical stance was consistently realist" (652). Gavrilyuk, Paul L. "The Retrieval of Deification: How a Once-Despised Archaism Became an Ecumenical Desideratum." *Modern Theology 25.4* (October 2009): 647-659. *EBSCO Host.* Web. 27.06.2012.

teristics are reason and will. Since these two features were completely corrupted after the fall, an individual is unable, according to such Protestant doctrine, to do anything for his salvation[44]. Thereby, the notion of synergy has vanished.

In contrast, the authentic Christian standpoint introduces the idea that, although the human person actually has undergone this corruption, he should not be reduced to the reason and will, as the image of God within an individual is his energy of self-government or self-determinism alone. This energy makes any individual a second participant in the act of salvation. Everything starts from faith in the salvation brought to humans by the incarnated Word of God, but this faith should be permanently proved by the act of the individual's self-determinism, and, though the good deeds are the fruit of the Holy Spirit, they must nevertheless be strengthened by the individual's self-determination[45]. Furthermore, Tselengidis asserts that Luther differs from the authentic Christian teaching in that he contends that, after baptism, ontological corruption still remains within our nature. Resting his contention with Paul's idea of the second law (Rom 8.2), Luther says that "the repentance lasts within Christians until their death, since repentance is connected with sin, which remains within the flesh, according to St Paul (Rom 7.23)" (Τσελεγγίδη, *Ή σωτηριολογία* 135). Hence, "even after being baptized, an individual, because of the remaining con-

44 The same sounds true for the Calvinist theology. In this context Neville says: "The [Calvinist] doctrine is that human beings, because of their sin, are utterly without power of their own to help themselves in the matter of salvation. For salvation they are utterly dependent on God (and if there is no God, they are utterly without hope of salvation, as existentialists and other disappointed Calvinists have declared). Furthermore, even if God 'offers' salvation, human beings are incapable of accepting or appropriating it except insofar as God moves them to do so." (87)

45 Gavrilyuk proposes the following relevant thoughts: "'Deification by grace alone through faith alone' has very little purchase in Eastern Orthodoxy. Most patristic authors simply refused to construe 'works' as engaged in casual competition with grace. The soteriological primacy and necessity of grace are not undermined by the fact that human acceptance of divine help involves much struggle and ascetic effort. But Luther's insistence on the passive acceptance of grace does not leave much space for the patristic paradox of human passivity and active cooperation of the free will with grace—a point at which Greek patristic and Lutheran anthropologies sharply part ways. Similarly, the emphasis on faith, while present in some patristic treatments of deification, is never meant to exclude the importance of other virtues. For the Greek Fathers, deification involves a life-long spiritual battle, the overcoming of vices and the climbing of the ladder of virtues (commonly cast in the language allowing both an Augustinian and a Pelagian reading). The anthropological assumptions and practices associated with deification in Luther are in a category of their own. As ecumenically fruitful as the discussion of *theosis* in Luther's version of participatory metaphysics might be, the profound shift in meaning of deification should not be ignored" (653). "The Retrieval of Deification: How a Once-Despised Archaism Became an Ecumenical Desideratum." *Modern Theology 25.4* (October 2009): 647-659. *EBSCO Host.* Web. 29.06.2012.

dition of sin, is, according to Luther, left ontologically sinful within the framework of the Church" (Τσελεγγίδη, *Ἡ σωτηριολογία* 135). Tselegidis brings an argument from St John Chrysostom to demonstrate that Luther misunderstood St Paul's statement about the second law. In interpreting the passage (Rom 7.23), St John Chrysostom states that St Paul's words about the second law that fights against his members has to do with an individual who was still under the servitude of sin during the time before the law of Moses and after that law was complete and valid. As to the passage (Rom 8.2), St John Chrysostom (PG 60.511-513) adds that the war of sin that was opposed to the law of an individual's nous, i.e., the natural law, was abolished by the grace of the Holy Spirit, after sin had been destroyed; whatever could not be done by the conscience of an individual or by the law of Moses was done by "the abundance of grace" (qtd. Τσελεγγίδη, *Ἡ σωτηριολογία* 135). This means, as St John Chrysostom says, that, after an individual has been released from sin and death, he can already "walk accordingly to the grace and not to the flesh" (PG 60.511-513). From here on, Tselengidis concludes that, "according to the Orthodox standpoint, within St Paul there is not any "remnant" of sin, which is opposed to the "law of the nous", and consequently, there is not such a "remnant" within any person who has been baptized" (Τσελεγγίδη, *Ἡ σωτηριολογία* 147). Consequently, this differentiates Protestant doctrine from Orthodoxy on the issue of the deification of the individual. According to Protestant doctrine, deification is the matter of doomsday, while within the Orthodox Church, deification starts, as Tselengidis (*Ἡ σωτηριολογία* 147) shows, in the present and will continue forever. It starts, for Tselengidis, from the moment of baptism when each believer becomes a "new creation" (*Ἡ σωτηριολογία* 147). Then, in the chrismation, each person receives the uncreated grace of the Holy Spirit, and, in Holy Communion, this process of deification is fed and grows (Τσελεγγίδη, *Ἡ σωτηριολογία* 147-8). All this presupposes that the believer freely remains within the mysterious body of Christ. This staying within the Church demands from an individual that he make the difficult attempt to keep the commandments of Christ with love (Τσελεγγίδη, *Ἡ σωτηριολογία* 148). Tselengidis (*Ἡ σωτηριολογία*) shows that, according to St Maximus' teaching, a particular individual who is deified keeps his natural characteristics, while he charismatically partakes in the uncreated deity, becoming "entirely God, in relation to his soul or body, due to the grace and the divine brightness of glory" (PG 91.1088c). The charismatic deification of the human being enriches his nature with uncreated deifying grace and thus, according to the St Maximus, "whatever God has, the deified individual has also, with exception of God's identity with relation to His nature" (PG 90.44d). Tselengidis quotes another passage from the St Gregory Palamas who says that "becoming God, the deified individual in his wholeness is God and he sees the glory of God and the divine light, something that guarantees that his theological teaching about God is true" (458). In addition, Tselengidis (*Ἡ σωτηριολογία*) points out that it is wrong to think that in the protestant doctrine the human will is perceived as completely corrupted, on the contrary, an individual keeps, according to Luther, the capability to manage his dealings within this world. If there is any talk of the complete incapability of will, it is said in relation to the work of salvation alone (Τσελεγγίδη, *Ἡ σωτηριολογία*). The fact that this corruption of human will pertains to matters of salvation alone explains the advanced progress of western civilization (Τσελεγγίδη, *Ἡ σωτηριολογία*). An individual actually "does not decide as to whether he will be saved or not, he only hopes for it because of his faith, and there is no intention to cooperate with God in transfiguring (*deifying*) this world, since it still retains the ontological residue of sin" (Τσελεγγίδη, *Ἡ σωτηριολογία* 149-50).

This reasoning is important because it seemingly produces a split between the Orthodox theologians — Thermos and Tselengidis. The locus of their discrepancy is, according to the foregoing reasoning, the issue of whether after baptism the ontological sin of human nature still remains or vanishes. Thermos builds up his arguments for the interaction with psychoanalysis on the point that one needs the aid of human science, since human nature is corrupted and sick. In this point, he seemingly repeats the Protestant idea of the "remnant" of sin within human nature even after baptism. Yet, it would be premature to identify his reasoning with that of Luther, because the latter reduced human being to his reason and will, which are completely unable to do something for salvation, while Thermos stresses that, even after the fall, an individual has kept his ability to determine himself, though this ability is influenced by the second law. Here, Thermos also differs from Tselengidis, who points out that, after the baptism, there is no second law within the believer. Perhaps Tselengidis misunderstands the essence of ontological sin that is swept away in the baptism? Maybe he adheres to a juridical understanding of original sin, as does the Roman Catholic theology? This is not the case. Tselengidis points out that the ontological sin abolished in baptism is the "corruption of our nature and death" (Τσελεγγίδη, Ἡ σωτηριολογία 39-40). In my opinion, Tselengidis apparently challenges the fundamental point in Thermos's reasoning, i.e., that the corruption of human nature accompanies every individual after baptism, and consequently that psychological problems stem from the corruption of nature and are by no means the result of personal sinfulness.

If we proceed from Tselengidis's reasoning, it becomes obvious that the flourishing of the psychological sciences was a natural consequence of a kind of isolation of metaphysics from our reality. Protestant theology could not provide believers *with* any guarantee of liberation from ontological servitude to sin and *with* the possibility of becoming a new creation in the present rather than on doomsday. Each suffering individual was virtually compelled to try to find his own means of obtaining freedom from ontological servitude. In this context, we can better understand St Macarius the Great's reproach— "... it is Christ that is the only Physician and Healer"— to one of his disciples who had resorted to the aid of drugs and medicaments (639-641). Obviously, the desert Fathers were aware of the close communication between the individual and God in the action of uncreated grace.

Seeing all these affinities between Thermos's standpoint and certain Protestant ideas, we could fairly ask whether Thermos did not undergo certain influences from this theology in relation to his contention that the corruption of nature remains within the Christian even after baptism. Maybe some unfavourable ideas have crept into his theological thought? The reader should be warned against any hasty categorical judgment, though, since it is possible to meet the same ideas within the works of certain famous Orthodox Fathers. For instance, St John Climacus, in writing about soul and flesh in his excellent book *The Ladder to Perfection*, refers to the latter sometimes as "spouse" and sometimes as "enemy". It is spouse as loved "due to natural kinship to the soul"; yet, it is simultaneously enemy as when it conceives and gives life to sinful inclinations, and, being born, these inclinations provoke death through despair" (Ἰωάννου τοῦ Σιναΐτου 215-218). Furthermore, St John calls his flesh "cooperator and rival, helper and contester, ally and enemy" (Ἰωάννου τοῦ Σιναΐτου 216). Kornarakis sees, in this text, a clear indication to the inner struggle or second law so expressively described by St Paul in his epistle to the Romans (Rom 7.23) (Κορναράκη, *Νείλου* 8-25). From here, St John deduces the necessity of vigilance or self-knowledge (introspection). Someone could object that these writings are in reference to the attacks of the devil, who is able to tempt every individual, even after baptism, and are not about the corruption of the energies of human nature. This could be right, but another Saint, Nilus Ancyranus, proffers other clarifications and says that, besides the spiritual attacks of demons, there are some hidden powers within the human being that set in motion "the passionate way of life" (Κορναράκη, *Νείλου* 8-25). He says that the only true spiritual guide is a person who can reveal "the hidden phenomena" within the human soul (Κορναράκη, *Νείλου* 8-25). Nilus Ancyranus says: "The spiritual guide who is supposed to be deeply competent in his work should be aware of all thoughts spread by the enemy; he should be able to show the hidden phenomena of those people who are entrusted to him, and after making known the sly character of these phenomena and having foresaid the attacks of the enemy, make, thereby, his flock able to attain victory in the easiest possible way and to get the laurels of winners. Yet, to find such a spiritual guide is a difficult task indeed" (PG 79.720-809).

All this reasoning is called on to show that Thermos did not build his standpoint on his own unfounded arguments or would-be Protestant ideas. On the contrary, there are Church Fathers who have underlined that Christians face a war within themselves even after baptism. Also important is the question of whether this convergence between certain of Thermos's and Luther's theological ideas, at least on the issue of perpetuating original sin, could be an important argument for more constructive dialogue among Orthodox and Protestant theology in the present. In addition, we could question Tselengidis: How does he actually explain the fact that Christians, who are supposedly devoid of the corruption of nature, fall sick somatically and / or psychologically? Why is each individual compelled to die with his own body, after he has died and risen in the sacrament of baptism? Certainly, the answer could indicate personal sins freely committed by every Christian after he has joined the Church, sins which produce natural death. These questions cannot be answered here since they would require a new project, one which is impossible within the current context. However, such a project is very important because it is only on the basis of scrupulous research that can we make a judgment concerning the discrepancy between Thermos's position and that of Tselengidis regarding the state of human nature after baptism and, consequently, establish the admissible limits of cooperation between Orthodox pastoral theology and psychoanalysis.

Psychotherapeutic techniques bear some of the responsibility for the loss of confidence in pastoral care within Western society. Here, the reasons seem to be clear. Every psychotherapeutic technique claims to have a vision of the human being that is scientifically founded. This point implies three things: firstly, nobody should oppose any methodological approach to the investigation and description of the human being without strong scientific counter arguments; secondly, every scientific method is already limited both by the angle from which it considers the human being, and by the example it provides for interpreting the investigated aspect of this human being; hence, thirdly, no psychological theory can express an opinion on the ontological content of existential phenomena because such theories do not have the appropriate means to do so. In regard to psychoanalysis, Ricœur states characteristically:

> In analysis, the primary thing is presented not by the thing that justifies or founds but by the things that precede. In psychoanalysis, genesis takes the place of basis. For this reason, nobody should demand that psychoanalysis solve the questions of radical origin, neither in the order of reality nor in values. In psychoanalysis, everything is defined in conformity with impulses, as well as the distortions and disguises that these impulses undergo. It is supposed that ideals and illusions will never be considered anything more than destinies of impulses …, creation and esthetic pleasure, ideals of moral life, illusions of religious sphere will never figure as something more than elements of the economic balance of impulse, as expenses in pleasure-displeasure relationship … On the other hand, we have to take into consideration the example used by psychoanalysis. In point of fact, psychoanalysis does not know the phenomena of culture, but only to the extent to which these phenomena may be considered as analogies of the 'fulfillment of desire' illustrated by the dream. (Ricœur, *De l'Interprétation* 174-186)

By saying that "today people visit the psychiatrist instead of the priest", Jung has established people's mounting desire to discover their hidden selves by way of psychiatry rather than of pastoral care (Κορναράκη, *Τό Πρόβλημα* 24). In doing so, Jung acknowledged that there are some problems that should be faced by pastoral care, but, because the borders between pastoral care and psychology became obscure, people started to search for help from the sciences that dealt with these problems (Κορναράκη, *Τό Πρόβλημα* 24). Yet, if someone (whether scholar or psychotherapist) intends to deal with existential human problems, he has to possess an all-embracing vision of the human being, knowledge which causes the scholar to overstep the limits of his scientific vision of the individual (Κορναράκη, *Τό Πρόβλημα* 24). Even in attempting this work, the scholar becomes more than a simple scholar; he becomes a philosopher (Bendaly, 1973; Herbart, 1993; Rosenberg, 2012). In this context, Jaspers has pointed out that "an individual always has the potential to discover more about himself than he might have known before, and therefore it is dangerous to present partial knowledge as an all-embracing understanding, since this leads to the narrowing of human image and consequently of the human being himself" (Dansereau 175). Simmel adds: "Every time any particular science tries to give answers that are universally applicable, i.e., answers that have to do with questions with relationship to the human being and the universe, it exceeds the bounds of its own scientific domain and talks nonsense" (qtd. Bendaly 1: 67). Thus, psychotherapeutic techniques compromise themselves when they set about to solve existential (i.e., religious and moral) problems, because in this way these techniques overstep the limits of their scientific possibilities and, consequently, inculcate erroneous ideas.

The social and cultural conjuncture outlined above was, according to Thermos, a favourable environment for the degeneration of psychotherapy. One may say that the responsibility for the emergence of an environment in which science interferes in existential issues can be attributed to both Protestant theology and psychotherapeutic techniques.

Thermos, too, describes the way this degeneration has been refracted in psychotherapeutic practice. The American style of life, along with its persistent belief in happiness, hopefulness and independence, incubated three trends within psychotherapy: 1) "techniques with scientifically inconsistent bases and ontology borrowed from the oriental religions (Buddhism, Hinduism); 2) techniques with humanistic content and 3) techniques with a Christian appearance but a secular spirit" (Θερμός, *Δύο πολιτισμικοί* 5-6).

Firstly, Thermos presents the destiny of psychotherapeutic techniques which degenerated in attempting to substitute their scientific base with the ontology of oriental religions. Thus, the limits between psychotherapist and guru became obscure. "These techniques use dialogism as a method to become calm; they refer to the undefined joining with the universe and its energy as the aim of therapy; chasing an indefinable 'inner truth', they look for the experience itself as self-aim" (Θερμός, *Δύο πολιτισμικοί* 2). These techniques are dangerous both "because they actually estrange an individual from God or absolute truth and because they may psychologically influence persons with lax borders, in the formation of their ego, even provoking psychosis" (Θερμός, *Δύο πολιτισμικοί* 4). Thermos puts his statement in perspective, by pointing to the famous New Age movement. Many persons involved in this movement were sincerely "willing to live in the emotions and the vitality of experience promised by these oriental religions" (Θερμός, *Δύο πολιτισμικοί* 4). These religions came up with a model of integrated personality and pretended to be psychological therapies (Θερμός, *Δύο πολιτισμικοί* 4). For Thermos, the problem with these oriental practices is that, "in lapsing into them, an individual loses not only God, but also his own self, because the human person, along with its basic ontological component — the communion of love, is determined as a collection of enjoyable experiences (be it pantheistic-sensuous or *cosmophobe*-nihilistic)" (*Δύο πολιτισμικοί* 4-5). Further, there are other kinds of damaging psychotherapeutic techniques, i.e., those with humanistic content. These look only to increase the power of the human ego and its competitiveness. They make appeals such as: "build up warmth and trust", "make your consciousness broader", "co-ordinate yourselves with yourself as well as your family", "capture your fears" (Θερμός, *Δύο πολιτισμικοί* 5). Such techniques became, according to Thermos (*Δύο πολιτισμικοί* 5), quite well-known and were often offered as a panacea. Here, the trap consists of the "erroneous assumption that human dynamics are without limits" (Θερμός, *Δύο πολιτισμικοί* 5). According to Thermos, "our desire will be always unsatisfied since it is predestined only for partial satisfaction here on earth" (*Δύο πολιτισμικοί* 5). The problem of these psychotherapeutic techniques stems from the denial of human limits. Thermos characteristically says:

> Such a "psychotherapy" will accept, without wondering, a provocative wastage, caring only about evoking no feeling of guilt (which is considered always as morbid and unwanted). It will accept any kind of client's sexual perversion within the framework of the post-modernist pluralism, limiting itself only to condemn the pederasty because it is illegal (in reality, it is not considered illegal because it is immoral, but as immoral because illegal). (*Δύο πολιτισμικοί* 5)

Even when psychotherapists, these representatives of such consumerist psychology, talk about the necessity of "sense" and "love", "they mean the fulfillment of emotional demands of the sick individual" (Θερμός, *Δύο πολιτισμικοί* 6-7). "Love" as self-sacrifice or "humility" as submission to the higher faith — all these sublimations are viewed, according to Thermos, "in the therapeutic sensibility as unbearably oppressive, insulting to common feeling and harmful for personal health and prosperity" (*Δύο πολιτισμικοί* 6-7). Psychological health means the "overcoming of inhibitions and the immediate satisfaction of each urge" (Θερμός, *Δύο πολιτισμικοί* 7). The most terrible part is that, "if success becomes the highest ideal, sin will be perceived only as failure" (Θερμός, *Δύο πολιτισμικοί* 7). Capps (3) says that "nowadays it is more probable that we live with our mistakes and experience feelings of shame rather than feelings of guilt" (qtd. Θερμός, *Δύο πολιτισμικοί* 7).

The last trend in degrading psychotherapeutic techniques is represented by techniques which have a Christian appearance but which are secular in spirit. Thermos points to Norman Peale, who was the forerunner of the psychological "gospel" of success. Peale wrote in 1937 that "the most important day in the life of each individual is when he begins for the first time to perceive himself. The power of positive thought: Trust yourself! Self-confidence leads to the acknowledgement of self and success. How to create your own success? Anticipate the best and take it" (qtd. Θερμός, *Δύο πολιτισμικοί* 8). Thermos points to Kurtz, who stated that "the movement of positive thought is unaware of the inner inconsistencies of self, ignores the necessity that people accept their limits, and presents religion simply as a crutch for personal benefit. It is about unceremonious secularism. The earth is the centre and heaven serves it. God exists, but the question is what God do we mean?" (qtd. Θερμός, *Δύο πολιτισμικοί* 8) There is a passage from Clapp (1996, 36-9) offering an interesting description of spiritual adversities within American Christian society:

> In America, there is a general understanding of faith as private issue, something that gives color to our private lives. Whatever I am thinking or feeling about God is between me and my consciousness. The "spirituality" is a shapeless, sometimes mercurial, a snag of isolated selves – of the human individual and of God – which, both are far from the world, time, place and community. American Christians of all kinds adopted easily and quickly a neutral, completely psychological faith; this faith unequivocally promises that God exists for "satisfying my own needs". We quickly recognize the syncretism of others but not our own…Yet, when Christianity becomes a psychological matter, the emphasis passes from the social change to the "adaptation" of the individual to the "status quo". (qtd. Θερμός, *Δύο πολιτισμικοί* 8-9)

Unfortunately, psychotherapy may also be involved in the very idea of immediate "pain-killing" activity, when it "faces the problems of a consumerist society, proceeding not from certain ontological values, but from the values of this society" (Θερμός, *Δύο πολιτισμικοί* 8). Thus, the problem of all these psychological techniques is, according to Thermos, that "they do not have an ontology, i.e., they concentrate obsessively on complacency about and complicity with subjective experience" (*Δύο πολιτισμικοί* 8).

The Romanian philosopher and psychologist Manzat directed even sharper rhetorical shafts against psychoanalysis by saying that it investigates "infirm specimens", and is able, therefore, to produce only an "infirm psychology" that loses sight of mature, creative, balanced and healthy personalities" (403).

4.2.2.2. Religious fundamentalism

The second difficulty concerning the interaction between Orthodox pastoral theology and psychoanalysis is, according to Thermos, connected to religious fundamentalism. The essence of fundamentalism is that it perceives modernity as a menace and therefore considers a return to the foundation as the only way to escape this menace (Θερμός, *Δύο πολιτισμικοί* 12; *Ἄνθρωπος* 303). This does not mean to say that modernity has never sponsored ideas dangerous to the truth (Θερμός, *Ἄνθρωπος* 303); quite the reverse, sometimes it was the high vocation of the religious mind to present insightful critique and to negotiate inter-mutual relations with certain theoretical bootstrapping on the side of modernity. Yet, Thermos says that, even when alternate pockets of understanding appeared to wrest important messages of divine revelation, religious fundamentalism was nevertheless not the adequate reaction to that (Θερμός, *Ἄνθρωπος* 303-4).

The reason that Orthodox fundamentalism[46] emerged lies, according to Thermos (*Δύο πολιτισμικοί* 12-15), in the fact that certain faithful and ecclesiastics veered into discussion of social problems without being able to develop a constructive Orthodox interpretation of those social challenges.

The main problem here is the unjustified reservation concerning the use of secular knowledge for new "unfolding" of revelation truth within the circumstances of present life (Θερμός, *Ἄνθρωπος* 305). For Thermos (*Ἄνθρωπος* 307), a constructive Orthodox interpretation consists in a continuous dialogue between the theology of church and new forms of material realities of this world with the purpose to preclude the absolutisation of any of such forms. On the other side, system of rule by a tradition witnesses "lack of self-critique, resistance to change, extraordinary emphasis on matters of little significance, the absolute authority of leaders, and the cultivation of an exaggeratory dependence on them" (Θερμός, *Ἄνθρωπος* 304-5). In other words, for Thermos (*Ἄνθρωπος* 305) the ineffectiveness of *παραδοσιαρχία* lies in the fact that this system of rule adopts an introverted and *cosmophobic* self-organization. As far as the dialogue with psychoanalysis is concerned, the theology of church should deny such a dialogue only in cases where the practices advocated by certain psychotherapists prove unsafe and fraudulent, or where certain psychotherapeutic trends promote extreme and dangerous deviations (Θερμός, *Ἄνθρωπος* 307).

4.3. Conclusions

In conclusion, Thermos has subjected psychoanalysis to critical scrutiny. As a result, he overcomes the shortcomings of Freud's psychoanalytic theory by presenting a transfigured psychoanalytic knowledge which points to the genetic

46 Thermos introduces here an alternate and *apparently* less obnoxious, to the Orthodox mind, term —"*παραδοσιαρχία*" or system of rule by a tradition (*Ἄνθρωπος* 304).

priority of the human instincts and the ontological priority of the human spirit. Thermos has managed also to present a persuasive and well-grounded Orthodox model of the human being. He has provided his reader with decisive support in the form of an adequate conceptual framework. Furthermore, Thermos has presented three strong arguments for an interaction between Orthodox pastoral theology and psychoanalysis; the argument of psychopathology seems to be the strongest and most persuasive. The argument connected with the issue of Orthodox hermeneutics seems to be less elaborated. It is all about the way in which an authentic Orthodox interpreter can be identified by the multitude of faithful. The last argument drawing upon the translation of Church truth into the language of contemporary gnoseology also seems to be sound, since in the early centuries the Christian credo signaled readiness for a change of language and concepts when this was considered expedient for the preservation and perpetuation of the divine message in time. The contemporary need to repair to psychoanalytic gnoseology and language lies in two realms: 1) the lack of any systematic patristic reasoning on the evolution of psychological components of hieratic vocation and 2) the need to make the Orthodox theological language more clear and exact. Finally, Thermos points out the difficulties arising from the interaction between Orthodox pastoral theology and psychoanalysis. These difficulties arose from the surreptitious shift of responsibilities, when psychotherapeutic techniques deviate from the sphere of their legitimate competence (human suffering caused by corrupted human nature) in order to inhabit the existential sphere (the corrupted human will of choice) which is the sole sphere and competence of pastoral care. In doing so, Thermos deduces that the conflict between Orthodox pastoral care and psychoanalysis should be explained by the failure to acknowledge the mutual lack of expertise in each other's respective fields, rather than by an inherent incompatibility. In the case of pastoral care, the area of competence is identified with issues originating in the corruption of human will of choice, whereas in the case of psychotherapy this competence may be demonstrated in issues concerning the treatment of the corrupted energies of human nature.

One serious problem in relation to Thermos's standpoint emerged when an attempt was made to establish the possible reasons for the qualitative decline in psychotherapeutic techniques within Western (mainly US) society. The point is that certain affinities emerged between the anthropological premises presented within Thermos's works and those of Luther's soteriological doctrine. These affinities lie in the concurrence of their outlooks in relation to the question of whether or not human nature keeps its corruption after baptism. Although it is wrong to reduce Thermos's views to the anthropology of Luther, it is a matter of fact nevertheless that both of them admit the persistence of corruption after baptism. The Orthodox theologian Tselengidis challenges the foregoing affirmation as being problematical since his perspective on the Orthodox soteriology brings forward the conviction that no remnant of ontological corruption stays within human nature after baptism. To solve the discrepancy between the two perspectives proffered by these Orthodox theologians seems impossible here, since this goes beyond the limits of this study.

5. Closing remarks

In this book, I have built certain scientific foundations to express an opinion about Fr. Basil Thermos's hypothetical paradigm concerning the interaction between Orthodox pastoral theology and psychoanalysis.

The general thesis statement of the present research, i.e., that Thermos presents a forcible and well-grounded paradigm of interaction between Orthodox pastoral theology and psychoanalysis, has proved to be right. Thermos has presented an adequate conceptual framework because of his knowledgeable and critical approach to psychoanalysis and Orthodox pastoral theology. Psychoanalysis is represented by a transfigured psychoanalytic knowledge that steps outside of the limits of Freud's scientific dogmatism and philosophical bias, while Orthodox pastoral theology and care are brought to the fore in the sense of a persuasive outline of an Orthodox model of the human being.

On the other hand, in dealing with the pastoral vocation problem, Thermos has kept the Chalcedonian mystery intact, despite his lopsided (psychoanalytic) approach to the issue. This manoeuvre was skillfully accomplished by his final acknowledgement that, although psychological maturity is a psychological analogue for the mature vocation for the priesthood, holiness, nevertheless, does not amount to psychological maturity and the lack of the latter is by no means an obstacle to salvation. In doing so, Thermos did not ignore the conviction of the Orthodox Church that ecclesiastical life is a mystery in which God through His uncreated divine grace works the salvation of the faithful without violating human freedom and self-determination. Importantly, Thermos provides forceful arguments to support the idea that the immaturity of candidates for priesthood and all the more of priests may condition the ineffectiveness of their pastoral ministry. This immaturity occurs because of the unsuccessful evolution of human instincts from an earlier stage of childhood up to the time when a particular person acknowledges a sense of vocation to the priesthood. Interestingly, the problem emerges from the complex structure of the human psyche, where, apart from consciousness, there is a deeper and more obscure sphere of the unconscious. Since instincts, or generally human desire, are supposedly concentrated within this sphere, the failures in the evolution of "desire" for the priesthood appear to be difficult to solve.

Thermos proceeds then to the case of the ineffectiveness of priests, and shows convincingly that the unconscious and self-knowledge are two important psychological factors that can determine each priest's effectiveness or ineffectiveness. He demonstrates that, if the unconscious sphere is not seriously balanced by a priest's introspection, it may lead to unpredictable consequences. In contrast, the skillful pastor seems to be the one who combines the spiritual life with attentive attitude toward his motives apprehended as products of the unconscious sphere.

Further, Thermos supplies his paradigm of interaction between Orthodox pastoral theology and psychoanalysis with careful reasoning about its advantages and disadvantages. Basically, he makes an attempt to show that this interaction is possible due to the two corruptions which occurred within the human being following the fall. Thus, the corruption of the human will of choice should be addressed by means of the spiritual knowledge accumulated by the discipline of pastoral care over many centuries; while the corruption of the energies of human nature must be faced through the expertise amassed within the psychological sciences. Thermos has reduced the essence of his arguments against the interaction to the incorrect management of psychotherapy instigated by the peculiarities of Western consumerist society. He concludes that the divergence between these two spheres of human activities should be perceived not as an incompatibility, but as a particular incapability to acknowledge the limits of their own competence. At one stage of this study an attempt was made to apprehend the probable reasons for Western society's increasing favouring of psychotherapeutic techniques to the detriment of ecclesiastical pastoral care. This trend seems attributable to the peculiarity of Protestant theology, anthropology and soteriology. After an examination of the main features of Protestant doctrine, certain affinities were *apparently* established between Thermos's and Luther's anthropological views in relation to the corruption of human nature after baptism. This position appears to be categorically rejected by the Greek theologian Dimitri Tselengidis, who contends that, according to the Orthodox soteriology, no remnant of the corruption of nature remains after baptism. No solution to this discrepancy between the two Orthodox theologians could be offered in the current research, since it would involve an extensive, new and difficult project. One may assert that this discrepancy between two contemporary Orthodox theologians cannot be easily reconciled because each position rests its standpoint on testimonies from the Orthodox theological and patristic tradition. The Ecumenical Orthodox Synod alone seems to have the appropriate authority to append an obligatory opinion on the issue, thereby settling the longed-for consensus between Orthodox theologians.

Finally, it could be said that the general aim of this research, i.e., to answer the question as to whether it is really possible and useful for Orthodoxy to promote cooperation between Orthodox pastoral theology and secular psychological sciences was thoroughly canvassed if not definitely met. It proved impossible to establish the admissible limits of cooperation between Orthodox pastoral theology and psychoanalysis, since the discrepancy between Thermos and Tselengidis targets the basic strands in Thermos's standpoint: the irreproachability of his model of the human being remains undecided; his assumption that the recourse to secular anthropological knowledge would not damage Orthodox anthropology is also questionable; and, finally, his arguments for the interaction between both spheres of activity appear to be frozen because they are built on the assumption of two corruptions within each individual.

6. Bibliography

Sacred texts

Septuaginta, id est Vetus Testamentum Graece iuxta LXX interpretes. Edidit Alfred Rahlfs. 1935. Editio altera quam recognovit et emendavit Robert Hanhart. Duo volumina in uno. Stuttgart: Deutsche Bibelgeselschaft, 2006. Print. Deutsche Bibelgesellschaft.

Biblia Hebraica Stuttgartensia. 5. verb. Auflage. Hrsg. Elliger K., Rudolf Kittel, und W. Rudolph. Stuttgart: Deutsche Bibelgesellschaft, 2001. Print. Deutsche Bibelgesellschaft.

Nestle-Aland Novum Testamentum Graece. 28th rev. ed. Ed. by the Münster Institute for New Testament Textual Research. Stuttgart: Privilegierte Württembergische Bibelanstalt, 2012. Print.

The Orthodox Study Bible. Ancient Christianity Speaks to Today's World. Annotated edition. Ed. St Athanasius Academy of Orthodox Theology. Nashville TN: Thomas Nelson Publishers, 2008. Print.

Patristic Texts

Ἁγίου Ἰωάννου τοῦ Σιναΐτου. *Κλίμαξ*. Ἔκδοση ἐνάτη. Ἀθῆναι: Ἱερά Μονή Παρακλήτου Ὠροπός Ἀττικῆς, 1995. Print.

Ἁγίου Κυρίλλου τοῦ Φιλεώτη. *Βίος καί διδαχαί*. Β΄ μέρος. Ἀθῆναι, 1987. Print.

Ἁγίου Μάρκου τοῦ Ἀσκητοῦ. *Τά 200 κεφάλαια περί πνευματικοῦ νόμου*. Εἰσαγωγή — μετάφραση ὑπό μοναχοῦ Θεοκλήτου Διονυσιάτου. Θεσσαλονίκη, 1974. Print.

Ἁγίου Νικοδήμου τοῦ Ἁγιορείτου. *Πηδάλιον*. Ἀθῆναι: Ἐκδόσεις Ἀστήρ, 1982. Print.

ΒΕΠΕΣ: *Βιβλιοθήκη Ἑλλήνων Πατέρων καί Ἐκκλησιαστικῶν Συγγραφέων*, Ἔκδοσις Ἀποστολικῆς Διακονίας τῆς Ἐκκλησίας τῆς Ἑλλάδος, Ἀθῆναι, 1955. Print.

ΕΠΕ: *Ἕλληνες Πατέρες τῆς Ἐκκλησίας*, Πατερικαί ἐκδόσεις «Γρηγόριος ὁ Παλαμᾶς», Θεσσαλονίκη, 1972. Print.

Φιλοκαλία τῶν ἱερῶν Νηπτικῶν Πατέρων. Θεσσαλονίκη: Πατερικαί Ἐκδόσεις «Γρηγόριος ὁ Παλαμάς», 1985. Print.

Μέγα Βασιλείου. *Εργα*. 6 τόμος. Θεσσαλονίκη: Ἐκδ. «Γρηγόριος Παλαμᾶς», 1973. Print.

PG: *Patrologiae cursus completus*, Series Graeca, ἐκδόσεις J-P Migne, Paris, 1857. Print.

Texts

Lutherisches Kirchenamt (Hrsg.). *Unser Glaube. Die Bekenntnisschriften der evangelisch-lutherischen Kirche* [Our Faith. Confessional Documents of the Evangelical Lutheran Church]. 1986. 5. Aufl. Gütersloh: Gütersloher Verlagshaus, 2004. Print

Works

Adamo, David. "Ruach in the Old Testament." *Δελτίο Βιβλικῶν Μελετῶν* Ιούλιος –Δεκέμβριος (1991): 27-37. Print.

Ἀυγουστίδης, Αδαμάντιος. *Ποιμένας καί Θεραπευτῆς* [Pastor and Therapist]. Ἐκδόσεις Ακρίτας. Ἀθῆναι, 1999. Print.

Becker, Jane F. "Formation for priestly celibacy: pertinent issues." *Journal of Pastoral Counseling* XXII. 1-2, (1987): 65-76. Print.

Beirnaert, Louis. «La révolution freudienne. [The Freudian Revolution]» *Sexualité humaine*. Paris: Lethielleux, 1966. 195-205. Print.

Bendaly, Constantin. «Images Paternelles et Attitudes Religieuses. [Paternal Images and Religious Attitudes]» 3 vols. Thèse en vue du Doctorat d´état en Lettres et Sciences humaines présentée à la Faculté de Philosophie de L´Université Jean Moulin. 1973. Print.

Blos, Peter. *On Adolescence: A psychoanalytic interpretation*. New York: The Free Press, 1962. Print.

———. "The Function of the ego ideal in adolescence." *The Psychoanalytic Study of the Child* 27, (1972): 93-97. Print.

———. "The genealogy of the ideal ego." *The Psychoanalytic Study of the Child* 29, (1974): 43-88. Print.

Cardwell, Sue Webb, and Richard A. Hunt. "Persistence in seminary and in ministry." *Pastoral Psychology* 28.2, (1979): 119-131. Print.

Cazacu, Petru. "Letter to the author." 10 February 2004. Email.

"Civil war.", "Abolitionists." *The Columbia Encyclopedia.* 6th ed. Ed. Paul Lagassé. New York: Columbia U P, 2000. Print.

Coombs, Marie Theresa, and Francis Kelly Nemeck. *Called by God: theology of vocation and lifelong commitment.* Collegeville, MI: The Liturgical Press, 1992. Print.

Crawford, Kenneth. "The minister's self-image and pastoral counseling." *Pastoral Psychology* 18.173, (1967): 49-54. Print.

D'Arcy, Paul. "Training for the priesthood based on freedom and responsibility." Eds. Michael J. O' Brien, and Raymond Steimel. *Psychological Aspects of Spiritual Development.* Washington, D.C.: The Catholic University of America Press, 1965. 80-91. Print.

Dansereau, Michel. *Freud et L'Athéisme* [Freud and Atheismus]. Paris: Ed. Desclée, 1971. Print.

David, Christian. *L'Etat amoureux. Essais psychanalytiques* [State Of Love. Psychoanalytic Essays]. Paris: P.B.P., 1971. Print.

Delacampagne, Christian. *Antipsychiatrie: les voies du sacré* [Anti-psychiatry: the roads of sacre]. Paris: Grasset, 1974. Print.

Dittes, James. "Research on clergymen: factors influencing decisions for religious service and effectiveness in the vocation." *Religious Education* (Research supplement) LVII, (1962): 141-165. Print.

Dunn, Ralph. F. "Personality patterns among religious personnel." *Catholic Psychological Record* 3, (1965): 125-137. Print.

Евмений, Игумен. *Пастырская помощь душевнобольным* [Pastoral Counselling to Mental Patients]. Иваново: Свет Православия, 1999. Print.

Φλωρόφσκυ, Γεώργιος. «Ἡ πορεία τῆς Ρωσικῆς Θεολογίας. [Ways of Russian Theology]» *Θεολογία, Ἀλήθεια καί Ζωή. Πνευματικόν Συμπόσιον.* Ἀθῆναι, 1962. Print.

Freud, S. *Correspondance de Sigmund Freud avec le pasteur Oskar Pfister.* 1909 – 1939 [Correspondence between Sigmund Freud and the Pastor Oskar Pfister]. Trad. de L. Jumel. Paris: Gallimard. 1966. Print.

———. *Psychopatologie de la vie quotidienne* [The Psychopathology of Everyday Life]. 1904. Trad. S. Jankélévitch. Paris : Petite Bibliothèque Payot, 1967. Print.

———. *Moïse et le Monothéisme* [Moses and Monotheism]. 1939. Trad. d'Anne Bermann. Paris: Gallimard, 1967. Print.

———. *Inhibition, Symptôme et Angoisse* [Inhibition, Symptom, and Anxiety]. 1924. Trad. de Michel Tort. Paris: Presses Universitaires de France, 1968. Print.

———. *Métapsychologie* [Metapsychology]. 1915. Trad. de Jean Laplanche et J. Pontalis. Paris: Gallimard. 1968. Print.

———. *Ma vie et la Psychanalyse* [My Life and Psychoanalysis]. 1925. Trad. de Marie Bonaparte. Paris: Gallimard. 1968. Print.

———.*Lettre à Ernest Jones. Le 3 mai 1928. La Vie et L'Œuvre de Sigmund Freud* [A Lettre to Ernest Jones. On 3 May 1928. The Life and Work of Sigmund Freud]. Tome 3. Ernest Jones. Trad. de Liliane Flournoy. Paris: Presses Universitaires de France, 1969. Print

———. *L'Avenir d 'une Illusion* [The Future of An Illusion]. 1927. Paris: Presses Universitaires de France, 1971. Print.

———. *Nouvelles Conférences sur la Psychanalyse* [New Conferences on the Psychoanalysis]. 1932. Trad. d'Anne Bermann. Paris: Gallimard. 1971. Print.

———. *Névrose, Psychose et Perversion* [Neurosis, Psychosis and Perversion]. 1924. Trad. de Jean Laplanche. Paris: Presses Universitaires de France, 1973. Print.

Gagey, Anne et Jacques. «Familles et vocation. [Family and Vocation]» *Jeunes et Vocations* 63, (1991): 5-16. Print.

Godin André. *The Psychology of Religious Vocations: Problems of the Religious Life.* Trans. and Ed. L. A. Wauck. Washington, D.C.: U P of America, 1983. Print.

Hanry, Pierre. *L'Inconscient à découvert* [The Unconscious Manifestly]. Paris: Editions Universitaires, 1972. Print.

Herbart, Johan Friedrich. *Lehrbuch zur Einleitung in die Philosophie* [A Textbook: Introduction to Philosophy]. Wolfahrt Henckmann. Textkritische revidierte Ausgabe mit einer Einleitung. Hamburg: Felix Meiner Verlag, 1993. Print. Philosophische Bibliothek, 453.

Houts, Donald C. "Ego identity and professional preparation for ministry." *Journal of Pastoral Care* 25.1, (1971): 12-24. Print.

Huber, W. «Psychanalyse et Psychologie. [Psychanalysis and Psychology]» *La Psychanalyse, science de l'homme*. Eds. Huber, W., Piron, H., et A. Vergote. Bruxelles: Dessart, 1964. Print.

Kaplan, Stanley M., and Roy M. Whitman. "The negative ego-ideal." *International Journal of Psychoanalysis* 46, (1965): 183-187. Print.

Kennedy Eugene, and Victor Heckler. "Report of the subcommittee on psychology." *Study on Priestly Life and Ministry*. Washington, D.C., 1971. 77-103. Print.

Kohut, Heinz, and Ernest Wolf. "The disorders of the self and their treatment: an outline." *Essentials Papers on Narcissism*. Ed. Andrew Morrison. New York: New York U P, 1986. 175-196. Print.

Κυριαζῆ, Δ., και Π. Σακελλαρόπουλου. «Ὁ ἔφηβος εἶναι ὁ ἄλλος; Κλινικές ἑλληνικές εἰκόνες.» *Ὁ ἔφηβος καί ἡ οἰκογένεια* ["Is Adolescent Another One? Greek Clinical Records." *The Adolescent and the Family*]. Ἀθῆνα: Ἑστίας, 1985. 271-299. Print.

Κορναράκης, Ἰ. Κ. *Σχιζοφρένια ἤ Ασκητισμός* [Schizophrenie or Asceticism]. Θεσσαλονίκη: Ἔκδοση Αδελφῶν Κυριακίδη, 1982. Print.

———. *Τό Πρόβλημα τῶν Σχέσεων Ποιμαντικῆς Φροντίδος καί Ψυχοθεραπείας ἐξ Απόψεως Ορθοδόξου* [The Problem of the Relationship between Pastoral Counseling and Psychotherapy Viewed from the Orthodox Standpoint]. Θεσσαλονίκη: Ἔκδοση Αδελφῶν Κυριακίδη, 1986. Print.

———. *Θέματα Ποιμαντικῆς Ψυχολογίας. Νείλου τοῦ Ἀσκητοῦ.Ψυχολογικές προοπτικές ὑπό τό πρίσμα σύγχρονων γνώσεων* [Issues Concerning Pastoral Psychology. Nilus Ancyranus: psychological perspectives through the lense of modern knowledge]. Θεσσαλονίκη: Ἔκδοση Αδελφῶν Κυριακίδη, 1991. Print.

———. *Θέματα Ποιμαντικῆς Ψυχολογίας. Ἡ «Κρίση ταυτότητος» κατά τόν ὅσιο Ἰωάννη τόν Σιναΐτη (τῆς Κλίμακος)* [Issues Concerning Pastoral Psychology. The "Identity Crisis" according to St John Climacus]. Θεσσαλονίκη: Ἔκδοση Αδελφῶν Κυριακίδη, 1991. Print.

———. *Ἐγχειρίδιον Ποιμαντικῆς Ψυχολογίας* [A Guide to Pastoral Psychology]. 3 τόμος. Ἀθήνα. 1993. Print.

———. *Ἐγχειρίδιον Ποιμαντικῆς Ψυχολογίας* [A Guide to Pastoral Psychology]. Θεσσαλονίκη: Ἔκδοση Αδελφῶν Κυριακίδη, 1993 (a). Print.

———. *Θέματα Ποιμαντικῆς Ψυχολογίας. Τό Ψυχολογικόν ἐπιχείρημα εἰς τήν ἑρμηνευτικήν μέθοδον τοῦ Ἰ. Φωτίου* [Issues Concerning Pastoral Psychology. The Psychological Argument in St Photius' Hermeneutic Method]. Θεσσαλονίκη: Ἔκδοση Αδελφῶν Κυριακίδη, 1998. Print.

Манн, Т. *Собрание сочинений. В 10-ти томах* [Mann's Collected Edition: in 10 Volumes]. Москва. 1961. Print.

Manzat, Ion. *Psihologia crestină a adâncurilor. Dostoevsky contra lui Freud* [Christian Depth Psychology. Dostoevsky vs. Freud]. Bucuresti: Ed. Univers Encyclopedic, 1999. Print.

Ματσούκα, Νικολάου Α. *Γένεσις καί ὀυσία τοῦ ὀρθοδόξου δόγματος* [The Genesis and the Essence of Orthodox Doctrine]. Θεσσαλονίκη: Πατριαρχικόν Ἵδρυμα Πατερικῶν Μελετῶν, 1969. Print.

———. *Ἐπιστήμη, φιλοσοφία καί θεολογία στήν Ἑξαήμερο τοῦ Μ.Βασιλείου* [Science, Philosophy, and Theology in the Hexaimeron of Basil the Great]. Ἔκδοση Β′. Θεσσαλονίκη: Ἐκδόσεις Πουρνάρα, 1990. Print.

———. *Δογματική καί Συμβολική Θεολογία. Ἐισαγωγή στή θεολογική γνωσεολογία* [Dogmatic and Symbolic Theology. Introduction to the Theological Gnoseology]. Θεσσαλονίκη: Ἐκδόσεις Πουρνάρα, 1996. Print.

McAllister, Robert J. *Living the Vows: the emotional conflicts of celibate religious*. San Francisco: Harper and Row, 1986. Print.

Milrod, David. "The ego ideal." *The Psychoanalytic Study of the Child* 45, (1990): 43-60. Print.

Минутко, В.Л. *Справочник Психотерапевта* [A Guide to Psychotherapy]. Москва, 1999. Print.

Mıtrī, Ṭāriq. *Al-ʿawlama wa-l-dīn: mawāqiʿ masīḥiyya fi-l-dīn wa-l-ʿawlama wa-taʿaddudiyya* [Globalization and Religion: on religion, globalization, and pluralism from the standpoint of a Christian]. Jāmiʿah Balamand: Markaz li-dirāsāt masīḥiyya wa islāmiyya, 2003. Print.

Μπαλογιάννης, Σταύρος Ι. *Ψυχολογία* [Psychology]. Θεσσαλονίκη: Ἐκδόσεις Πουρνάρα, 1993. Print.

Μπρατσιώτου, Νικολάου. *Ἀνθρωπολογία τῆς Παλαιάς Διαθήκης: ὁ ἄνθρωπος ὡς Θείον δημιούργημα* [The Anthropology of the Old Testament: human being as divine creature]. Ἀθῆναι, 1989. Print.

Neville, Robert Cummings. *A Theology Primer*. New York: S U of New York, 1991. Print.

O' Doherty, E. F. *Religion and Personality Problems*. New York: Alba House, 1964. Print.

Πετρούτσου, Μαρίας. «Ψυχολογία τῆς κλήσεως. [The Psychology of Vocation]» *Ἑλληνοχριστιανική Ἀγωγή*. Ἀθῆνα, 1959. 11-15. Print.

Quinlan, Timothy. "The novitiate." *The Way* 15, (1972): 44-53. Print.

Ricœur, Paul. *De l'Interprétation. Essai sur Freud* [Freud and Philosophy: An Essay on Interpretation]. Paris: Seuil, 1965. Print.

———. «La Psychanalyse et le Mouvement de la Culture contemporaine. [The Psychoanalysis and the Movement of Contemporary Culture]» *Traité de Psychanalyse*. 1 vol. Paris: Presses Universitaires de France, 1965. 79-109. Print.

Rosenberg, Alex. *Philosophy of Science. A Contemporary Introduction*. 3rd ed. New York [a.o.]: Routledge, 2012. Print. Routledge Contemporary Introductions to Philosophy.

Rulla, Luigi M. *Depth Psychology and Vocation: a psychosocial perspective*. 1971. Chicago: Loyola U P , 1983. Print.

Rulla, Luigi M., Joyce Ridick, and Franco Imoda. *Entering and Leaving Vocation: intrapsychic dynamics*. Chicago: Loyola U P , 1976. Print.

Rycroft, Charles. *A Critical Dictionary of Psychoanalysis*. Penguin Books, 1968. Print.

Sakellariou, Ioannis. «La formation au ministère sacerdotal dans les «écoles ecclésiastiques» en Grèce contemporaine.» [The Formation of Sacerdotal Ministers in the Church Schools of the Modern Greece] Thèse de doctorat de «3ème cycle» U de Strasbourg, 1981. Print.

Στανιλοάε, Δημητρίου. *Τό ἀνθρώπινο σῶμα* [Human Body]. Τόμος 4. Ἀθήνα: Σύναξη, 1982. Print.

Σταυροπούλου, Αλεξάνδρου Μ. «Ἱερατικές κλήσεις.» *Στιγμιότυπα καί περιπλανήσεις σέ δρόμους ποιμαντικῆς διακονίας* ["Sacerdotal vocations." Snapshots and Wanderings on the Roads of Pastoral Ministry.]. Ἀθῆνα, 1983. Print.

Stern, Karl. *Refus de la Femme* [The Denial of Womanhood]. 1965. Tours: Ed. Mame, 1969. Print.

Strunk, Orlo. "Men, motives and the ministry." *Religious Education* 54, (1959): 429-34. Print.

Θερμός, Βασιλείου. *Ποιμαίνοντες μετ'ἐπιστήμης* [Pastoral Counseling by Way of Integrating Modern Psychological Thought and Method]. Ἀθήνα: Ἐκδόσεις Αρμός, 1996 (a). Print.

———. *Ὁμοιοπαθείς ἄνθρωποι / Ζητήματα Ποιμαντικῆς Ἀυτοσυνειδησίας* [Kindred Human Beings: pastoral self-awareness issues]. Ἀθήνα: Ἀποστολική Διακονία, 1996. Print.

———. *Ἀναζητώντας τό πρόσωπο: Ὁ αληθῆς καί ὁ ψευδῆς ἑαυτός τοῦ ἀνθρώπου κατά τόν ψυχαναλυτῆ Donald Winnicott καί κατά τόν Ἅγ. Γρηγόριο Παλαμά* [Seeking the Human Essence: the true self and the false self according to D. Winnicott and St Gregory Palamas]. Ἀθήνα: Ἐκδόσεις Αρμός, 1997. Print.

———. *Ἡ Ἱερατική κλίση ὡς ψυχολογικό γεγονός* [The Hieratic Vocation as Psychological Event]. Ἀθήνα: Ἔκδοση Ι. Μητροπόλεως Θηβῶν καί Λεβαδείας, 1998. Print.

———. *Τά ὀφφίκια τῶν πρεσβυτέρων* [The Priests' Duties]. Ἀθήνα: Ἐκδόσεις Ἀκρίτας, 1999. Print.

———. "Πρός μία θεολογική προσέγγιση καί κατανόηση τῆς ψυχοπαθολογίας καί τῆς θεραπείας [Toward a New Theological Approach and Understanding of Psychopathology and Therapy]." *Θεολογία καί Ψυχιατρική σε διάλογο.* Ἀθήνα: Ἀποστολική Διακονία, 1999. Print.

———. "Προλεγόμενα στήν ἀνάγνωση τῶν Πατέρων κατά τήν εἴσοδο τῆς νέας χιλιετίας [Foreword to the Reading of Fathers at the Advent of the New Millenium]." *Νέα Κοινωνολογίας* 30, (2000): 24-35. Web. 11.02.2013. http://de.scribd.com/doc/36566027/νεα-κοινωνιολογια-30

———. "Δύο πολιτισμικοί κίνδυνοι γιά τήν ψυχοθεραπεία [Two Cultural Perils for the Psychotherapy]." Εἰσήγηση στό Διεθνές Συνέδριο Ορθόδοξης Θεολογίας καί Ψυχοθεραπείας. Ἰ. Μητρόπολη Θηβῶν καί Λεβαδείας, τόν Οκτώβριο τοῦ 2003. Print.

———. "Θεολογία, Νεωτερικότητα καί ἐπιστήμες τοῦ Ψυχισμοῦ [Theology, Modernity and Psychiatry, Psychology, and Psychotherapy]." (Εἰσήγηση). Ἀθήνα, 2003. Print.

———. *Thirst for Love and Truth: Encounters of Orthodox Theology and psychological Science.* Montréal: Alexander Press, 2010. Web. 28 Sep. 2012.

———. *Ἄνθρωπος στόν ὁρίζοντα! Προσεγγίζοντας τή συνάντηση Ὀρθόδοξης Θεολογίας καί ἐπιστημών τοῦ ψυχιψμοῦ* [Human being on the horizon! Approaching the meeting point between Orthodox Theology and Psychiatry, Psychology, and Psychotherapy]. 2005. Ἀθήνα: Εκδόσεις Γρηγόρη, 2011. Print.

Tollefsen, Torstein Theodor. *Activity and Participation in Late Antique and Early Christian Thought.* First published. Oxford [a.o.]: Oxford U P, 2012. Print. The Oxford Early Christian Studies.

Τσελεγγίδη, Δημητρίου. *Ἡ σωτηριολογία τοῦ Λουθήρου* [Luther's Soteriology]. Θεσσαλονίκη: Ἐκδόσεις Πουρνάρα, 1998. Print.

Walsch, Thomas. "The age of choice." *The Way* 15, (1972): 36-43. Print.

Ware, Kallistos, Metropolitan of Diokleia. *Man, Woman and the Priesthood of Christ.* Genève: World Council of Churches Publications, 2000. Print.

Wick, Robert J. "Practical Psychological Aspects of Self-Examination in the Spiritual Formation of Seminarians." *Journal of Pastoral Counseling* XXII.1-2, (1987): 1-10. Print.

Winnicott, D. W. *L'Enfant et sa famille* [The Child and Its Family]. Paris: Petite Bibliothèque Payot, 1971. Print.

Волков, А. А. *Курс руской риторики* [Course of Russian Rhétorique]. Москва, 2001. Print.

Ζηζιούλα, Ἰωάννου, Μητρ. Περγάμου. *Ἡ κτίση ὡς εὐχαριστία* [Creation as Eucharist]. Ἀθήνα: Ἐκδόσεις Ἀκρίτας, 1992. Print.

Zilboorg, G. «Freud et la Religion.» [Freud and Religion]. *Supplément de la Vie spirituelle* 50, 3 ème trimestre (1959). Print.

Ziller, Robert. *The Social Self.* Oxford: Pergamon Press, 1973. Print.